CONTENTS

INTRODUCTION

What is *Blueprints Physical Education?*

Blueprints Physical Education is a practical classroom resource written to fulfil all the requirements of the National Curriculum for Physical Education at primary school level. It is intended to be used flexibly, either as an ideas bank for individual teachers or as a workable core resource for a whole school's scheme of work in Physical Education.

Blueprints Physical Education consists of a teacher's resource book for each of the primary key stages. Together they provide a coherent spiral curriculum for primary Physical Education.

Blueprints Physical Education and the National Curriculum

Physical Education is a foundation subject within the National Curriculum. It comprises six areas of activity outlined in the Key Stage 2 Programme of Study:

Athletic activities
Dance
Games
Gymnastic activities
Outdoor and Adventurous activities
Swimming.

This book covers all six areas. It aims to provide you with a complete scheme of work for Key Stage 2 Physical Education. This is provided by units of work which give you outline lesson plans and by an activities bank for each area of Physical Education. However, you will find that the coverage is weighted towards Dance, Games and Gymnastics, as these are the core PE activities.

The material is structured so that there is progression from Years 3/4 through to Years 5/6. The material also follows on from *Blueprints Physical Education Key Stage 1*. The lesson plans for Years 3 and 4, 5 and 6 have been designed together so that you and your colleagues can decide how you present your activities. In Years 5 and 6 some activities may be grouped together in blocks and in Years 3 and 4 some activities may extend over two terms.

For each area of activity you will find a structured bank of materials, comprising the following:

About the area of activity: an introduction giving you essential information about the area of Physical Education being covered.

National Curriculum requirements at Key Stage 2: this reproduces the content of the National Curriculum exactly and provides an at-a-glance guide to the coverage of that particular area of activity.

Teaching the area of activity at Key Stage 2: this provides you with a clear strategy for breaking down and tackling the area of Physical Education into key themes which provide the basis for the units of work which follow. It gives you important teaching points to watch out for in teaching the area of PE. You will also find that it provides you with a model lesson which takes an example from the lesson plans that follow and explains in detail teaching strategies for teaching that area of PE.

Activity bank: there is a bank of activities for each area of PE. These banks provide progressive activities basic to each area. You will find these continuously referred to in the lesson plans.

Lesson plans: these are provided for Years 3/4 and Years 5/6. They provide you with a complete outline scheme of work for Physical Education. As you will see, most lessons have the same structure in terms of Introduction, Development and Conclusion. (In the Dance section the lessons also have a three-part structure, although different headings are used). This layout ensures a sound progression of the theme throughout the lesson.

A time allocation has been made for each area of activity based on a realistic assessment of the time available and the needs for Physical Education, as follows:

	Years 3/4	Years 5/6
Dance	24 lessons	24 lessons
Gymnastics	24 lessons	24 lessons
Games	24 lessons	24 lessons
Athletics	12 lessons	12 lessons
Outdoor/Adventurous	12 lessons	12 lessons
Swimming	12 lessons	

You will notice that not all the activities have an equal allocation of time. The areas of Gymnastics, Dance and Games have a greater emphasis as they provide the foundation for all basic movement and understanding.

When planning your timetable of activities, it is important to give breadth and balance so that the Programme of Study is completed by the end of Key Stage 2. The way in which these activities are planned into your timetable will depend on the facilities and equipment available. It is important that you do provide the opportunity for all of your pupils to have the experience of the activities as identified in the National Curriculum at Key Stage 2. If the foundation skills have been provided at Key Stage 1, where the children have been given the opportunity to learn by doing and moving, then at Key Stage 2 the children will be able to develop their knowledge, understanding and skill.

At this age the child's motor skills, control and overall co-ordination will have developed and they will need time in their lessons to refine them. You will notice in the lesson plans that opportunities are given so that the children have time to practise movements/skills. For children to have this time will enhance their understanding as well as improving their ability. At this age the children enjoy the challenge of working with, and competing with, their peers. They are also more inventive and their actions are more spontaneous than at Key Stage 1.

At Key Stage 2 you should, wherever possible, give the pupils opportunities to plan and make decisions for themselves. However, they must be guided in terms of tasks so that they are provided with a learning situation. For example, in a games lesson if the task has been developing the skills of receiving and sending in threes, an extension of this is for the children to devise a game, which involves basic rules and a scoring system, using the skills developed. They will have to select the equipment to be used, select and identify the rules and be given time to explore the tactics of the game.

As well as planning, the performance of the activity needs thought when structuring material. The area of performance does not mean being able to produce a skill, but rather how this skill is applied in a variety of practical situations. You need to give your pupils the opportunity to improvise and compose as well as adapting and refining their movements.

Managing PE at Key Stage 2 ▷

Physical Education has a major role to play in the development of young children. It is an integral part of the total education of any child and is closely allied to other creative and learning experiences and skill acquisition. It makes a significant contribution to the all-round harmonious development of the mind and body. Therefore, the planning and management of the Physical Education curriculum in schools should always have children as the focus of attention, with the overall purpose of providing rich and varied learning experiences. The provision of a broad, balanced and well-differentiated programme of physical activities is a major responsibility of the primary school, in order to promote a healthy active lifestyle and love of the open air. Primary teachers therefore need to ensure that sound teaching methods are used and that they build upon the children's learning experiences and areas of competence already gained at Key Stage 1.

Cross-curricular links

The class teacher is usually responsible for Physical Education and because of this has the opportunity to provide links with other subject areas. Linking up with the other National Curriculum Attainment Targets will ensure deeper understanding of the subject matter. The area of space, for example, can be related to Physical Education and different topics such as symmetry and asymmetry can be related to gymnastics. The development of language is also important, both in understanding the meaning of words and in the ability to recap a performed sequence or to express ideas when devising a small game in a group.

The role of the PE Curriculum Leader

Many schools have teachers in charge of Physical Education (often called Curriculum Leaders) and they are responsible for co-ordinating the Physical Education curriculum. The Curriculum Leader needs to have enthusiasm for the subject and a sound understanding of Physical Education, as well as an ability to take a leadership role in planning, teaching and evaluating the Physical Education programme. The Curriculum Leader will not take every class within the school but should be able to assist colleagues with guidance and advice. The key factor in developing a sound Physical Education curriculum is for the Curriculum Leader and class teacher to seek and maintain strong support from the Headteacher. Appropriate time and funding are critical to the maintenance of a balanced programme of activities, and to the provision of opportunities for all children whatever their age or ability.

If Physical Education is to be fully accepted in the primary school there must be recognition by all staff of its value as an essential part of the whole curriculum. The programme should be varied, involving a variety of physical experiences which are both enjoyable and demanding for the children. These experiences should be continually assessed and adapted so that skills can be developed according to the individual's capabilities. Physical Education has a major contribution to make in the life of every individual. The primary years are a critical phase for physical development.

The Curriculum Leader has a major role to play in promoting Physical Education and in developing the confidence of inexperienced teachers or those teachers who feel ill-equipped for, or even dislike, the teaching of the subject. The Curriculum Leader acts as a resource for other teachers as well as taking responsibility for equipment and resources. The impact that the Curriculum Leader can have on the school is of paramount importance if the subject is to respond to an ever-changing society. Links between feeder schools, both pre-primary and post-primary, are of great importance so that there is continuity in the development of movement competence. The development of good relationships between the primary school and the appropriate secondary schools will ensure a much easier transition for the pupils and enable continuity of Physical Education learning experiences to be maintained. Teachers from these schools need to clarify and discuss the whole notion and process of continuity through an agreed network structure.

In managing the curriculum, the Curriculum Leader needs to implement sound practice in the overall Physical Education curriculum. This would include planning, implementing and evaluating content and teaching strategies, and being aware of equal opportunities and special needs provision. Ensuring adequate time allocation for the various activity areas and making sure a balanced curriculum is being developed is also vital. The organisation of the timetable, facilities and resources, plus the school events that are curricular or extra-curricular, need to be co-ordinated. The use and organisation of equipment needs to be continually addressed so that procedures are uniformly followed by pupils and staff. Checking changing facilities for Physical Education for health, hygiene and safety factors is also very important.

Promoting Physical Education, e.g. by the use of notice boards publicising clubs and team practices, should be the responsibility of the Curriculum Leader, as should informing school staff and pupils as well as parents and governors of school events. Periodic use of bulletins can assist in transmitting information on school events. Pupils' work should be displayed in main corridors for all to see.

With demands from other areas of the curriculum and lack of appropriate facilities, there is often not enough opportunity for children to participate in a full range of physical activity during the school day. Therefore, extra/extended curricular activities are beneficial as they help increase opportunities for children.

New initiatives are taking place where community involvement is becoming a part of the extended school curriculum. Identified in the National Curriculum is the area of Partnerships, Physical Education and Sport, whereby sports leaders, coaches and dance animateurs assist during curriculum time. These personnel are not intended to substitute for the teacher, but to provide support. It is therefore important that the teacher has the overall responsibility for the planning, organisation and evaluation of the curriculum so that the pupils have a sound and coherent experience. There are many agencies that could provide support to the Curriculum Leader. It is up to the Curriculum Leader to find out from the local agencies what opportunities are available, so that children, whatever their age or ability, can participate in a range of activities associated with Physical Education, sport and dance.

Closer working relationships between primary and feeder secondary schools can be beneficial in terms of ease of transition for pupils at Key Stage 2. There may also be opportunities for further support between staff. Partnership is about coming together to share opportunities with others. The school needs to determine which partnerships to develop. The national Curriculum highlights the following list for schools to identify:

- the needs and priorities of the pupils
- the gaps in provision (facilities, teaching, training)
- the extent to which the development of partnerships will benefit pupils, individually and collectively.

PLANNING, MONITORING AND EVALUATING PHYSICAL EDUCATION

SCAA (1995) has identified three levels of planning; long-term, medium-term and short-term. Each of these has been considered below and presented in an easy-to-follow guide to planning.

LONG-TERM PLANNING ▶

LONG-TERM PLANNING is:
Planning a key stage

↓

STATUTORY REQUIRFMENTS

General Requirements   Programmes of Study   End of Key Stage Descriptions

The following headings must be considered at this stage:

CONTENT	APPROACHES TO TEACHING	HEALTH & SAFETY
• PoS • Progression • Continuity • Breadth and balance between activities	• General Requirements – make lessons active – develop positive attitudes – understand success and limitations in performance – plan, perform and evaluate • Methods of delivery – teaching strategies – differentiation	• Understand importance of safe practice

MAPPING THE CURRICULUM

↓

Considerations
- Time available/Number of lessons
- Allocation of time available for each lesson
- Statutory requirements
- Placement of activities depending on seasonal factors
- Availability of hall/indoor space(s)
- Religious/cultural celebrations

Below are a number of tables to assist with planning the physical education programme. Examples have been provided, although it is accepted that each school will have individual needs, and therefore adaptation of each table will be necessary according to the school's situation.

Mapping the curriculum

	GAMES	GYMNASTICS	DANCE	ATHLETICS	OAA	SWIMMING
YEAR 3	30 LESSONS	18 LESSONS	18 LESSONS	12 LESSONS	6 LESSONS	24 LESSONS
YEAR 4	30 LESSONS	18 LESSONS	18 LESSONS	12 LESSONS	6 LESSONS	24 LESSONS
YEAR 5	36 LESSONS	24 LESSONS	18 LESSONS	12 LESSONS	18 LESSONS	
YEAR 6	36 LESSONS	20 LESSONS	24 LESSONS	12 LESSONS	18 LESSONS	

Figure 1 **Mapping the curriculum.** This table shows the number of lessons per year allocated to each area of activity within the key stage. Games, gym and dance must be taught during each year of the key stage; OAA, swimming and athletics are taught at appropriate points throughout the key stage. Ideally there should be a minimum number of three lessons per week. Each lesson should be 30 minutes in duration, not including the time taken for changing.

Activity programme planner

	AUTUMN TERM		SPRING TERM		SUMMER TERM	
YEAR 3	GAMES DANCE ATHLETICS	GAMES DANCE SWIMMING	GYMNASTICS DANCE SWIMMING	GAMES GYMNASTICS SWIMMING	GAMES GYMNASTICS SWIMMING	GAMES OAA ATHLETICS
YEAR 4	GAMES DANCE ATHLETICS	GYMNASTICS SWIMMING GAMES	DANCE SWIMMING GAMES	DANCE SWIMMING GYMNASTICS	GAMES SWIMMING GYMNASTICS	GAMES OAA ATHLETICS
YEAR 5	GAMES GYMNASTICS DANCE	GAMES GYMNASTICS DANCE	GAMES GYMNASTICS DANCE	GAMES OAA GYMNASTICS	GAMES OAA ATHLETICS	GAMES OAA ATHLETICS
YEAR 6	GAMES GYMNASTICS ATHLETICS	GAMES GYMNASTICS DANCE	GAMES GYMNASTICS DANCE	GAMES OAA DANCE	GAMES OAA DANCE	GAMES OAA ATHLETICS

Figure 2 **Activity programme planner.** Here the information from Figure 1 has been translated onto this table. Each activity is allocated a half-term slot in line with current practice, and presuming that each half-term is six weeks in duration.

Weekly planner: Autumn term

	MONDAY	TUESDAY	WEDNESDAY	THURSDAY	FRIDAY	MONDAY	TUESDAY	WEDNESDAY	THURSDAY	FRIDAY
YEAR 3	GAMES		DANCE	ATHLETICS		GAMES		DANCE	SWIMMING	
YEAR 4		GAMES	DANCE		ATHLETICS		GYMNASTICS	SWIMMING		GAMES
YEAR 5	GAMES			GYMNASTICS	DANCE	GAMES			GYMNASTICS	DANCE
YEAR 6	GAMES	GYMNASTICS	ATHLETICS			GAMES	GYMNASTICS	DANCE		

Figure 3 **Weekly planner.** This demonstrates where each lesson is placed during the week for each group. (This will be more complex in a school situation as there is more than one class per year.) Here teachers will be able to see at a glance the activity that they are to teach. This example is of the autumn term, although one for each term will be needed.

x

Facility planner: Timetable for Hall/Yard/Field

	MONDAY	TUESDAY	WEDNESDAY	THURSDAY	FRIDAY
9.00–9.30					
9.30–10.00					
10.00–10.30					
10.30–11.00					
11.00–11.30					
11.30–12.00					
1.00–1.30					
1.30–2.00					
2.00–2.30					
2.30–3.00					
3.00–3.30					

Figure 4 **Facility planner.** A facility planner should be reproduced for each space available for physical education, usually by the Curriculum Leader. In the past the hall space has been allocated to classes in larger blocks. Consequently appropriate use of the time and space has not always been made. By using this method, each class is allocated a half-hour slot, and the hall should therefore be in constant use, with one class lining up outside waiting for the previous group to vacate the hall. (This has implications for children changing as well as being able to put out/clear away apparatus efficiently.)

MEDIUM-TERM PLANNING

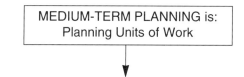

MEDIUM-TERM PLANNING is:
Planning Units of Work

Each year group has a programme of activities
(see figure 2)

Year 3: Games, Gymnastics, Dance, Athletics, OAA and Swimming
Year 4: Games, Gymnastics, Dance, Athletics, OAA and Swimming
Year 5: Games, Gymnastics, Dance, Athletics, and OAA
Year 6: Games, Gymnastics, Dance, Athletics, and OAA

When planning units of work the following issues must always be addressed:

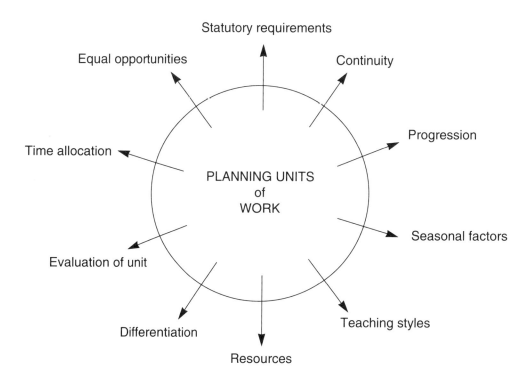

Physical Education Unit of Work

Key Stage: Year: Number of sessions

Aims of unit: Unit number

Intended learning outcomes:

a) Plan

b) Perform

c) Evaluate

Activities to be covered	Opportunities to evaluate pupils' progress (In relation to learning outcomes)

Resources

The definition of each of the terms used within the Unit of Work is essential.

Aims: These identify what is to be learned in the unit. They should draw on statements from the Programmes of Study and also make reference to the General Requirements from the Statutory Orders.

Intended Learning Outcomes: These extend from the aims of the unit. They should be presented in relation to knowledge, skills and understanding and attitudes that pupils will acquire after being taught the unit. Each learning outcome has been divided into planning, performing and evaluating learning outcomes to highlight the process model of the National Curriculum Physical Education.

Activities to be covered: These show what the pupils will actually do within the unit. They should include activities related to the four phases of a lesson. It is essential that activities are appropriate for the intended learning outcomes presented.

Opportunities to evaluate pupils' progress: Within each learning activity there will be an opportunity for a teacher to evaluate closely pupils' progress in relation to the intended learning outcomes.

A sample Unit of Work for Games is presented here for guidance.

Physical Education Unit or Work

Key Stage: 2	Year: 5	No. of Sessions: 8
		Unit No. 3 of 3

Aims of Unit:
- To develop pupils' understanding and play small-sided games of cricket.
- To improve the skills of sending, receiving and striking the ball in cricket.
- To develop pupils' positive attitudes by teaching them to observe the conventions of fair play, honest competition and good sporting behaviour as individual participants, team members and spectators.

Intended learning outcomes

Pupils will be expected to demonstrate

a) Plan:
(i)   an awareness of basic fielding positions in order to prevent the batter from scoring runs.
(ii) an understanding of when to run between the wickets in situations both with and without a partner.

b) Perform:
(i)   increased accuracy in aiming a ball using a bat at a target.
(ii) stopping a ball using the hands as well as demonstrating competence in both throwing and catching a ball.
(iii) methods of bowling the ball at the batter using underarm and/or overarm.

c) Evaluate:
(i)   evaluating preferred methods of field placing.
(ii) where the ball should be placed in order to score maximum runs.

Activities to be covered	Opportunities to evaluate pupils' progress (In relation to learning outcomes)
1. Protect target using different body parts/bats	b) (i)
2. Bowler bowls to batter, who aims to direct the ball at a variety of different targets.	b) (i) (iii)
3. Make up, play and refine practices and small-sided cricket games involving principles of striking and fielding games.	a) (i) c) (i) (ii)
4. Small-sided games involving a batting side and a fielding side	a) (i) (ii) c) (i) (ii)

Resources

Small, medium and large balls, different coloured cones, cricket shaped bats, bean bags, baskets, sectors made up of markers, hoops.

The following Physical Education year-planning framework for units of work (Figure 5 and Figure 6) are provided as a checklist when Units of Work are being produced. This framework meets the statutory requirements of the National Curriculum. These requirements are broken down into specific activities whilst concentrating on the pupil's ability to plan, perform, evaluate, work safely and understand the effects of exercise.

Category		Year 3 Programmes of Study		Year 4 Programmes of Study	
They can work safely alone and with others		Work alone and with others in co-operative and competitive tasks	☐	Work with another person or small group in small competitions/activities and adapt good sporting/group behaviour	☐
They can sustain energetic activity and have an understanding of what is happening to their body.		Recognise the short-term effects of exercise on their bodies	☐	Sustain energetic activity over appropriate periods of time	☐
They can make judgements of their own performance and suggest ways of improving		Suggest ways of improving their own and other's performance	☐	Make simple judgements about the effectiveness of the performance of themselves and others	☐
They practise, adapt, improve and repeat longer and more complex sequences of movement	Swimming	Be aware of basic water safety and hygiene requirements in swimming baths	☐	Understand water safety and hazards for open water	☐
		Develop water confidence and achieve propulsion through water	☐	Develop a variety of means of propulsion using either arms, legs or both	☐
	Outdoor pursuits	Undertake simple outdoor and adventurous activities in one type of outdoor environment, demonstrate basic skills in the activity undertaken.	☐	Undertake simple outdoor and adventurous activities in one of two different environments, demonstrating the skills undertaken	☐
		Participate in challenges of a problem solving nature	☐	Plan, participate and evaluate challenges of a problem solving nature in small groups	☐
	Activities	Practise basic actions in running (over shorter and longer distances and relays), jumping and throwing	☐	Practise basic actions in running, jumping and throwing	☐
				To measure and improve their own performance	☐
	Gymnastics	Develop the themes of turning, balancing, swinging and climbing both on the floor and using suitable apparatus	☐	Practise and refine the themes of rolling, jumping, swinging, balancing and taking weight on hands both on the floor and using suitable apparatus	☐
		Explore longer sequences on the floor and suitable apparatus	☐	Explore, practise and refine longer sequences on the floor and apparatus and repeat them	☐
		Explore changes of speed, shape and direction	☐	Develop changes of speed, shape and direction	☐
	Dance	Create simple dances with clear beginnings, middles and ends	☐	Improvise on given stimulus and make appropriate selections to create simple dances	☐
		Express moods and feelings through movement of the whole body and parts of the body	☐	Create simple dances based on a dramatic theme	☐
		Create simple character within dances	☐	Vary the range of movements through altering shape, size, direction, speed, weight and rhythm	☐
		Improve the content and quality of movements by varying shape, size, direction and speed	☐	Copy simple movement sequences and learn set dances	☐
	Games	Further develop the skills of sending, receiving, striking and travelling with the ball, individually/partner/small group	☐	To explore and understand common skills and principles in invasion, striking/fielding, net/wall and target games	☐
		To make up, play and refine their own games with guidance from the teacher	☐	Further consolidate games making, including practices, within prescribed limits	☐
				Play small-sided conditioned games in a variety of contexts and understand ideas as member of a team	☐
They make appropriate decisions quickly, plan in different environments, explore and make up activities		Select movement and link them together	☐	Select effective responses to a variety of tasks and situations	☐

Figure 5   Physical Education year planning framework for units of work Year 3 and Year 4

		Year 5 Programmes of Study		Year 6 Programmes of Study	
They can work safely alone and with others		Develop and appreciate the different roles within a team or group situation	☐	Recognise the strengths and weaknesses of each team/group member and take into account when planning tactics/activities	☐
They can sustain energetic activity and have an understanding of what is happening to their body.		Understand the value and demonstrate sustained activity over appropriate periods of time	☐	Prepare the body for different physical activities	☐
They can make judgements of their own performance and suggest ways of improving		Recognise what they and others are doing and make simple suggestions about how it can be improved	☐	Compare, and if appropriate, evaluate two performances, indicating the differences	☐
They practise, adapt, improve and repeat longer and more complex sequences of movement	Swimming	Further develop swim strokes on front and back	☐	Swim competently, unaided, for 25 metres.	☐
		Develop basic survival skills	☐	To be able to plan, perform and evaluate their own performance effectively	☐
	Outdoor pursuits	Undertake outdoor and adventurous activities in one or more different environments, demonstrating further skills in the activities undertaken	☐	Have developed outdoor and adventurous activities in one or more different environments, demonstrating the skills necessary for the activities undertaken	☐
		Plan, participate, record and evaluate challenges of a problem solving nature in small groups	☐	Participate in challenges of a problem solving nature using suitable equipment, including planning, recording and evaluating whilst working in small groups	☐
	Activities	Experience competitions including those made up themselves. Develop and practise basic actions in running, jumping and throwing	☐	Develop and practise basic actions for running, throwing and jumping	☐
		To measure, compare and improve their own performance	☐	Measure, compare, improve their own performance. Experience competitions including those made up.	☐
	Gymnastics	Adapt, practise and refine different ways of rolling, jumping, swinging, balancing and taking weight on hands both on the floor and using suitable apparatus	☐	Practise, refine and develop more difficult ways of rolling, jumping, swinging, balancing and taking weight on hands both on the floor and using suitable apparatus	☐
		Select, practise and refine increasingly difficult movements on the floor and using apparatus	☐	Select, refine and repeat longer sequences of more difficult movements both on the floor and using suitable apparatus	☐
		Choose appropriate changes of shape, speed and direction	☐	Emphasise changes of speed, shape and direction	☐
	Dance	Begin to compose longer dances involving improvising, exploring and selecting content	☐	Choreograph dances individually or as part of a pair or small group	☐
		Improvise and create structured dances using a wide range of stimuli with a decreasing level of help from the teacher	☐	Create characters and express narratives in movement	☐
		Select simple choreographic principles to give a dance interest and variety	☐	Perform set dances from different times and cultures	☐
				Create dances using the dance forms from different periods in history and from other cultures as a stimulus	☐
	Games	To practise and apply the common skills and principles involved in invasion, striking/fielding, net/wall target games	☐	Explore and understand common skills and principles in invasion, net, striking, fielding and target games	☐
		To create their own games and develop their own rules and scoring systems	☐	Improve the skills of sending, receiving, striking and travelling with a ball in the above games	☐
		Play simplified versions of recognised invasion, striking/fielding and net games	☐	Make up, play and refine their own games practices within prescribed limits considering and developing rules and scoring systems	☐
				Develop an understanding of and play small-sided and simplified versions of recognised invasion, net/wall and striking/fielding games	☐
They make appropriate decisions quickly, plan in different environments, explore and make up activities		Select effective responses to changing situations		Select effective responses, taking account of their own level of skill and that of others	☐

Figure 5   Physical Education year planning framework for units of work Year 5 and Year 6

After each Unit of Work has been taught it is essential that the Unit as a whole is evaluated as well as the pupils' progress. Figure 7 offers a monitoring and evaluating pro forma sheet, that should be attached to each unit taught. The top half of the sheet identifies issues in relation to evaluating the unit. Here comments can be made for monitoring of future Units of Work. The bottom half of the sheet is provided to record pupils' progress in relation to learning outcomes. There are two spaces provided: the names of those pupils 'working within' the learning outcome should be identified here, as should those pupils who are 'working beyond' the learning outcome. The remainder of the class are assumed to have 'achieved' the specified learning outcome. This will be the majority of the class in most instances, therefore it is not necessary to detail all names. In future the information may be transferred on to provide details of pupils to assist them with their Physical Education planning.

Figure 7 may also form the basis of any reports that are presented to parents. Together with the End of Key Stage Descriptions they can provide the framework for final report on a child's progress in Physical Education.

Activity Unit _____ Class _____ Teacher _____

UNIT EVALUATION

Were all learning outcomes delivered effectively?

Was unit appropriate to needs and ability of pupils?

Specify areas to be re-visited:

Identify aspects that were inappropriate:

PUPILS' PROGRESS

*Identification of pupils who have not achieved learning outcomes or those working beyond these outcomes

Learning Outcomes	Working Within	Working Beyond
LO 1		
LO 2		
LO 3		
LO 4		
LO 5		
LO 6		
LO 7		

Figure 7 Monitoring and evaluation pro forma sheet

SHORT-TERM PLANNING

> SHORT-TERM PLANNING is:
> Lesson Planning

This book provides many examples of lesson plans.

A LESSON PLAN should contain the following phases:

- Introductory activities — include here an activity based warm up
- Development phase — here is the major aspect of the lesson
- Concluding activity — the 'climax' of the lesson should occur here.
- Warm down — the pupils should be allowed time to bring their heart rate back to resting

Figure 8 is included to assist teachers in presenting a series of lesson plans to ensure that progression and continuity are addressed.

	Lesson Structure	Lesson 1	Lesson 2	Lesson 3	Lesson 4	Lesson 5	Lesson 6
	Introductory activities						
	Development						
	Concluding activity						

Area of Activity

Year

Number of Lessons

Title of Unit

Figure 8

The National Curriculum for Physical Education is a single attainment target encompassing all the end of key stage descriptions, which incorporate the processes of planning, performing and evaluating. Throughout the document the focus is on activity and performance. The programmes of study provide the teacher with a planning base plus information about how the skills and processes will enable children to achieve the attainment target as defined by the end of the key stage descriptions.

There are two parts identified in the programmes of study:

- General requirements, which apply to the teaching of physical education across all key stages.
- Key Stage 2 programme of study, which refer to each area of activity taught within this key stage.

General requirements

Physical Education involves pupils in the continuous process of planning, performing and evaluating. The greatest emphasis should be placed on the actual performance. The general requirements reflect good practice, so they need to be at the forefront of planning lessons.

Key Stage 2 programmes of study

These provide the content of PE and are the areas which will provide the framework when planning the PE programme. Pupils should be taught six areas of activity. During each year of the key stage pupils should be taught Games, Gymnastic Activities and Dance. At points during the key stage pupils should be taught Athletic Activities, Outdoor and Adventurous Activities and Swimming. Highlighted in the Non-Statutory Guidance of the National Curriculum are the following cross-curricular elements.

Health
Safety
Personal and social skills.

Health

Each activity plays a part in promoting a sound and healthy attitude to PE. The end of key stage statements and programmes of study (general) provide a framework for relating exercise to its effects on the body. This is where you as the teacher should make sure that each lesson involves the children in activities that involve whole body movements. The children need to understand the importance of changing for PE lessons and develop a positive awareness of hygiene principles, as well establishing good habits in how they use their bodies and adopting good posture.

Safety

In the programmes of study, particular attention is drawn to the area of safety. It is your responsibility as the teacher to make sure that the environment is a safe place to work in and that the children are appropriately dressed for the activity and are able to move freely. All jewellery needs to be removed so that there is no danger of pupils catching or damaging themselves or others.

It is important that the children learn to handle equipment safely when lifting, carrying and placing it. Children should be made aware of their own safety and that of others in all the activities, and should readily respond to your instructions and signals. It is necessary at this age that routines are established in terms of codes of practice and rules. If these habits are formed early in the children's PE activities then they will gain the benefit of a good life-long attitude to safety.

Personal and social skills

From Key Stage 1 and through to Key Stage 2, PE needs to promote children's understanding of how to present themselves in a co-operative manner when working individually or as a group. They must be allowed the opportunity to understand themselves and the attributes and capabilities they possess. Children also need time to practise social skills through different strategies in terms of teaching and learning styles.

All PE activities should promote equal opportunities. The PE curriculum should give all children the opportunity to develop their full potential in a balanced curriculum. Individual needs, abilities and interests should be catered for through a well-planned and progressive programme. If this is the case, then the children will develop enjoyment and satisfaction from planning, performing and evaluating a balanced range of movement activities.

General requirements for physical education: key stages 1–4

Physical education should involve pupils in the continuous process of planning, performing and evaluating. This applies to all areas of activity. The greatest emphasis should be placed on the actual performance aspect of the subject. The following requirements apply to the teaching of physical education across all key stages.

- **1.** To promote physical activity and healthy lifestyles, pupils should be taught:

    a to be physically active;

    b to adopt the best possible posture and the appropriate use of the body;

    c to engage in activities that develop cardiovascular health, flexibility, muscular strength and endurance;

    d the increasing need for personal hygiene in relation to vigorous physical activity.

- **2.** To develop positive attitudes, pupils should be taught:

    a to observe the conventions of fair play, honest competition and good sporting behaviour as individual participants, team members and spectators;

    b how to cope with success and limitations in performance;

    c to try hard to consolidate their performances;

    d to be mindful of others and the environment.

- **3.** To ensure safe practice, pupils should be taught:

    a to respond readily to instructions;

    b to recognise and follow relevant rules, laws, codes, etiquette and safety procedures for different activities or events, in practice and during competition;

    c about the safety risks of wearing inappropriate clothing, footwear and jewellery, and why particular clothing, footwear and protection are worn for different acivities;

    d how to lift, carry, place and use equipment safely;

    e to warm up for and recover from exercise.

Key stage 2 programme of study

Pupils should be taught six areas of activity. During each year of the key stage pupils should be taught Games, Gymnastic Activities and Dance. At points during the key stage pupils should be taught Athletic Activities, Outdoor and Adventurous Activities, and Swimming unless they have already completed the programme of study for Swimming during Key Stage 1. If aspects of the Swimming programme have been taught during Key Stage 1, pupils should be taught Key Stage 2 Swimming programme starting at the appropriate point.

Throughout the key stage, pupils should be taught:

■ how to sustain energetic activity over appropriate periods of time in a range of physical activities.

■ the short-term effects of exercise on the body.

AREAS OF ACTIVITY

Pupils should be taught:

■ 1. Games

a to understand and play small-sided games and simplified versions of recognised competitive team and individual games, covering the following types – invasion, *eg mini-soccer, netball,* striking/fielding, *eg rounders, small-sided cricket,* net/wall, *eg short tennis;*

b common skills and principles, including attack and defence, in invasion, striking/fielding, net/wall and target games;

c to improve the skills of sending, receiving, striking and travelling with a ball in the above games.

■ 2. Gymnastic activities

a different means of turning, rolling, swinging, jumping, climbing, balancing and travelling on hands and feet, and how to adapt, practise and refine these actions, both on the floor and using apparatus;

b to emphasise changes of shape, speed and direction through gymnastic actions;

c to practice, refine and repeat a longer series of actions making increasingly complex movement sequences, both on the floor and using apparatus.

■ 3. Dance

a to compose and control their movements by varying shape, size, direction, level, speed, tension and continuity;

b a number of dance forms from different times and places, including some traditional dances of the British Isles;

c to express feelings, moods and ideas, to respond to music, and to create simple characters and narratives in response to a range of stimuli, through dance.

■ 4. Athletic activities

a to develop and refine basic techniques in running, *eg over short distances, over longer distances, in relays,* throwing, *eg for accuracy/distance,* and jumping, *eg for height/distance,* using a variety of equipment;

b to measure, compare and improve their own performance.

3

Pupils should be taught:

■ **5. Outdoor and adventurous activities**

a   to perform outdoor and adventurous activities, *eg orienteering exercises,* in one or more different environment(s), *eg playground, school grounds, parks, woodland, seashore;*

b   challenges of a physical and problem-solving nature, *eg negotiating obstacle courses,* using suitable equipment, *eg gymnastic or adventure play apparatus,* whilst, working individually and with others;

c   the skills necessary for the activities undertaken.

■ **6. Swimming**

a   to swim unaided, competently and safely, for at least 25 metres;

b   to develop confidence in water, and how to rest, float and adopt support positions;

c   a variety of means of propulsion using either arms or legs or both, and how to develop effective and efficient swimming strokes on the front and the back;

d   the principles and skills of water safety and survival.

4

DANCE

ABOUT DANCE ▶

Dance is a part of the cultural heritage of all people, whether it is a social experience (for example, the disco) or a theatrical experience (for example, a visit to see a professional company). The kind of dance that is performed varies with time and place (for example, the dances of Tudor England are not those of today and the dances performed in Ghana are not the same as those of Bali). Wherever dance occurs, and in whatever form, the following strands of involvement can be found: the performer/dancer, the maker/composer and the observer/audience; in Western cultures the spectator role often predominates but if all those who go to discos are included there is also a very large performer role. Today British society consists of people from very varied cultural (including dance) traditions, and each of these has a part to play in the development of dance in the 1990s; at times styles retain their distinctiveness (for example, Lancashire morris) and at others new styles emerge as aspects of several different dances are brought together.

Whatever the particular characteristics of any dance, there is always movement organised in time and space. Creators of dance shape and structure these elements in the ways most appropriate for their purpose (for example, to enliven a festive occasion, to communicate some universal truth or to fulfil a religious function). Movements are selected because they make pleasing lines or rhythms or for their contribution to the idea being expressed.

Dance in schools should introduce pupils to, and develop understanding of, this diversity. This can be done by providing opportunities for pupils to dance, to make dances and to watch the dance of others including professional works. In these ways pupils can be led to express their own ideas through dance, to share these ideas with others and to see their own endeavours in the wider context of the adult world.

Children at Key Stage 2 have already begun to acquire the vocabulary of dance through the work they have engaged in during their first two years of school. They have already begun to master changes of bodily action, tension, timing, fluency and simple spatial orientation. They have experienced what it feels like to respond to a variety of stimuli and have learned to structure their responses into phrases which, when linked together, form the building blocks of dance. At Key Stage 2 they need to be helped to enrich their dance vocabulary, increase their understanding of the relationship between idea and movement, develop further their knowledge of the conventions of dance and

become better able to talk and write about both the experiences they have had and the works they have seen. This can be done by developing their understanding of the three strands of dance education: composing, performing and evaluating, or quite simply: making, doing and describing what they and others have done.

Progression

In dance there is not a simple line of development where one skill is a prerequisite for another. Indeed, in each of the units of work and within an individual lesson, children will be having several different experiences. For example, in unit 2, lessons 1–2 of this area they are:

- responding to music
- acquiring skill in controlling the action
- making precise pathways
- being helped to develop rhythmic responses by keeping in time
- learning to repeat and to practise.

It is also the case that some experiences will be repeated later in the key stage but that there will be greater expectations in terms of pupil response. For example, in unit 1, lesson 2, pupils are given a clear movement framework (i.e. wriggle and pounce) and are asked to make their movements like a kitten. In unit 3, lesson 2, pupils have a much more complex task, to interpret the words 'crack and grow' in the context of the description of ice given in the poem. They have to exercise greater independence as they are not given the movement structure within which to work.

Progression can take several forms; for example, throughout Key Stage 2 it should be possible to see the following:

1 Increasing control over the action, quality and spatial orientation of the movement.
2 Increasing sensitivity when dancing with others.
3 Greater clarity of phrasing, i.e. the design of the action between moments of stillness.
4 Responses which derive more appropriately from the stimulus.
5 Use of structural devices which demonstrate wider understanding of the conventions of dance.
6 Greater ability to describe and interpret what they and others have done.
7 A move from dependence on the teacher to greater independence in both initiating the dance and carrying it through to completion.

NATIONAL CURRICULUM REQUIREMENTS AT KEY STAGE 2

Physical Education should involve pupils in the continuous process of planning, performing and evaluating. This applies to all areas of activity. The greatest emphasis should be placed on the actual performance aspect of the subject. The following requirements apply to the teaching of physical education across all key stages.

1. To promote physical activity and healthy lifestyles, pupils should be taught:

   a to be physically active;

   b to adopt the best possible posture and the appropriate use of the body;

   c to engage in activities that develop cardiovascular health, flexibility, muscular strength and endurance;

   d the increasing need for personal hygiene in relation to vigorous physical activity;

2. To develop positive attitudes, pupils should be taught:

   a how to cope with success and limitations in performance;

   b to try to consolidate their performance;

   c to be mindful of others and the environment.

3. To ensure safe practice, pupils should be taught:

   a to respond readily to instructions;

   b to warm up for and recover from exercise.

The programme of study (area of activity) identifies the content of these experiences.

Pupils should be taught:

a to compose and control their movements by varying shape, size, direction, level, speed, tension, and continuity;

b a number of dance forms from different times and places, including some traditional dances of the British Isles;

c to express feelings, moods and ideas, to respond to music, and to create simple characters and narratives in response to a range of stimuli, through dance.

TEACHING DANCE AT KEY STAGE 2

The emphasis at this key stage is on consolidating and developing further the experiences that pupils have had at Key Stage 1. They still need opportunities to respond to a wide variety of stimuli, to structure these responses into simple dances with clear beginnings, middles and ends, and time to practise these so that they can be performed fluently and with confidence. In particular, there should be an increasing emphasis on the need for pupils to make very clear the connection between the movements being made and the stimulus which motivated them. As with all other aspects of the physical education curriculum it is important that the pupils are involved in the three processes of making decisions about what they are going to do, carrying out the actions and thinking about how successful they have been. Often one simple instruction embodies more than one activity; for example: 'Show me how a spider moves' requires a judgement about what a spider actually does, decision-making about what the body should do to achieve this and then carrying through the plan in performance.

The lesson plans

It would be inappropriate to isolate the requirements of the programme of study into discrete units. Any dance lesson requires stimulus for movement and attention to the the action, dynamic and spatial content; therefore each lesson contains work in which all of these come together. Two principles underlie the selection of content: firstly the need to develop understanding of the material out of which dances can be formed and secondly the need to make dances. Both are equally important and in practice this is merely a question of emphasis, at times on content itself, at others on its use to fulfil a particular purpose.

Therefore most lessons have two themes: the stimulus (expressive content) and the vocabulary (dance content). Whilst this is a totally artificially division it is felt to be helpful to the teacher. The stimuli for the lessons are representative of a range of different starting points from which dances can be made. They include: pictures, poetry, prose, events and objects. In addition, they take account of the need both to make links with the National Curriculum for art and for music and to include dances which arise from material relevant to the wide variety of cultural traditions present in today's society. Where music has been suggested from a particular source it is because these tapes provide, in addition to the given piece, many others useful for the dance teacher. The ideas presented are neither exhaustive nor definitive; many other starting points could equally well have been chosen. The important factor is whether the starting point is motivating for the pupils and also has potential for dance, i.e. action is an integral part of the idea.

In following the lessons these points should be kept in mind:

1 Pupils and teacher need the security of a clear movement framework.
2 In the early stages of learning, the action should always be accompanied by some audible rhythm.
3 Pupils need to have their attention drawn to what the movement is saying as well as to how it is being performed. This can be done in several ways, for example by using words such as 'creep' instead of 'walk', by giving illustrations such as 'like a feather' and by providing concrete images.
4 Sections should be repeated several (perhaps four) times without a pause, then pupils can be given advice followed by further repetition.
5 There is a need for balance between increasing the range of vocabulary pupils have to use and increasing their skill in using it.

All of the above have been assumed in writing the lesson plans, although in the model lesson they are made explicit.

Within a unit, material has been presented in groups of lessons; the amount of material included for each group of lessons is based upon the mythical average Key Stage 2 pupil, but any particular class of pupils may take a shorter or longer time to cover the same content. Within each group of lessons material has been arranged under three headings:

Introducing the theme
Developing theme and dance vocabulary
Developing the dance structure.

These are not lesson equivalents, and while it is necessary to do some sections of 'Introducing the theme' prior to embarking on 'Developing theme and dance vocabulary' it is by no means necessary to do all of them. Similarly, it is unlikely that there will be time to work through all the developmental ideas prior to 'Developing the dance structure'. It is important that pupils do finish a unit with a completed piece of dance, however small; to ensure this it may (and probably will) be necessary to omit sections en route. Teachers should choose parts from each of the three sections as is appropriate for the age, maturity and prior experience of their classes. The model lesson will illustrate this further. In all cases, the sequencing does assume knowledge of material included in previous lessons. Lessons are linked together where continuity of these is essential.

The units are supported by the Dance Activity Bank; this provides material which will help in implementing lesson content. Firstly it provides further details of the stimulus and accompaniment and secondly it provides additional information to assist the development of pupil learning either in respect of particular skills or in making the connection between movement and meaning.

The model lesson

The lesson chosen as the model has been selected because of the way in which it exemplifies aspects of good dance teaching. These aspects are neither definitive nor exhaustive, but should be considerations when planning all dance lessons.

The distinguishing feature of a dance lesson is the use of movement either to 'say' something or as a response to a particular stimulus. The main focus of this lesson is to help pupils look more closely at one section of a poem and then to explore its meanings through their movement. The teacher helps the pupils by drawing their attention to specific aspects of the poem, e.g. the ice and the way it cracks, growls, roars and howls. The provision of structured questions, e.g. 'What do these words mean?' 'What movements might you use to show them?', helps develop pupils' interpretive skills. On several occasions in the lesson pupils are asked what it feels like to move in different ways or how they might feel in certain circumstances, e.g. being surrounded by ice. These questions help pupils to make connections between the words of the poem and their own feelings and emotions; this lays the basis for interpreting the words in dance.

Use of accompaniment is an important feature of dance work. In the lesson, each time the pupils are asked to move, the teacher provides accompaniment on the tambourine; this should reflect the quality of the action that the children are trying to achieve. In providing this accompaniment the teacher is both giving a very clear structure to the movement, i.e. beginning, middle and end, and also employing a very good control mechanism, i.e. there is no doubt when pupils should be moving and being still. Appropriate patterns of behaviour are established within the dance convention of phrasing rather than having to be imposed from the outside.

In order that the responses pupils make have dance-like qualities, they always need to be encouraged to phrase the movement. At this stage of their experience they will need a lot of help in organising their ideas into appropriate phrase structure. The teacher can assist this by providing the outline, e.g. 'crack, crack, crack, growl'. This provides a clear sequence of actions which already includes contrast of quality. The tasks are capable of achievement at many different levels of ability; therefore all pupils are given the opportunity of success.

Once the pupils have begun to respond to the words they will need help to both extend and improve what they are doing. This can be done in several ways: firstly by reminding them of the possibilities open to them (e.g. 'Have you tried lying, sitting, kneeling?', secondly by isolating one part of the action (e.g. 'it crack'd'), thirdly by asking questions which require answers within the phrase (e.g. 'Are the links between movements smooth?'), fourthly by reminding them of the images which they are trying to interpret (e.g. 'Is the crack different from the growl?') and fifthly by using a good demonstration, drawing attention to important aspects of composition and performance.

In lessons where pupils are being asked to interpret an idea in their own way, decision-making is an important aspect of the lesson. Note the use of leading questions which require pupils to check their own response against the poem (e.g. 'Can I tell the difference between crack and growl?'). Only the pupil can decide whether they intended there to be a difference, but the teacher can help the pupil make that difference evident in the dance. Pupils have to choose all the way through the lesson, firstly what to do and secondly, out of all the possible ideas they have tried, those which make the best interpretation.

Evaluation is an important feature of all lessons. In this example, the whole lesson is about making judgements as to whether or not the movements that are being made are a real response to the poem. Pupils are asked to think about what the poem contains and to assess whether their movements are a good interpretation of it. They are asked to check their own movements for whether they meet expectations (e.g. 'Do roar and howl differ?'). Then they have to make judgements about what constitute the 'best' responses. Note that pupils' thinking and judgements are closely channelled by the nature of the questions asked.

The way the lesson material has been developed allows the pupils to warm up and to recap on last week's ideas, including reminders about safety, before the introduction of new material. As one of the main purposes of the lesson is to get pupils to provide their own dance interpretations, this section begins with the poem, asks pupils for ideas which might be translated into dance, and then gets them to show these ideas in movement. Further ideas are introduced only after pupils have made an initial response; the teacher builds from the pupils' material rather than giving movements as a starting point. The main section of the lesson involves the teacher in helping pupils to extend and improve their ideas. The lesson ends with a 'performance' of the phrase as far as it has progressed

and a cool down, preparing the pupils physically and mentally for the next lesson.

Do not forget the importance of cross-curricular links. In this lesson there is a very obvious link with English and others that might be made with Science and Geography. The starting point for the lesson is an extract from *The Rime of the Ancient Mariner* by Coleridge. While it is not the intention to deal with the complex literary and ethical issues raised by the poem, pupils should be able to appreciate the vivid nature imagery, the feelings of the sailors at the mercy of the elements and the enormity of the killing of the albatross. The images of a region dominated by ice could link with a study of countries which are ice-bound and the ways in which animals and people survive in such areas. Pupils might investigate how ice behaves under particular circumstances, and why 'crack', 'growl' and 'roar' might be appropriate words to describe ice. The whole process of the lesson links with the English AT1, Speaking and Listening. Pupils are required to talk about what they hear in the poem and how their movements fit with aspects of it. They need to listen carefully to what the teacher and other pupils say. Throughout the lesson they have to respond to increasingly complex instructions and questions from the teacher. In addition there are abundant opportunities for increasing vocabulary, both in order that pupils understand the tasks set and by encouraging them to use a wide range of words in their replies to questions.

One aspect of good practice not illustrated by this lesson is the inclusion of opportunities to see dances in the professional repertoire. This is often not easy, as videos are not always available and it is difficult to take pupils to see live performances. Where it is possible the impetus it brings to pupils' work is tremendous and such provision should be encouraged.

Model lesson: unit 1, lesson 2 ▷

Theme: *The Rime of the Ancient Mariner;* contrast in quality of movement

Purpose: PoS a, c

Activity bank: Activities 1, 2, 3, 4, 5, 11, 22

Resources: Poem: *The Rime of the Ancient Mariner* by Coleridge; tambourine/drum; music: sections from *Heaven and Hell* by Vangelis or music by Clannad; pictures of sailing ships, seascapes, icebergs, snowfields, albatross; art works, e.g. *Calais Pier: an English Packet Arriving* by Turner

Activity	Organisation	Teaching points
Introducing the theme Pupils warm up by practising some of the movements from previous lesson.		
Pupils start 'closed in' and spread like the fog, then swirl back in to close. Repeat four times without pause.	Pupils in their own space. Accompany with drum rhythm: 1 2 3 4 5 6 7 8 s p r e a d and swirl in	Feel the action getting larger and larger. Make the action go to the end of toes and fingers. Fill all the beats of the drum.

Activity	Organisation	Teaching points
Repeat the phrase, spreading into the space behind the body. Repeat four times without pause.	Repeat rhythm as above.	Try to make your movements fog-like; think what quality this needs and show me as you dance. Use different levels as you spread. Fill as much of the space as you can.
Get into a space of your own and show me the movements you did for the storm.	Check pupils do have enough space.	Remember to be careful as you land, feet down before you roll over. As soon as you go down think about having to get up again.
Practise all together: fall, roll over and rise again.	Accompany on drum: & 1 & 2 & 3 & 4 leap, land, roll over & rise	Make sure you curl up tight as you roll over, tuck your feet right underneath you so that you can rise up quickly, push up strongly through your hips, look up. Make sure you get up again on the beat.

Developing the theme and dance vocabulary

Activity	Organisation	Teaching points
Read the section of the poem about the ice.	Pupils sit down near teacher. Check that pupils understand the words used.	Ask who has seen icebergs? What did they look like? How did they move? How would you feel if you were in a land of ice?
Read again the line, 'It crack'd and growl'd, and roar'd and howl'd'.		Ask pupils what kind of movements these words suggest. Ask them to say how the movements they make could be different. What kind of sound might accompany the action?
In their own space, pupils show movements which might suggest 'It crack'd'.	Accompany with sharp rhythm: ~ ~~~~~~ ~ ~~~~~~ it crack'd it crack'd ~ ~~~~~~ ~ ~~~~~~ it crack'd and pause	Show me a starting position. Make your movements fit the rhythm. Can I see where the 'crack' happens? Is it the whole body or just part of the body that cracks? Can you make the action sharper? Have you tried kneeling, sitting, lying, standing?
One pupil demonstrates the phrase.	Continue to play rhythm.	What makes this example good? Are the cracking movements clear? Someone describe one of these.
All pupils practise their phrase.	Continue to play rhythm.	Make your 'cracks' as good as those in the demonstration.
Repeat the phrase four times more, adding a 'growl' instead of a pause.		Make the 'growl' very different from the 'crack'. Can I see the change?
Pupils show movements which are like 'roar'd and howl'd'.	Accompany with drum roll.	Make these movements very different from the 'crack' and 'growl' movements. Is the 'howl' the same as the 'roar'? Can you make them different?
Pupils try to say in words how they might make the actions different. They try to explain how the feeling of each might be different.	Pupils stand still in their own space.	Encourage use of wide vocabulary.
Pupils repeat the roaring and howling movements.		Remember how you said the actions would feel. Can I see this in your movement? Have you tried lying, sitting, kneeling and standing? Have you used all the space?

9

Activity	Organisation	Teaching points
Developing the dance structure		
In your group, make a short dance for the whole phrase: crack, crack, crack, growl, crack, crack, crack, growl, crack, crack, crack, growl, r o a r and h o w l.	Pupils get into threes, each group in its own space.	
Listen to the music for this section.	Pupils sit and listen to the music. Then allow them a short time to talk about what they might do.	Think about how your movements can match both the words and the music.
Show me the group starting position. When the music starts, show the 'crack, crack, crack, growl' phrase. Repeat it lots of times.	Put on music. Keep on returning music to the beginning of this section. Move round to each group in turn, and at the same time put some of the questions to the whole group.	Does it remind me of ice? Can I see it is cold? Are all the group members doing the same thing? Can I see the difference between 'crack' and 'growl'? Think about the shape the whole group makes. Are all the cracks the same size? Can I tell it is ice that is cracking? Have you tried out lots of different ideas?
Group chooses the movements that best say, 'crack, crack, crack, growl'.	Put on the music.	Check that you have used different levels and directions, that the 'cracking' movements are clear and sharp, that the whole group is working together and that there is a difference between 'crack' and 'growl'.
Listen to the music for 'roar and howl'. In your group show me how you will dance this phrase.	Play appropriate section of the music.	Think about how your movements could match both the words and the music. Can I see the difference from the first phrase? Are all the group members working together, or one after the other?
Pupils explore the possibility of each member of the group 'roaring' in turn.	Set a rhythm to keep all the pupils together.	Watch carefully until the one before you has just finished before you start. Is each one of you doing exactly the same movement? Do you all use the same speed, level, direction?
Groups choose their best ideas for 'roar and howl'. Practise to improve.	Put on music.	Make your shapes very clear. Check where one person's movements are in relation to others in the group.
Groups link together both phrases. Repeat several times.	Put on music.	Make the difference between the different movements clear. Make the transition smooth. Where is the most important part of each phrase?
Pupils perform the phrase all together for the last time this lesson.	Put on music.	Make your phrases as good as you can this time. Remember to stay still at the end until I say 'Relax'. Show me in dance, not in words, what the poem says.
Stretch out as far as you can. Gradually close up small, then rebound to the stretch.	Pupils stay where they are, but move a little away from each other.	Imagine you are being crushed. You try to resist it, but you are forced into a small shape. As you reach that very small shape, the pressure goes and your body stretches out again.
Repeat several times, gradually slowing down both crushing and spreading actions.	Pupils end standing very quietly.	

DANCE ACTIVITY BANK ▶

Activity 1: Safety

Spacing

It is always necessary to ensure that the pupils have enough space around them in which to move without contacting other pupils, unless this is the purpose of the lesson. They should from the very first lesson look around themselves and check that they are not too near other pupils. This is especially important when travelling from one place to another. Speed should be contained within limits compatible with safety. When the dance requires that children 'dash' away, this section should first be practised at slow speed with awareness of the spacing and then put into the dance context. Particular care needs to be taken when the pupils are being encouraged to travel backwards. They should look in the direction in which they are travelling.

Landing and falling to the ground

Falling is an exciting dance image for children, as for example in unit 3, lessons 1–3 where the dance requires that pupils leap into the air, fall to the ground and roll over to create the feeling of a storm. It is, however, also an action which requires great attention to the safety aspects, particularly at this age, otherwise pupils could very easily bang their heads. It is suggested that the pupils practise this skill in the following stages:

• ensure pupils can land safely on their feet
• land and then sit down carefully on the floor, as skill increases gradually decrease the gap between landing and sitting.
• from sitting, roll backwards and shake feet in the air (be sure to check children are rounding their backs); return to sitting.
• join the above together with a pause between each section and gradually decrease the length of the gap
• as pupils become proficient add the leap to the beginning of the phrase.

General warning

There are many actions which are performed in the dance context which would be very unsafe if performed outside the controlled conditions of the lesson, e.g. staging a fight or swinging in the manner of a mobile. It is important that on every such occasion pupils are reminded that they are on no account to practise the actions elsewhere.

Activity 2: Working for poise

From the very earliest stages pupils should be encouraged to work for good quality dance action. The following may help in achieving this; it should be an expectation, if not an achievement from the very first lesson.

In all the pupils' movement look for the things shown in the picture, i.e. the way the action goes all the way to the toes, the middle of the body is held firm, the head is looking at the hands and there is a lot of concentration.

This picture illustrates some more points that may help to improve the pupils' action. Look for the aliveness of the action right through to the fingertips, the way the head is in line with the body and the eyes are looking outwards, the way the tummy is held well braced, and the way the back leg is fully involved in the action. There is full concentration on the movement.

Activity 3: The phrase

This is a sequence of movement with a clear beginning, middle and end. In the early stages of developing an idea it is important that the action is accompanied by audible rhythm such as percussion or music.

Example from unit 1, lessons 1–3

Use the voice, or a drum, to indicate the rhythm below:
'wriggle and pounce,   wriggle and pounce,
 wriggle and wriggle and wriggle and pounce'.

It is helpful to make phrases around two or three action words, e.g. toss, punch, spin, whirl, creep, dart, explode, spring, freeze, hover. The choice of such words immediately helps pupils in three ways, with the action,

11

the quality and the feeling towards which they are working.

Activity 4: Extending the pupils' responses to the stimulus

Whatever task the pupils are working on, they need to have their attention drawn to the ways in which they can develop their ideas beyond those which they first thought of, and/or to make the movements they began with become more dance-like. They need to try out lots of ideas before they choose the one which is the best solution for the particular problem. The following suggestions may help pupils do this for any task, although there will be additions which will be very specific to any one given problem.

Pupils should be asked:

'Have you tried the action in lying, sitting, kneeling and standing positions?'

'Have you used different parts of the body? Have you used the whole body?'

'Have you used travel, turn, stillness, jumps and gestures?'

'Have you used changes of speed, of tension and of fluency?'

'Have you used different levels, directions and a variety of shapes?'

'Have you tried different beginnings and endings?'

'Have you thought of lots of different ideas about the item which was the stimulus for the dance?'

'Have you thought of lots of different ways you might have felt about or reacted to the stimulus?'

'Have you tried to show these in your dance?'

As the pupils are practising their dance the teacher should select that which is going to be most helpful at a particular moment for the particular pupils. It is most helpful to give the pupils just one or two things to think about at a time.

However, it is vitally important to note that whilst it is important that the teacher asks these questions of the pupils, (and eventually hopes they will ask them of themselves) it may not be appropriate that any one pupil includes all, or indeed any, of the above in the response they finally choose. It is possible that the most appropriate response is at one speed, at one level, uses just one body part and continues smoothly. What is essential is that this is a conscious decision to 'do it this way' and not merely the result of not knowing what alternatives there were.

Activity 5: Improving the pupils' responses to the stimulus

Whatever task the pupils are working on they need to be encouraged to improve the quality of both performance and composition. In performance they always need reminding to make sure that:

- the action goes right through to the ends of the limbs
- the tummy and buttock muscles are appropriately gripped
- the actions are controlled and rhythmic and spatial design is clear

- focus is where it is intended to be
- there are no extraneous movements, e.g. pushing hair back, pulling down vests
- actions are performed so that they capture the mood, feeling or idea of the stimulus.

In composition it is less easy to pre-specify points relevant to all situations but pupils will always need reminding that:

- the starting position must prepare them for that which follows
- the ending position should be held perfectly still for a little while after the end of the dance
- the movements they choose must relate very clearly to the stimulus (not all movements will be acceptable)
- some parts of the dance should be more important than others
- there need to be moments of contrast.

Activity 6: Poem: *Jump and Jiggle*

The following poem by Evelyn Beyer appears in the *Puffin Book of Funny Verse* compiled by Julia Watson:

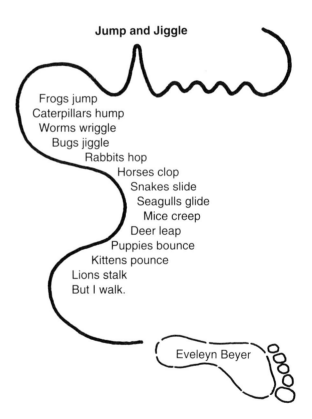

Jump and Jiggle

Frogs jump
Caterpillars hump
Worms wriggle
Bugs jiggle
Rabbits hop
Horses clop
Snakes slide
Seagulls glide
Mice creep
Deer leap
Puppies bounce
Kittens pounce
Lions stalk
But I walk.

Eveleyn Beyer

Pupils listen to the poem and talk about the animals it includes. For example, ask if have pupils seen these animals moving, either live or on television. How would they describe their actions? What words are used in the poem to describe the actions? Check pupils know what the words mean.

Activity 7: *Tales of Beatrix Potter* (Royal Ballet)

This video is available from most music and video shops. Pupils watch one section from the video, e.g. that of

Jeremy Fisher. After viewing it they could either describe or show in movement some of the important movements. Ask pupils to say why the movements were frog-like. Ask pupils what they thought was the best/worst part of the dance. Encourage them to say why they think this; in particular try to get them to give reasons which have their basis in the dance, e.g. 'His landings were light like the frogs I have seen in the garden', rather than 'I do not like frogs'.

Activity 8: Improving the stretch
Ask pupils to practise the movement shown opposite. Draw pupils attention to the need to:

- feel the stretch right through the middle
- pull out of the floor with the hips
- grip buttock and tummy muscles
- feel as if the body is being pulled in two directions at once
- make all the muscles work really hard, as if stretching a very strong piece of elastic.

Pupils should be encouraged to feel the difference between a very extended position and the release into a rounded position. Try to get them to imagine there is a strong piece of elastic attached between the extremities of the body and they have to stretch this to get into the extended shape.

For example, ask them to try these movements:

13

Activity 9: The vibrating exercise

8 counts	Cross arms across the body and vibrate hands on top of the arms as if very cold
8 counts	Drum feet on the floor
8 counts	Nod head very rapidly with very small actions
8 counts	Vibrate whole body as if a pneumatic drill

Activity 10: Rama and Sita

This dance draws particularly upon the following ideas from the traditional story:

Rama had been banished to the forest and his wife, Sita, insisted on accompanying him. In the forest they were searching for a safe place to stay. Ravenna (another king) also wanted Sita, and was determined to capture her. He knew that to do this he would have to use his magical powers. He sent a magnificent deer to dart through the forest so that it could be seen by Rama, who fell into the trap and pursued the deer, leaving Sita behind. Whilst he was gone, Ravenna captured Sita and made her a prisoner. Rama had lots of monkey friends who found out where Sita was being held and then helped him make an enormous bridge across the sea. A terrible battle followed which Rama eventually won because he had a special weapon. A great celebration was held to give thanks for the return of Sita.

Activity 11: Turning a story/poem into dance

It is rarely the case that a story or poem will be interpreted word for word in dance. Dance is not a good medium for conveying details of events, but is an excellent medium for communicating feelings associated with these events.

It is much more likely that some aspect/s is/are selected for the dance, e.g. particular images, sections or underlying themes. One way of approaching the task or turning words into the language of dance is outlined below.

- Identify the sections of the story you are going to use in the dance; give each section a name.
- How many of the class will be involved in each section? What formations will be used? For example, everyone scattered, circles, lots of little groups, lines, blocks.
- For each section, draw a plan showing the formation. Here is an example for travelling through the forest:

- Match each of the sections to a piece of the music. Use the number of bars or the numbers on the tape-recorder to identify sections. Time each section.
- Look carefully at the words of the story/poem. Are there any that immediately suggest movements, e.g. in the story of Rama and Sita the deer darts from one place to another, in *The Rime of the Ancient Mariner* the fog spreads. Choose a few of these to form the basis of the dance.
- For the words selected for each section, what kinds of movement will the pupils need to do? Think in terms of action and quality (energy, timing, use of body space or shape). Write these by the box for this section, e.g. running away section:

action – travel and stop, twisted body shape
quality – careful and searching
Use of space clear pathway, level and direction change.

- Decide how many lessons you think you want to spend.
- Decide how much you think you can do in each lesson. Remember to leave enough time to perform the dance lots of times at the end, and to talk with the pupils about how successful you all thought it was.
- Think up a warm-up that would be appropriate. This should prepare the pupil's bodies for movement and should give them the opportunity to practise some of the movement skills they will need later.
- Practice the accompaniment you will use for this dance.
- For each section, look at the kind of movement you have identified for the pupils to do. Think of ways in which you could introduce the pupils to this kind of movement. Remember you may want them to find their own way of moving within the framework. Make up some outline phrases (sequences) within which the pupils can use their own ideas.
- Decide how the sections will be joined together. How will you help the pupils to achieve this?
- Decide how you will help the pupils remember and perform the whole dance.
- Decide what form the performance will take, within the class (perhaps bringing other pupils or parents in to watch).
- Decide how the pupils can be best helped to evaluate their work.

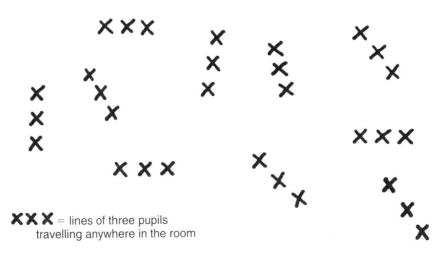

✗✗✗ = lines of three pupils
travelling anywhere in the room

Activity 12: Improving spikey and curved shapes

These diagrams show the features you should encourage pupils to aim for when making spikey or curved shapes.

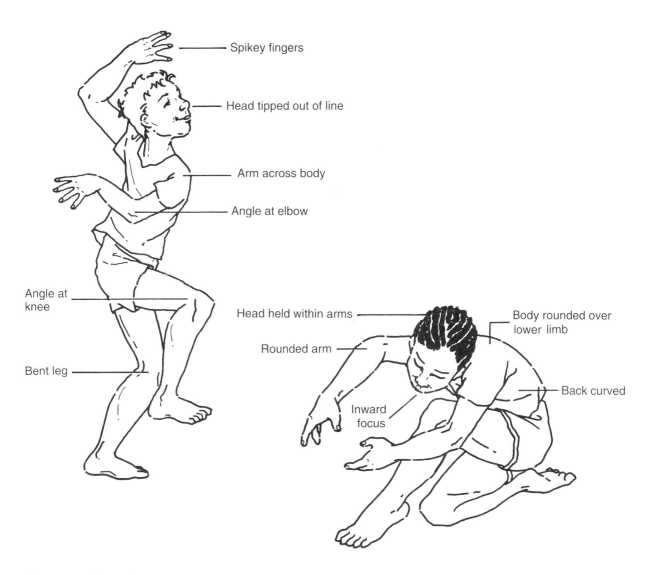

Activity 13: Pathway dance

The simplest structure for a pathway dance would be:

Section 1 Pupils start on their own in a space and dance to the first 12 bars of the music making angular and curving pathways of their own choice. The task could be further restricted by requiring that at some point they have to include an anticlockwise and a clockwise turn. At the end of this section they finish with a partner.

Section 2 With their partners, they make phrases based on the shapes of letters. Then one follows the other as they travel on curving or angular pathways to meet in fours.

Section 3 The fours choose some of the ideas on which they had worked before; they should include advance and retreat, going round the circle and making at least one angular and one curving shape. The group should work out a good ending for the dance.

Activity 14: Improving quality of movement in 'Ragtime for robbers' (unit 2, lessons 3–5)

For the 'dash', pupils should:

- look at the spot towards which they are travelling,
- get there as quickly as possible,
- use lots of little steps,
- keep the arms close to the body,
- go straight to the spot they are aiming for.

15

For the 'freeze', pupils should:

- grip all the body,
- push the feet hard into the floor,
- be like a statue,
- hold their breath,
- fix their eyes on one spot in the room,
- hold the tummy muscles tight.

For the 'spring as if startled', pupils should:

- bounce lightly off the floor,
- keep the eyes on the landing point,
- reach for the floor with the toes,
- bend the knees as they are landing,
- be ready to take off again.

For the 'creep', pupils should:

- place the feet or other parts of the body very carefully on the floor,
- grip the tummy muscles to keep balance,
- look where the foot is about to touch the floor,
- keep very quiet.

For the 'swerve', pupils should:

- lean the body as if going round an object,
- keep the action continuous,
- move smoothly and swiftly as if trying to escape,
- take small steps with feet.

Activity 15: Tudor context

The dance 'Lord of Misrule' is set in the context of Tudor England and is most likely to be successful when pupils are studying this period for their history curriculum.

There is little direct evidence for the style of dancing appropriate for England in the late sixteenth century, but it is known that the ability to dance well was a necessary accomplishment for the gentleman and his lady. The instructions for the given dances have been taken from: Arbeau, T. 1588, *Orchesographie*, Translation by Evans, M. S., edited by Sutton, J. (Dover, 1967). This is available from Dance Books, Cecil Court, London WC2N 4EZ. More detailed instructions for the given dances and some others plus a cassette of music to accompany the dances can be obtained from Mr I. Gatiss, Liverpool John Moores University, I. M. Marsh Campus, Barkhill Road, Liverpool L17 6BD. Further background to the period can be found in *Junior Education*, August 1993.

The Lord of Misrule was an important figure in the Christmas and New Year celebrations in Tudor and Stuart England. He presided over the events and often the occasion was used to mock authority. It was an opportunity for the less important, e.g. students at the Inns of Court, junior members of a household, to make fun of their superiors. The person who played this character was often chosen because of his prowess in dancing, and from the time he was appointed he could make other people do as he wished for the duration of the event. Dancing was an important feature of the celebrations and often special performances (masques) took place. These were usually designed to show off the power of the person who had commissioned them and dancing, both of performers and audience, was an integral part of their design.

Activity 16: Characteristics of, and steps for, Tudor dance

Conventions

Steps should always be smaller rather than larger; a good guide is the length of the dancer's foot. The body should be carried upright, but should not be rigid. The head should be well lifted and the back straight; the tendency to bend from the hips should be avoided. The knees should be kept fairly straight. The arms should be held by the sides; unless otherwise indicated, the arms do nothing. Combinations of steps normally begin on the left and are then repeated on the right. Floor patterns are usually symmetrical. The man tends to take a dominant role.

The reverence

The reverence was a very important action and was a form of official greeting; those of lesser importance would almost always have used this as a mark of respect for their superiors.

For the man: Step back smartly on the right foot, bending the knee. The left foot should stay in place with the leg straight. Remove the hat whilst stepping back. Continue the bend and bring the hat to the side of the thigh. Do not lower the head. Straighten the body and replace the hat whilst bringing the right foot back to its place beside the left.

For the lady: Start with the feet placed with the heels together and the toes about 90° apart (like a ballet first position). Slowly bend the knees, keeping the heels on the ground. Keep the body upright, but the eyes can be lowered somewhat. Slowly rise again.

Steps

Most of the dances require only two basic steps: the single and the double. Any sequence of these usually starts on the left foot. In addition, it is necessary to do the reverence, which was performed at the beginning and the end of the dance.

The single: This may be done forwards, backwards and sideways and basically consists of a step on one foot followed by the other foot joining it, e.g. step forwards on the left and then join with the right foot.

The double: This takes twice as long as the single; it may also be done in any direction. It basically consists of three walks and a joining of the feet on the fourth beat.

A second single or double would usually be performed on the other foot.

Galliard

Beat 1   hop on right foot, raising left foot smartly forwards

Beat 2   leap on to left foot, raising right foot smartly forwards

Beat 3   leap on to right foot, raising left foot smartly forwards

Beat 4   leap on to left foot, then spring up high from this one foot, with right leg swinging forward vigorously

Beat 5   in the air

Beat 6   land on two feet with right foot slightly behind left

Jumps (sauts)

These can be done straight or with turns; the body, however, should be kept upright and the landing should be controlled. Jumps would normally land on two feet but the take-off might be from one or two feet. They can also be done with capers or caprioles, this is when the legs are moved around one another whilst in the air.

Activity 17: 'Washerwomen's Branle'

The 'Washerwomen's Branle' ('Branle des Lavandieres', Arbeau, 1588) is mimed branle in which the clapping of the hands represents the beating of clothes by washerwomen beside the Seine. The dancers usually begin in a circle, facing inwards, men and women alternating. The lady on the right is the man's partner.

Perform four doubles sideways, beginning with the left foot to the left, then right, then left, then right again. End facing partner.

Perform two singles, first to the left and then to the right.

Repeat the singles.

During the first two singles the women put their hands on their hips and the men shake their fingers at them.

During the repeat men put their hands on their hips and the women shake their fingers at them.

Perform three doubles, beginning to the left with the left foot, then right, then left again. On the doubles to the left, dancers clap their hands.

Perform three little springs, kicking the free leg slightly in front and jump with the feet together. In doing these, each individual should turn through a full circle, turning anticlockwise.

Activity 18: Actions for coopers

Pupils could mime the action of a cooper as he uses his mallet to hammer the iron hoops into position round the staves (as shown). Other examples of actions to mime are trussing up a barrel or putting the boards or staves within a hoop.

Iron hoops which need to be hammered down to hold the wooden staves in position

Mallet for knocking the iron hoops into place

Activity 19: 'Lord of Misrule': dance structure

Any music of the Tudor Period could be used to accompany this dance. London Pro Music publish a good selection suitable for school use (available from 15 Rock Street, Brighton BN2 1NF). A cassette of music edited for this dance by Mr I. Gatiss can be obtained from him at Liverpool John Moores University, I. M. Marsh Campus, Barkhill Road, Liverpool L17 6BD.

The lengths of phrases given here are as on the cassette, but could easily be adjusted for other music.

Section 1: Entry

The music is repeated twice in total. During this time all the children make an entry into the dancing space, either singly or in small groups (some could enter before the others). They could choose their own steps, but should be discouraged from using a plain walk. They could use singles or doubles instead, or they could simply skip in time.

Each child could choose an occupation from Tudor times and they could mime some of the actions of their job, e.g. hoeing the field or sweeping the floor. This will require them to exercise judgement about the appropriateness of the kind of tasks they choose for the period. Looking at some of Breugel's paintings might well provide other ideas.

By the end of this section they should end up in small circles ready for Section 2.

Section 2: The mimed branle

This music is also repeated twice. It has two sections: A is eight bars long, B is four bars long.

The children begin in small groups in circles, like those that they used for the Washerwomens' Branle (see Activity 17).

In the A section of the music the children choose their own combinations of singles and doubles, going around the circle, and in the B section they make up a series of mimed actions that show the audience that they are coopers (see Activity 18 for ideas).

The dance is repeated twice.

Section 3: Competition

Repeat the music from Section 1.

The children dance out of the circles and practise their own sequences for the competition to choose the Lord of Misrule.

A possible structure for this would be to have a general practice for the first time through the music, when the children all show their best jumps and most fancy steps. They should be encouraged to maintain their period character and avoid the 'football dive'!

When the music is repeated, small groups could perform at a time and the Lord of Misrule can be selected.

Section 4: Procession

The music for this section should be slower, to allow the dancers to try to show the way the courtiers might have acknowledged their new Lord, but because this is misrule odd things can happen. The newly appointed Lord of Misrule could be crowned with a crown of feathers and given a carrot to carry, for example, and there is ample opportunity for mocking gestures from the crowd following.

In this section the other children should perform many 'reverences' to the Lord of Misrule.

The piece could end with a celebratory circle dance which everyone joins in.

Activity 20: Other ideas associated with Tudor Dance

Watch a video of dances as they might have been performed at the time, for example, *The Manner of Dauncying*, available from the Audio Visual Department, University of Leeds, Leeds LS2 9JT.

Watch some relevant TV programmes, for example *Timelines – Tudors and Stuarts* on Channel 4.

Learn to play the music for some of the dances. A collection of music is available from London Pro Music (see Activity 19 for address). Instructions/tape and sheet music (arranged for children) are available from Mr I. Gatiss, Liverpool John Moores University, I.M. Marsh Campus, Barkhill Road, Liverpool L17 6BD.

Look at some other English country dances. Videos are available from The Folk Shop, Cecil Sharp House, 2 Regents Park Road, London NW1 7AY. Instructions and music for the dances are also available from this source. Perhaps you could teach some other English country dances.

Use an English myth or folk tale as the basis of another dance, thus giving pupils a chance to respond to a different kind of stimulus.

Watch a local festival, for example at Helston, where they dance The Furry Dance. Find out something about the origins of the dance. Other areas of the country can provide some equally good examples.

Watch dances in the professional repertoire where folk dance patterns are used, e.g. section of *La Fille Mal Garde* (available from Dance Books, 9 Cecil Court, St Martins Lane, London WC2N 4EZ). Encourage pupils to identify the patterns they recognise and give them some background to the piece.

Activity 21: *The Rime of the Ancient Mariner*

The full text of the poem *The Rime of the Ancient Mariner* by Samuel Taylor Coleridge can be found in *The New Oxford Book of English Verse*, Gardner, H. (ed.), OUP, 1972. The following section was chosen for the dance:

'And now the storm blast came, and he
    Was tyrannous and strong;
He struck with his o'ertaking wings,
    And chas'd us south along.
With sloping masts and dripping prow,
As who pursued with yell and blow
Still treads the shadow of his foe,
    And forward bends his head,
The ship drove fast, loud roared the blast,
    And southward aye we fled.
And now there came both mist and snow,
    And it grew wondrous cold;
And ice, mast-high, came floating by,
    As green as emerald.
And through the drifts the snowy clifts
    Did send a dismal sheen;
Nor shapes of men nor beasts we ken –
    The ice was all between.

The ice was here, the ice was there,
    The ice was all around;
It crack'd and growl'd, and roar'd and howl'd,
    Like noises in a swound.
At length did cross an Albatross,
    Through the fog it came;
As if it had been a Christian soul,
    We hailed it in God's name.
It ate the food it ne'er had eat,
    And round and round it flew,
The ice did split with a thunder-fit;
    The helmsman steered us through.'
And a good south wind sprung up behind;
    The Albatross did follow,
And every day, for food or play,
    Came to the mariners' hollo!
In mist or cloud, on mast or shroud,
    It perched for vespers nine;
Whiles all the night, through fog-smoke white,
    Glimmered the white Moon-shine.
'God save thee, ancient Mariner,
    From the fiends, that plague thee thus! –
Why look'st thou so?' – 'With my cross-bow
    I shot the Albatross.'

Read this extract from the poem to the pupils and discuss with them the images it contains. Encourage them to try to imagine what it would be like to have been in this situation: how would they have felt and what would they have done? Ask them to select from the poem some words which might be useful as a starting point for the dance.

Activity 22: Body shape phrase

Link the following shapes (as shown in the diagrams below) together to form one continuous phrase: flat, twisted, rounded and narrow. Join the shapes together so that some of the transitions are much faster and more vigorous than others. Pupils could join the shapes together for themselves, but when they do this they often tend to choose to do movements already familiar to them or rely on less demanding combinations. By setting a prescribed manner of performance the teacher can encourage the pupils to learn a different vocabulary and is beginning to establish the bases for the kind of discipline they will need at Key Stage 3.

Activity 23: Transforming characters/animals into dance

Whenever pupils are required to make a dance phrase around any character (animal or imaginary person), the following questions will help them to transform the real thing into the actions and qualities of the dance.

What do they look like and how do they move?
Using the example of spiders and their webs ask the pupils to show you in their movement the answers to the following questions. *What do they look like? How are the limbs placed on the floor? How do the legs move? What is the body like? How are the limbs jointed? How do the legs move?*

What do they do?
Continuing with the above example, answers to this question might be 'Spiders crawl up the bath'; 'They spin webs'. Ask pupils what shapes webs are (e.g. tunnel, tube and sheet). You could point out that webs are attached to other things, e.g. walls, curtains and lights, and that other insects are caught in the webs. Spiders move very fast across the floor, up and down walls.

How do they make people feel?
You could point out that while many people are afraid of spiders, other people keep them as pets. Ask pupils how they feel about spiders.

Pupils then make short dance phrases which try to show the things that have been discussed through their movement.

Activity 24: Tarantulantics dance

Section 1
Some pupils start on the stage facing away from the audience. These pupils are stretched in spider-like

shapes and may move very slightly. Other pupils rush in from the sides of the dancing area using cartwheels and leaps. These pupils are also facing away from the audience and arrive behind those already on stage and take up spider shapes.

Section 2
Everyone stretches and closes three times. On the last stretch, all turn to face the audience.

Section 3
Some pupils from the back of the group leap forward and weave in and out of the others. A few more rush in and out with spider-like movements and a few more from the back advance and drop to the floor.

Section 4
All perform the spider fall phrase (see p. 33). Then one or two pupils begin to jump, first to one side and then the other, and everyone else joins in. At the end of this, everyone, except for one group, falls to the floor. The group still standing performs their travel phrase, at the end of which they hold a spider-like shape. Each group performs in turn. When all groups have danced their travel phrase, everyone spins wildly and suddenly stops, as if looking at a fly.

Section 5
Each group then makes its own web, after which there is the group action of looking into and out of the web.

Section 6
The class decides how the dance should end.

Activity 25: 'The Quest' 1: Introduction
The 'heroes' set out through the 'enchanted forest' to search for their 'trapped comrades' who are held prisoner by the four 'barriers' they have to overcome. Success in overcoming the last of these will release their comrades. Each group of 'heroes' has three means of overcoming the 'barriers', each of which may only be used once. These are: begging/pleading/negotiating,

power, or magic/clever tricks. Pupils should first of all establish the identity of, and give names to, the 'heroes', the 'barriers' and the 'enchanted forest'. They should establish what each looks like, how it moves and what it does (see Activity 23).

Activity 26: 'The Quest' 2: Chance categories
Each of the following words and drawings could be numbered and then pupils select a number which determines what they do, or alternatively the words and drawings could be copied onto cards and pupils select a card which tells them what to do. (You could add words of your own choice to each category.)

Body part	*Shape*
arms	long
shoulders	thick
hips	straight
legs	twisted
feet	round
whole body	symmetrical
head	asymmetrical

Action	*Space*
jump	forwards
spin	backwards
wave	sideways
pause	hip level
travel	low level
lie down	medium level
punch	
stride	*Quality*
hover	quick
whirl	slow
	flowing
	staccato
	sharp
	strong
	gentle

Pathway (as shown below)

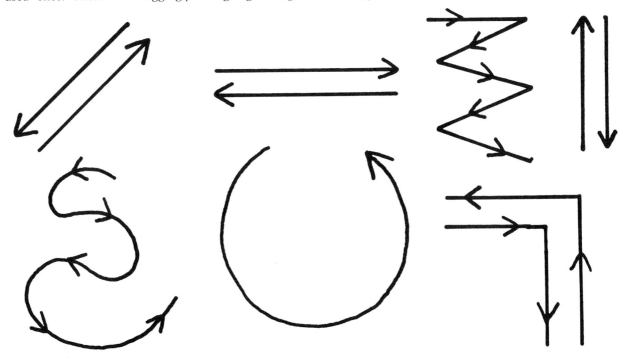

Activity 27: 'The Quest' 3: How to determine the order of events

There are three major points in this dance at which it is necessary to determine the order in which things happen. These are: the order in which the small groups confront the 'barrier', the order in which the 'barriers' appear, and the order of the phrases created by each group to overcome the 'barriers'. The decision-making could be undertaken by the teacher, or in consultation with the pupils, or by chance. In the latter case each 'barrier' and each group could be given a number and the order is then decided by, for example, throwing a dice.

Another method could be used to determine the order of the phrases used by each of the small groups to confront the 'barrier'. Pupils could be asked to judge which of the phrases any group has made has the best chance of being successful in overcoming the 'barrier'. The teacher guides the pupils' decision-making by providing appropriate criteria and by asking pupils to give reasons for their choice. Appropriate criteria might be: the precision of the movements, the way the different categories have been combined, or how convincing the performance is. In each case, pupils should be asked to explain what they say by refering to something that has happened in the movement they saw.

Activity 28: 'The Quest' 4: The 'barriers'

The 'barriers' need to be very clear shapes that provide obstacles to the travel of the 'heroes'. The shapes of the 'barriers' are made by groups of pupils. Pupils can take their own shape within the barrier, but once there they need to remain very still. Examples of 'barriers' are:

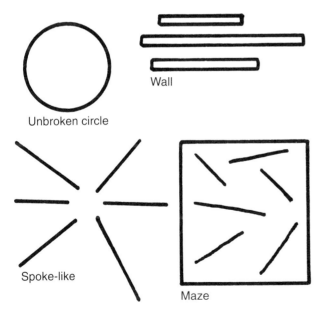

Unbroken circle

Wall

Spoke-like

Maze

Activity 29: Describing and interpreting the dance 'The Firebird'

A video of 'The Firebird' choreographed by Glen Tetley can be obtained from Dance Books, Cecil Court, London WC2N 4EZ. It is important to note that the pupils should not, at this stage, be asked to copy the movements of this dance. By showing them a work in the established dance repertoire they are helped to set their own work into the context of the public world of dance. There is a connection between the underlying theme of the pupils' dance and that of 'The Firebird'. The pupils could see the whole dance in one viewing or they could see the work one section at a time, like reading a chapter in a book. In either case, it is suggested that pupils view the work after making their own dance, because one of the aims of the lesson is to get pupils to respond to the category of movement they have chosen by chance, rather than to reproduce something they have seen.

It is helpful to focus pupils' attention by asking them specific questions, for example: 'What were the first movements the firebird made?' 'How did the story compare with your own?' 'What magic 'weapon' secured the release of the chief of the maidens?' 'Describe the part of the dance you found most exciting.' 'What happened in the movement to make it exciting?'

Activity 30: Carnival: the background

An excellent source book on carnival is *Festival Carnival* by Kerven, R., Commonwealth Institute and Macmillan Education, 1986. Further information, including a video entitled 'Caribbean Music Village', can be obtained from the Commonwealth Institute, Kensington High Street, London SW1Y 4PH. A film entitled 'Carnival' can be obtained from the High Commission of the Republic of Trinidad and Tobago, 42 Belgrave Square, London SW1X 4NT.

Carnival traditionally occurs on the Monday and Tuesday immediately preceding Lent; such events in this country now tend to happen during the summer but contain many similar features. One of the major aspects of carnival is the traditional parade of costumes accompanied by the music of steel drums and 'jumping up' or lively dancing. The most exciting element is the parade of bands (the Mas). Each band is accompanied by a large crowd of people from the neighbourhood where it is based. Each band adopts a theme and is elaborately costumed to suggest the theme; the nature of the costumes is a strictly guarded secret until Carnival day.

Whilst there are traditional Mas characters, modern themes most usually have a social or political message. There is a competition for the best band and for the best individuals in costume, usually referred to as 'kings' and 'queens'. Possible themes could be: Rain Forest, Flower Power, Rice Bowl of Asia, Outer Space, Noah's Ark, Save the Whale, Greenpeace, No Nuclear Fuel Here, Peace not War, or Glitter not Litter (the example used in this book and a theme used recently in the Trinidad Junior Carnival).

Activity 31: Carnival: procession and celebration

Pupils need to have a common step pattern for the procession and the dance ends with a section in which all pupils do very similar movements. These movements could be taken from the film of an actual carnival, could be taught by someone with some specialist knowledge of the Caribbean (there may well be a parent of a pupil in the school who has taken part in a Carnival celebration) or the class teacher can give the pupils some simple movements in the appropriate style. Any traditional calypso music could be used to accompany the dance.

The following movements are suggested for guidance only and should be modified to meet the needs of a particular class.

Procession

The basic movement is a walk with a slight bounce and a swagger of the hips. The feet should be kept fairly flat on the floor but not rigid and the knees should be resiliently bent. The whole body should move with the foot action.

Beats 1 2 3 and 4	Three steps forward beginning with right foot, a quick step on the ball of the left foot and transfer the weight on to the right again (this action is almost like a flat Scottish setting step and is referred to hereafter as 'ball change step'). As this is happening, both arms swing up above the head

Repeat all this, beginning on the other foot and bringing the arms back down to the sides.

Beat 1	One step forward on the right
and 2	'ball change step' left on to right
3	One step forward on the left
and 4	'ball change step' right on to left
Beats 1 2 3 4	Four steps, turning around in a small circle anticlockwise.

Repeat this pattern as often as is needed. The steps going forwards need to be bigger than those going backwards in order to progress. To cover more ground, all steps could be taken forwards.

This basic pattern could be broken by a series of four or eight skips which, whilst keeping the bounciness of a skip, do not lift high off the ground.

Celebration dance

This begins with the same step pattern as above, but with all the pupils facing the audience in one big group. The phrase should be repeated at least twice before any other elements are added.

The phrase can be extended in the following ways: take three steps to the right side and replace the 'ball change step' with two claps. Repeat this to the left side.

Perform pivot turns, keeping the rhythm of the music, on the spot anticlockwise or clockwise, with hands raised above the head.

Take four little jumps forwards with the stomach leading and hands held loosely by sides of the body. Retreat with eight tiny runs backwards.

These steps and any others that are appropriate could be performed in any order. The most important aspect of the dance is to capture the liveliness of the occasion yet retain a feeling of 'earthiness', the feet are never far from the ground although the feeling of bounce pervades the whole body.

Activity 32: Carnival dance structure

Throughout the dance, the teacher decides the amount of music to be used for each section. The dance as given below focuses on one theme only, i.e 'Glitter not litter'. It would be possible to present the dance with several 'bands' each with their own message and have the whole still linked by the parade part of the procession.

Glitter not litter

Section 1 All pupils process into the dancing area and continue to parade round the room, using the steps given in Activity 31.

Section 2 The litter 'kings' and 'queens' (a small group of five or six pupils) emerge. The rest of the pupils spin away into a space and hold a litter shape. The litter 'kings' and 'queens' perform the following phrase: three leaps and finish on the feet, bend low to the floor and roll over, first to the right then to the left, rise to the feet and spin around. This is repeated twice, then everyone else joins in with their own phrase of leap, roll and spin.

Section 1b Repeat the parade part of the procession.

Section 3 Perform the litter phrase in small groups. Groups are organised so that all the dancing space is used.

Section 1b Repeat the parade part of the procession.

Section 4 Work in pairs, as litter and sweeper. Pairs are organised so that the whole space is used.

Section 5 Perform the celebration dance (see Activity 31). It would be appropriate for the procession to be repeated and the pupils to use the given step pattern to lead off the dancing area.

Activity 33: Describing and interpreting the carnival dance

Pupils should watch a video of their own performance and be guided by the teacher to describe and interpret some aspects of it. They should look at their own performance of the step pattern for the procession and talk about how accurately they performed it. The teacher could ask questions, for example, 'Did you have the correct number of steps?', 'Were you in time with the music?' and 'Were you performing with conviction?'. They should look at the small group work for the litter, and answer questions such as 'Were all the sections present?' 'Was it possible to distinguish the different parts by the way the movement was done?' 'Were the movements litter-like?'. In each case, pupils should be encouraged to give reasons for their answers by referring to what actually happened in the movement.

Pupils should compare their own dance with the pictures, film or video they have seen of a real Carnival and assess how well they have captured the atmosphere of Carnival.

Activity 34: Other activities associated with carnival

Carnival is an excellent cross-curricular theme. Pupils could learn about the geography and culture of the Caribbean islands. As a topic, it provides a very positive image of the Caribbean culture yet also allows for the exploration of some of the issues which have adversely affected the development of African cultures.

Costume design and music are essential elements of the presentation. The making of costumes offers opportunities for creative design to enhance the messages. There is traditional music to listen to, calypsos to write and the excitement of the strong rhythmic beat to generate interest in playing an instrument.

The idea of the bands having a message allows for exploration of social, environmental and moral issues.

The book *Festival Carnival* (see p. 21 for details) includes many different activities in which to involve the pupils.

LESSON PLANS FOR YEARS 3 AND 4

Unit 1, lessons 1–3

Theme: *Jump and Jiggle,* combining action and quality

Purpose: PoS a, c

Activity bank: Activities 1, 2, 3, 4, 5, 6, 7

Resources: Tambourine; music: *Fossils* from *Carnival of the Animals* by Saint-Saens, poem: *Jump and Jiggle* by Evelyn Beyer, video: *Tales of Beatrix Potter* (Royal Ballet)

Introducing the theme:
Pupils practise different ways of hopping and jumping accompanied by drum played by teacher, e.g. a phrase of eight jumps from two feet to two feet on the spot followed by eight springs from one foot to the other travelling around the room. Pupils are encouraged to travel forwards, sideways and backwards. Repeat the whole phrase many times. Remind pupils about good take-offs and landings. Pupils practise hopping on one leg and then the other. Encourage pupils to change the position of their arms as they hop. Pupils talk about what kinds of creature hop, jump or spring. Encourage them to describe how the action takes place; for example, robins are very light and delicate in their movements, and frogs jump up suddenly and stop. Pupils choose one of these creatures and show in their movement both the action and the quality of the movement.

Pupils start by reaching high into the air and then glide down to settle on the floor without travelling. After settling briefly, pupils soar back up to standing. For example, a phrase of:

g l i d e down and settle, s o a r up and hold.
shake of tambourine ～～～～★   ～～～～～～～★

Encourage pupils to achieve smoothness of the glide, gentle landing in a definite shape and swift, even lifting upwards again. Repeat the whole phrase, including travel.

Pupils talk about what kinds of creature travel by gliding and sliding. Repeat the process given for hopping and jumping.

Pupils practise creeping and walking. Step in time to the drum beat; for example, a phrase of

1	2	3	4	5	6	7	8
creep,	creep,	creep,	creep,	run	away	and	pause

Encourage pupils to place feet very carefully on the floor, to be ready to stop at any moment and to look around as if uncertain of what might happen. Pupils explore the possibility of using other body parts on which to creep (e.g. hands and feet). Pupils talk about what kinds of creature travel by creeping and walking. Repeat the process given for hopping and jumping.

Developing theme and dance vocabulary:
Read the poem to the pupils and help them to talk about the different images it contains, e.g. check that they know what the creatures are, encourage them to talk about what they understand by such words as 'pounce' and 'stalk', get them to show in movement what these words might look like, ask pupils what it feels like to wiggle or to stalk and then help them to show the difference in their movement. Where possible, pupils should watch some suitable creatures in action, either live or on video. Pupils could watch a section of *Tales of Beatrix Potter* and observe the ways in which the animals' actions have been interpreted in dance.

Pupils choose one idea for the whole class to interpret in their movement. Guide the development into a phrase

(e.g. 'kittens pounce'). Give drum accompaniment for: wriggle and a pounce, wriggle and a pounce, wriggle and a pounce and pounce and pounce. Pupils explore different body parts on which wriggle can be made, possible directions for pounces and making pounces of different sizes. While they are doing this, help pupils to land resiliently and take off energetically, remind them to focus clearly on the spot towards which they are pouncing and help them to achieve the difference in quality between wriggle and pounce. Pupils choose their best ideas and repeat these many times. Remind them of how to make them better. The above should be repeated with all the pupils for at least one contrasting activity (e.g. 'bugs jiggle').

Developing the dance structure
Pupils listen to the music, identify the repeated section and the two other sections. In twos, pupils listen to the first section of the music and choose sections from the poem that fit the music. One section will have to be repeated three times; make this the most important part of the dance. In their twos, pupils work on each section in turn, showing a clear starting position, choosing move-

ments appropriate for the image and being encouraged to repeat these as accurately as possible and to end each section clearly. Help pupils to make links between sections and to make the quality of the movement in each section different from the others. Remind them to be really still at the end of the phrase. Half the class watches the other half. Those watching try to decide which creatures those dancing have chosen.

Unit 1, lessons 4–6

Theme: Elastic; combining action and quality

Purpose: PoS a, c

Activity bank: Activities 1, 2, 3, 4, 5, 7, 8, 9

Resources: Tambourine; piece of elastic

Introducing the theme:

Show pupils a piece of elastic being stretched and recoiling. Encourage pupils to talk about what happens, especially the changes of tension and timing. Pupils take up a starting position from which they can stretch. On given accompaniment, e.g. tambourine, they stretch as far as they can, continuing throughout the sound; then to a given sharp sound they curl up again. Repeat several times. Repeat, making vocal sound to accompany; ensure sound and action match. Pupils practise to improve the stretching action by learning a stretching exercise (e.g. Activity 8).

Pupils watch elastic vibrate. Encourage pupils to talk about what happens. Pupils take a starting position from which they can vibrate. Start with hands, then use other parts of the body including middles and hips. Give accompaniment. Repeat several times, with pupils making their own vocal sounds. Pupils practise to improve the vibrating action by learning a vibrating exercise (e.g. Activity 9).

Developing theme and dance vocabulary:

Pupils practise the stretching idea. Repeat this many times from standing, lying, sitting and kneeling. Work especially on balancing on one leg. The stretching should be started with different body parts and go in different directions. The recoil can cause the trunk to curl over forwards, sideways and backwards. Remind pupils to make the action go to the ends of the toes and the fingers.

Pupils watch what happens when, having been stretched, the elastic is released altogether. Pupils show this in their movement. Encourage them to get the feeling of explosiveness in the action. Pupils accompany the action with their own sound.

Pupils practise the vibrating action: using just one body part, using the whole body, with the limbs near the body and far away, slow or fast, gentle or vigorous, changing the size during the vibration. Pupils accompany the action with their own sound.

In twos or threes, pupils start close together and one pupil moves first to pull the others into a line like a stretched piece of elastic. The pupil at the other end has to remain still as if being held. Recoil like a piece of elastic. Remind pupils to think about the shape made when recoil is complete. Repeat many times, changing the leader. Remind pupils to make the action like the elastic. Pupils accompany with vocal sound. Make the sound match the movement.

In twos or threes, pupils stand near each other in a line. The first pupil starts to vibrate, the next is 'infected' and then the last until the whole line is shaking. Start very gently and get more vigorous as the other pupils join in. Ask pupils to decide how they will make the vibration stop. Pupils accompany with vocal sound. Make the sound match the movement.

Developing the dance structure:

Here is one suggestion for organising the whole class dance: first the whole class stretches so that it looks like one piece of elastic. Then two or three small groups perform their own small dances at the same time. Repeat until all have shown their dance. After this the whole class stretches and recoils together. Pupils accompany with own sound. Pupils practise stretching for the opening phrase, using recoiling action to split into small groups.

Pupils compose their own dance in twos or threes. This must involve (in any order) stretch, vibrate and recoil. Help pupils to perform these better and advise on how

to make the transitions smooth. Together with pupils, decide on the order in which these should be performed. Ask pupils what those who are not the main performers should do (e.g. take a stretched or recoiled shape and hold). After last group has performed, all pupils stretch together and make one last recoil. Repeat many times, making vocal sound match movement. Remind pupils to make some of the stretches more important than others and to be still when not dancing.

Half the class watches the other half dance. Those watching identify those who had really good stretches, who were still when not dancing and who kept their concentration all the way through the dance.

Unit 1, lessons 7–9

Theme: 'Miraculous mobile'; making movements which capture shape and mood

Purpose: PoS a, c

Activity bank: Activities 1, 2, 3, 4, 5

Resources: Variety of percussion instruments; painting *Harlequins Carnival* by Joan Miro

Introducing the theme:
Show the picture to the pupils. Ask pupils questions to help them 'see' the detail in the painting, e.g. 'Tell me about one creature. What does it look like? What is it doing? If you were that creature how might you feel? Can you see a sad creature? Describe it. Describe a creature very different from this one. How does it differ? What other kinds of things can you see in the painting?'

Pupils choose one creature and make a shape that is like it. Repeat, varying body part, direction or level. Pupils explore many ways in which their creature could move on the spot, e.g. it shakes, wriggles, rises and falls, twists and turns, surges and soars, flies. Ask pupils what it feels like to move in these ways. What moods could these movements suggest? Give action phrase and accompaniment on percussion, for example:

surge & pause, surge & pause, travel with turns, be still
    & 1 &2 **&3** &4 **&5 &6 &7 &8**
drum beats ★★   ★★   ★★★★★★★★

Alternatively, pupils choose one starting position. To the given rhythm they gradually fold up and then recoil to the original shape.

Pupils decide how their creature might move. It must have a starting and finishing position and quick and slow movements. Ask questions while the pupils are working, e.g. 'Does your creature have a change of level and direction? Does it move strongly, gently, smoothly or jaggedly? What kinds of mood is it in? How can I tell?'. Pupils look again at the picture so they can relate their own work to what they see.

Pupils choose the phrase which best captures the feeling initiated by their their creature and practise it many times. They could begin to make vocal sound to accompany their movements. In twos, one pupils watches the other. Ask those who are observing to see if they can guess what the creature is and to say how the performance tells them this.

Developing theme and dance vocabulary:
Pupils looks at some mobiles. Ask questions about how the hanging objects can move (e.g. swing, sway, turn around). Pupils could make their own giant mobile. Pupils take a starting position that is like one creature, but a different one to the creature used before. Show in the starting position the effect of hanging as in a mobile. Give rhythmic accompaniment for pupils to perform the action phrase: swing and swing and turn around. Encourage pupils to keep the action flowing, to make the swings gradually bigger and to maintain the shape and feel of their creature. Actions can be performed with single body parts or the whole body.

Pupils find 'eyes' in the painting, take the shape of the creature with the eye and explore different ways of looking: high, low, towards the back, underneath one body part, quickly, slowly, dartingly. Accompany with rhythm. Pupils explore the possibility of 'eyes' on

elbows, knees, shoulders, backsides, stomachs etc. Pupils use the creature phrase they developed previously and add to it 'eyes' on a particular body part. Remind pupils to keep to the rhythm and to decide where the eyes should focus.

Pupils work on making sounds which match their movements. Ask pupils to choose one creature in the painting and together make an appropriate sound. Pupils explore different sounds for the same creature. Pupils are encouraged in all their actions to make sound which matches their movement.

Pupils look again at the painting, select a creature which might be doing something and then show that action in their movement. Accompany with rhythm. Encourage pupils to think about how the action could be done differently (e.g. on the spot, travelling or as if on a mobile). What other things might the creature do?

Developing the dance structure:
Discuss with pupils how they could make a dance from the painting, and/or select some of the best ideas explored previously. Agree a dance structure with pupils, e.g. everyone looks round, this section ends by focusing in stillness on the 'sad creature', a few pupils in turn (starting with the 'sad creature') show their creatures, then everyone joins in to make one large mobile.

Help pupils to select and refine the movements for each section in turn.

Section one, the 'looking' section: pupils choose the

creature they like best, select a starting position to convey it and decide which body part the 'eye' will be on. Pupils develop their own 'looking' phrase between two stillnesses in the same shape. They accompany the phrase with their own vocal sound. Help pupils refine their work by checking that they have quicker and slower movements, changes of supporting body part, 'looks' which go behind the body, up into the air, down to the ground. Give one teaching point on each series of repeats, as pupils perform their phrase many times. This section ends by all pupils focusing on those who have chosen to move like the 'sad creature'.

Section two, a few pupils working in turn: pupils develop phrases and accompaniment for their own choice of creature. Set the structure for these, e.g. move on the spot, travel, do something the creature might do and hold. Help pupils refine the phrase by asking questions, e.g. 'Are you using lots of different body parts? Are you using changes of speed, direction and level? Can I tell what your creature is doing? Could your quick movements be quicker, the slow one slower? Are the links between actions smooth? Can you repeat the phrase exactly?'. Pupils perform their phrases four or five at a time.

Section three, making the mobile: pupils all do the swinging phrase learned previously and accompany themselves with vocal sound. Start the movements very slowly and smoothly and gradually increase the energy until everyone's actions are as big as they can be. Pupils decide with the teacher how the dance should end. Practise this.

Pupils practise the whole dance with sound many times. Give one point to think about on each repeat. Half the class performs for the other half. Observers try to match performers' actions with creatures in the painting and identify pupils who show interesting phrases.

Unit 1, lessons 10–12

Theme: 'Rama and Sita'; making phrases to interpret a story in movement

Purpose: PoS a, c

Activity bank: Activities, 1, 2, 3, 4, 5, 10, 11

Resources: Tambourine, cymbal, music: extracts from Race Apart, New Asian Dance Theatre, 198 Albert Road, Teddington, Middlesex TW11 0BD; available by ringing 0181 969 9488.

Introducing the theme:
Read the story to the pupils (see Activity 10). Talk with them about the different parts of the story and how these could be turned into movement. Agree with the pupils the ideas to be used. Provide opportunities for the pupils to suggest movements which might be appropriate, and encourage them to talk about actions, quality and spatial orientation. Listen to the music and ask the pupils which sections might be used for which parts of the story.

Developing theme and dance vocabulary:
Pupils practise different ways of travelling. Encourage change of level and direction. Ask pupils what they might have to do if they were like Rama and Sita travelling through a forest, e.g. go round fallen trees, stoop under branches or climb over obstacles. Pupils repeat travelling, including some of these ideas. Ask pupils what they would need to do if they were looking for a safe place to hide, e.g. travel as if frightened, pause and look around as they stand still. Accompany phrase with tambourine, e.g. travel, travel, travel and p a u s e. Repeat this phrase many times. Ask the pupils what it would feel like to be Rama and Sita travelling in the forest. Repeat the phrase, trying to show this feeling in their movement.

Pupils explore some movements which could be used for the section where Rama chases the magic deer, e.g. darting from one place to another, running swiftly with rapid changes of direction, twisting and turning at speed. Ask pupils to imagine what it might feel like if they were trying to escape. What kinds of things might they do to avoid capture? Repeat the phrase, trying to include some of the ideas. Accompany with tambourine, e.g. a long rapid shake and single beat for a pause.

travel   pause   travel   pause   travel   pause

Repeat the phrase many times. On each group of repeats remind pupils to change direction and level, and to look around when they pause.

Pupils explore ideas which might be used to show the capture of Sita, e.g. at the sound of the cymbal each pupil becomes trapped in an individual magic net. Encourage them to push against the netting with different body parts, to try to escape from underneath or to try to climb out of the top. Start fairly slowly and gradually become more frantic in the struggle to escape.

On their own, pupils try out some ideas for interpreting the fight between Rama and Ravenna. Pupils practise leaping into the air and landing with feet wide apart and knees bent. Accompany with rhythm: and leap, and leap, and leap, pause. On landing, tense legs, push feet into the floor, make a fist with the hands, look fierce. Pupils practise punching into space. Remind them to keep in their own space. Give the rhythm: and punch, and punch, and punch, and punch. Encourage pupils to use different directions and levels in space, and to punch with different body parts. Make the actions short, sharp and jabbing. Look in the direction of the punch. Pupils practise fighting actions in slow motion. Remind pupils to keep the actions clear and to perform them so slowly that it looks as if they are hardly moving.

Developing the dance structure:
Pupils work through each section of the dance in turn. Encourage them to be very still at the beginning and end of the phrases. For each section of the dance, pupils should be led through the following process:

Pupils repeat some of the exploratory work undertaken earlier. Pupils choose the movements which best fit the idea. Pupils check that the movements they have chosen have appropriate variety of direction, level and quality, and that they have used different body parts. Pupils

practise these phrases so that they can be repeated, with actions fitting the rhythm and the pupils conveying the appropriate feeling.

Help pupils to link the sections together and thus to remember longer and more complex sequences. Prompt the action by use of words or percussion. Pupils then perform the dance several times. Pupils talk about the dance, describing some parts, discussing what it felt lie, and making suggestions for improvement.

Unit 2, lessons 1–2

Theme: Pathway, level and direction

Purpose: PoS a, c

Activity bank: Activities 1, 2, 3, 4, 5, 13

Resources: Drum, tambourine; music: *March of the Mods*

Introducing the theme:
Pupils learn the basic steps and floor patterns.

Pupils march on the spot to the drum beat for 8 counts, then are still for 8 counts. Repeat many times. Pupils advance for 8 counts, then retreat for 8 counts. Pupils practise travelling sideways, e.g. by galloping or stepping to the side. Make sure they remain facing to the front. Pupils march, making a box shape on the floor. The end should be exactly where the action started, e.g. march forward for 8 counts, to the right for 8 counts, backwards for 8 counts, to the left for 8 counts. Repeat, but marching forwards all the way

round the box. Repeat marching sideways and backwards. Pupils draw a big zig-zag in the air, then make the same shape as they march around the room. They make a very sharp movement every time there is a change of direction. Pupils skip around the room using curving pathways, loops and circles, accompanied by a skipping rhythm on the drum. Pupils face the teacher and walk around in a small circle anticlockwise, then clockwise. Repeat, skipping.

Pupils choose some of these ideas and perform them to the music.

Developing theme and dance vocabulary:
Pupils use the shapes and pathways practised above in new situations. All the following examples should be accompanied by either drum or music.

Pupils trace in the air the first letter of their name. Repeat this several times, placing the letter to the side of and behind the body, using different body parts to trace the action, supporting the body on different body parts and changing level and direction. Give one teaching point on each group of repeats. Pupils choose another letter with a contrasting shape and repeat the above.

Working in pairs, pupils choose a three-letter word. One traces the first letter while the other stands still. They exchange roles for the second letter, then make the third letter together. Explore many different ways of tracing the letters. Add turns, jumps and pauses. Choose the best ways and repeat many times. Ask pupils whether they have jumps, turns, changes of direction and level and whether they have used different body parts.

In pairs, pupils advance forward for 8 counts, then divide away from each other, taking a further 8 counts to return to meet where they started. Ask pupils whether the turn was clockwise or anticlockwise.

Pupils join hands in fours in a line with a leader at one end. The leader travels carefully around the room making curving or angular pathways, with the others following, like thread in a needle. Change leader and repeat. The leader takes the line into a spiral and out again. The leader takes the line into a space, then the first two pupils make an arch and the others pass underneath.

Pupils in groups of four travel anticlockwise and clockwise round a circle, using different levels and directions. Advance and meet in the centre of the circle, part and retreat. Pupils in groups of four explore other patterns they could make.

Developing the dance structure:
Pupils dance to the music *March of the Mods*.

Work through each section of the dance in turn; pupils should choose some of the best ideas from the work previously explored. For each section, pupils should

select ideas appropriate to the task and then practise these to clarify the action and check that they have the required variations in pathway, shape, level and direction. Each section should be repeated many times to the music.

Unit 2, lessons 3–5

Theme: 'Ragtime for robbers'; combining pathway and quality

Purpose: PoS a, c

Activity bank: Activities 1, 2, 3, 4, 5, 13, 14

Resources: Drum, tambourine; music: *Stoptime Rag* by Scott Joplin; one copy of Workcard 1 (see p. 38) per pupil

Introducing the theme:
Pupils look at the floorplan (Workcard 1) and talk about the patterns shown on it. Encourage wide use of vocabulary. Pupils walk each section of the pattern in turn. Discuss how these pathways might be used in dance about robbers escaping. Ask pupils to suggest words which might capture some of the feelings of the robbers as they travel along the pathway. Ask pupils to suggest the kinds of places robbers might be in if they were travelling along such pathways as these.

Developing theme and dance vocabulary:
Pupils explore vocabulary appropriate for the theme.

Pupils focus on another place in the room, dash as quickly as possible to it and freeze on arrival. The teacher gives drum accompaniment. Repeat many times. Pupils change direction of travel, distance covered, shape and level of the freeze. Ask pupils to describe what it feels like when dashing and when freezing. Repeat without accompaniment, so that pupils can vary the length of time they dash and/or freeze.

Pupils swirl around the room as if avoiding objects which are close together (e.g. as in slalom) or further apart. Give accompaniment to phrase the action, e.g. by shaking a tambourine and varying the length of time between stops. Ask pupils what other ways they might have to avoid objects. Ask them to show these ways as they travel. Practise many times, asking pupils to keep continuity, repeat the pathway exactly and make the action clear.

Pupils take slow careful steps as if very unsure of where they are going, while the teacher accompanies with the drum, e.g.

1	2	3	4	5	6	**7**	**8**
							very loud
step	step	step	step	step	step	?	?

Ask pupils what they might do on the loud beats. Ask them to show this in their movement. Practise many times, asking pupils to place their feet very carefully on the ground, to make the rest of the body help them keep balanced and to ensure they are looking where they are going.

Pupils learn to jump from two feet to one, and then from one foot to two. Accompany giving rhythm, e.g. six jumps and stop. Practise many times, asking pupils to make landings light and controlled.

Developing the dance structure:
Pupils make a dance (as an individual, in twos or as a small group) based on the given floor plan. Ask pupils to recall some of the ideas they talked about in relation to the floor plan and to suggest movements they might use for these ideas. Firstly, for each section of the dance pupils should explore a variety of ways of showing, in movement, the given idea. Secondly, pupils should choose the ways that best convey the idea. Thirdly, they should practise these so that action, quality and pathways become clearer. In particular, make sure there is a good ending. Practise each section and the whole dance with the music.

Pupils perform the dance several times. Half the class observes the other half perform. Ask observers to describe the pathways used, to say how the actions differed from section to section, to say which parts they liked best and to say whether there was a good ending.

Unit 2, lessons 6–12

Theme: 'Lord of Misrule'; a dance in the style of Tudor England

Purpose: PoS a, b, c

Activity bank: Activities 1, 2, 3, 4, 5, 15, 16, 16, 17, 19, 20

Resource: video: *The Manner of Dauncying* (see Activity 19) pictures and stories about Tudor England (see Activities 15 and 20)

Introducing the theme:
Pupils learn the posture, and some steps and patterns, characteristic of dance in Tudor England.

'Washerwomen's Branle':
Standing in a circle, pupils learn the double step sideways (see Activity 16 for details of the dance steps).

Practise with the music (A). Ask pupils how they would have to stand if they were wearing Tudor clothes. Repeat the steps, stressing upright posture. Pupils learn the single steps facing the partner. Practise with the music (B). Link (A) and (B). Pupils add the last three double steps and learn the spring step, all facing the centre of the circle (C). Repeat the spring step, with pupils turning around anticlockwise. Practise with the music.

Perform whole dance twice through with the music (see Activity 17). Repeat many times. Each time, the teacher provides one more point to think about, stressing the need for correct posture and accurate timing.

Pupils learn the reverence (see Activity 16). Perform the whole dance with a reverence at the beginning and the end.

'Galliard':
Pupils jump four times on the spot, counting 1, 2, 3, 4, then stand still for 5, 6. Make the rhythm very precise. Practise with the music. Repeat, but instead of standing still do one more large jump, landing on beat 6:

1	2	3	4	5	6
jump	jump	jump	large jump	in the air	land

Repeat the first exercise, replacing the first four jumps with springs from one foot to the other:

1	2	3	4	5	6
spring	spring	spring	spring	stand still	

Pupils stand on one leg with the other leg raised slightly in front, spring into the air and land on two feet. Now include this as the large spring on the fourth beat:

1	2	3	4	5	6
spring	spring	spring	large spring	in the air	land on two feet

This last sequence forms the galliard step (see Activity 16). Make sure pupils understand that this whole sequence of six beats is just one galliard step.

Pupils practise performing one galliard step and then standing still for the equivalent of one step.

Pupils work in pairs; one of the pair performs four galliard steps while the other observes and helps the performer to do the steps better. Repeat changing roles.

Practise the following sequence with the music: both pupils perform a reverence; pupil A does four galliard steps; pupil B does four galliard steps; both pupils perform a reverence.

The Tudor context:
Pupils learn about what it might have been like to have been alive in Tudor England, e.g. by visiting an historic house or a 'living history' event, watching a video or looking at pictures of life at the time (see Activities 15 and 20 for more ideas). Ask pupils what the people wore and how they stood and walked. Had they seen any of the steps they had learned? Ask pupils about the ways in which Tudor people moved/behaved/danced that were different from present-day equivalents. Could they suggest reasons for the differences? Ask pupils what it might have been like to have been a lord or lady of a manor or a peasant working in the fields. Ask pupils to show these differences in the way they stand and walk.

Developing theme and dance vocabulary:
Pupils use the material already learned to make up their own dances.

Pupils discuss work that might have been done in Tudor England, e.g. haymaking, sweeping, barrel making. Pupils, with direction from the teacher, mime some of the actions used in these tasks.

Pupils work in groups of six to make their own mimed branle. The group chooses any one work action. Repeat three times and be still for the equivalent of the fourth. Repeat using a different work action. Practise so that the action can be recognised, use the whole body and keep to the beat. Practise with the music and provide one point to think about on each repeat. Pupils listen to the music and identify the two sections. Pupils use their own mimed action for Section B, and practise with the music. Watch groups in turn, and other pupils try to identify what tasks are being mimed. Pupils make suggestions as to how this part of the dance could be improved. All groups practise many times with the music. Add Section A of the branle: this is eight doubles. Variations could be made by more able groups.

Galliard competition:
Pupils practise the basic galliard step. Ask pupils what is important about the actions.

Pupils learn some variations on the basic step, e.g. hopping one one leg and swinging the other forwards and backwards near the ground. Teacher reminds pupils that there must be only four swings followed by the last jump to land on beat six:

1	2	3	4	5	6
hop	hop	hop	hop	in the air	land on two feet

Pupils choose their best variation and practise to improve posture and timing

Pupils practise turning while jumping: starting from two feet, take off and turn in the air before landing on two feet. Add this to the end of the galliard sequence. Remind pupils that in order to perform the turn safely they need to take off from two feet on beat four. Ask pupils what else they need to do to ensure that they land safely on their feet. Pupils perform their chosen variation four times, and on the fourth time only they add a turn to the final jump. Pupils work in pairs. One observes the other and gives advice on improvement. Together they decide how well each has done.

Developing the dance structure:

For the entry, pupil start off-stage in the small groups used for their branle and dance into the hall using a very clear pathway, finishing in a circle in their small group. Ask pupils what it would feel like if they were going to a celebration and ask them to make their actions show this. Practise many times with the music so that pupils clarify pathway, posture, timing and mood.

Pupils practise their own mimed branle. Ask pupils to make the link between the entry and the branle very clear. Remind pupils about points to improve (one or two points only for each repetition). Practise from the entry into the branle many times with the music.

Using basic galliard steps, pupils dance out of the circle making a very clear pathway to finish in a space of their own. Small groups in turn perform their competition galliard variation. Ask pupils what might make a winning entry. Practise the link between the end of the branle and the galliard competition.

The Lord of Misrule is elected. Practise the dance several times from the entry to this point. Add the last section. Ask pupils to show in their movements some

difference between the entry and this final procession. Practise to improve posture, timing and pathway. Practise the whole dance many times from the beginning, concentrating on smooth links between sections.

Pupils perform the dance, preferably with some appropriate dress, and have the opportunity to observe other pupils dancing. Half the class could watch the other half, or, if a video camera is available, the whole class could watch a video of themselves.

Ask pupils to talk about, for example:

what it felt like to move in ways different from those of today,

similarities and differences between people's behaviour then and now,

which parts of the body they used in the mimed branle actions,

whether the actions were quick or slow, strong or gentle.

which parts of the dance still need improving, and how might this be done.

LESSON PLANS FOR YEARS 5 AND 6

Unit 3, lessons 1–3

Theme: Rime of the Ancient Mariner; contrast in quality of movement; making some parts more important that others	*Resources:* Poem: *The Rime of the Ancient Mariner* by Coleridge; tambourine/drum; music: sections from *Heaven and Hell* by Vangelis or music by Clannad; pictures of sailing ships, seascapes, icebergs, snowfields, albatross; art works, e.g. *Calais Pier: an English Packet Arriving* by Turner
Purpose: PoS a, c e2	
Activity bank: Activities 1, 2, 3, 4, 5, 11, 12, 21	

Introducing the theme:

Pupils explore some action phrases which might later be useful for the fog section of the dance. Accompany with rhythm on drum, e.g. pupils start in a tightly closed shape and 'spread and spread and spread and hold, and swirl swiftly in again'. Encourage pupils to fill up more and more space gradually and smoothly, to extend into many directions at once, to look outwards, to take the action right through to the end of the limbs and then recoil swiftly.

Pupils explore some vocabulary which might later be useful for the storm section. Here are two examples:

Example one, tossing: pupils start sitting on the ground and practise forwards and backwards actions of the body. The try these ideas also standing, kneeling and lying. Start with small actions and gradually increase the size. Increase the energy of these actions so that body parts or the whole body are being tossed backwards

and forwards. Again gradually increase the size. The most important moment comes as most energy is used.

Example two, exploding and retreating: pupils start on the feet, leap and expand into the air and land on the feet. Encourage pupils to control their weight on landing and to throw themselves energetically into the leap. Repeat, but after landing take a few steps backwards. Give rhythm, e.g. 'and leap, land and step back again'. Repeat the phrase several times, gradually increasing the size of the leap. Repeat the phrase, trying to add the feel of the tossing action into the leap.

Pupils explore some vocabulary which might later be useful for the ice section. Pupils choose any spikey shape as the starting position and practise changing from one spikey shape to another. Accompany the phrase with the tambourine, e.g. 'shape, shape, shape, and shiver all over'. Encourage pupils to change the supporting body part, the level and direction of the shapes. Remind pupils about making shapes spikey (see Activity 12): make lots of angles in the body, make knees and elbows important, make sharp changes, make some shapes bigger and more important than others. Pupils start in a wide-spread spikey shape and are squeezed into a small space, then spring out again as the pressure is released. Encourage pupils to resist the squeeze, i.e. they need to grip muscles, push feet into the floor, hold tummy muscles tight and show the difference when the force is released. Make the release important. Explore possibilities of only one side of the body being squeezed and of springing out into a different spikey shape.

Developing theme and dance vocabulary:
Read the chosen extract from the poem (see Activity 21) with the pupils and discuss with them some of the images it contains (e.g. storms at sea, the feel of fog and the chill of ice). Together with the pupils, identify some of the important images (e.g. 'tyrannous and strong', 'chased us south along', 'treads the shadow', 'it crack'd and growl'd', 'The ice did split with a thunder-fit'). Discuss with the pupils storms at sea. What might it feel like to be in a storm? Compare with being outside on a cold, wet and windy day. Show pictures/videos of storms at sea.

Ask pupils to talk about the movements experienced previously. For which sections of the poem could they be used? Ask pupils to suggest other dance vocabulary that might be useful. Ask for ideas about how the dance could be structured (e.g. individuals, twos or small groups working; beginning and ending; most important parts).

Develop some phrases which could be used for the dance. Here are three examples: Example 1, for the storm:

&	1	&	2	&	3	&	4
and	leap	and	leap	and	leap	and	leap
&	5	&	6	&	7	&	8
and	fall and roll over,			stand up		and retreat.	

Ask pupils to make the last leap bigger and more vigorous than the others.

1	2	3	4	5	6	7	8
crack,	crack,	crack,	growl;	crack,	crack,	crack,	growl;
9	10	11	12	13	14	15	16
crack,	crack,	crack,	growl &	r o a r	&	h o w l	

Remind pupils to think about the pictures they have seen and what it might feel like to be there. They should try to capture this in their phrases. Ask pupils to make each group of four beats a bit bigger and more vigorous than the previous one and to make the roar and howl very important.

Example 3, for the fog, in threes, from a starting position where all are in closed shapes, close together, spread out until they only just maintain contact and then swirl in together again:

1	2	3	4	5	6	7	8
s p r e a d - - - - - - - - - - -					and	swirl	in.

Make a new phrase, spreading out one after the other and then becoming compressed in again:

1	&	2	&	3	&	4
swirl	and	hold (No. 1)	swirl	and	hold (No. 2)	
5	&	6	&	7	&	8
swirl	and	hold (No. 3)	and	come	back	in

Help the pupils to get the feel of expansion to fill all directions round self and group, to be sensitive to others in the group and to keep the actions very gentle. Remind pupils to try to keep the feel of the fog and to make the still moments as if frozen and the shapes like vast icicles.

In each case help the pupils to both expand and improve the phrase.

Developing the dance structure:
Discuss and agree with pupils an appropriate structure, e.g. storm, fog, ice, arrival of albatross, splitting of ice, shooting of albatross. Pupils use the phrases worked on previously to show the storm, fog and ice sections. Encourage pupils to select the best ideas and then to refine and improve their performance. Pupils should repeat sections many times making sure they are exactly the same each time.

Work on the transitions between sections. Remind pupils to think about what each section might feel like and to try to capture this in the movement. Encourage pupils to achieve the change in quality (e.g. to control the weight at the end of the storm section, to hold the breath and gradually move into the fog section).

Pupils work together on the final section. Encourage pupils to remember pathways and focus, particularly at the end. Pupils practise the whole dance several times. Review the whole dance with the pupils and agree where the most important moments should occur (e.g. at the arrival of the fog after the storm, when the ice splits, when the albatross is shot). Pupils discuss how these moments can be made important in the dance (e.g. by a large increase in speed or tension, by suddenly freezing the action or by a rapid change in direction). Pupils practise the whole dance many times. Give one teaching point on each repeat (e.g. keeping the pathways the same, making each action go right through the body).

Half the pupils watch the other half, and are then encouraged to talk about changes in quality of movement and whether important moments could be identified. Always encourage pupils to give reasons to support what they say.

Unit 3, lessons 4–6

Theme: An energetic dance; partner work, especially mirroring, copying, leading and following

Purpose: PoS a, c

Activity bank: Activities 1, 2, 3, 4, 5

Resources: Drum; music: *Russian Dance* from *The Nutcracker Suite* by Tchaikovsky; video of the ballet *The Nutcracker*

Introducing the theme:
Pupils mirror teacher (i.e. teacher faces class) making wide, elongated, rounded and twisted shapes. Pupils learn a phrase containing these shapes, composed by the teacher. Pupils mirror teacher's actions. Pupils repeat the phrase, copying the teacher's phrase (i.e. teacher has back to class). Encourage pupils to refine the shapes. Ask pupils to explain the difference between mirroring and copying. Pupils repeat the phrase twice without a pause, the first time mirroring the action, the second copying (i.e. the pupils will be doing the actions first with one side of the body and then with the other).

Pupils explore different ways of making elongated shapes by varying the body part forming the support, the body part initiating the action, the direction and the level in space. All pupils should practise using the space to the side and behind and taking different lengths of time to arrive in the space (e.g. shooting into the space or arriving gradually). Repeat the above for rounded, twisted and wide shapes.

Pupils choose three contrasting shapes and practise shooting into these to fit the rhythm:

1	2	3	4	5	6	7	8
shoot,	hold	-	-	shoot,	hold	-	-
9	10	11	12	13	14	15	16
shoot,	hold	-	-	hold	-	-	-

Each pupil shows the phrase to a partner who checks that the three chosen shapes are in contrast to each other.

In twos: one stays still while the other marches eight steps around the room (accompany on drum). The other now follows exactly the path taken. Repeat, changing the leader. Repeat many times, varying the action taken (e.g. run, skip, glide or creep). The second pupil has to follow exactly the actions and pathways of the first.

Developing theme and dance vocabulary:
Pupils repeat the phrase of three 'shoots' to the rhythm as given above, but on the fourth repetition, instead of 'hold', whizz around:

1	2	3	4	5	6	7	8
shoot,	hold	-	-	shoot,	hold	-	-
9	10	11	12	13	14	15	16
shoot,	hold	-	-	whizz around	-	-	-

Repeat the whole four times.

In twos, pupils designate themselves A and B, observe each other's phrase and choose the one which has the most interesting body support and use of space. Both pupils learn this phrase. Pupils perform the first sequence of the dance, A does the phrase, B does the phrase and all this is repeated. Pupils decide whether they are copying or mirroring. The pupil who is not active holds the first position of the phrase.

Listen to the first section of the music and visualise the phrase. Ask pupils to say where their phrase fits the music. Encourage the pupils to match the energy of the music and to keep the beat. Repeat the whole sequence many times.

Developing the dance structure:
Pupils practise the first section of the dance, clarifying shapes, working to arrive on time and making sure that the one not performing remains 'alive'.

Pupils develop the second section of the dance from the ending position of the first phrase. B scurries, weaving around the dancing area and becomes still at the end of the music phrase. A copies exactly what B has done and follows precisely the pathway taken. Practise to get a swift pattering foot action, to clarify the pathway and to eliminate any 'extra' movement. Finish this section ending face to face. Pupils link first and second sections together and practise.

Pupils listen to the third part of the music and identify the rhythm. Help them by playing the drum. Pupils together make shapes which mirror or copy in time to the music. Pupils make up the last section of the dance. They could either repeat the first section or vary this. Practise the whole dance many times. Encourage pupils to clarify the action and to capture the energetic mood of the music.

One pair shows another pair their dance. After observing, viewers talk about the dance, e.g. 'Was there any contrast in the movement? Were moments of copying and mirroring obvious? Did the dancers keep in time? What was the most exciting moment in the dance?'

Pupils view the *Russian Dance* from the ballet *The Nutcracker*. Pupils talk about the dance, e.g. 'What was the mood of the dance? What makes you say this? What actions were the dancers performing? Were some actions repeated more often than others?'

Unit 3, lessons 7–11

Theme: 'Tarantulantics'; making and sustaining the dance image

Purpose: PoS a, c

Activity bank: Activities 1, 2, 3, 4, 5, 23, 24

Resources: Drum, cymbal; music: *Uranus* from the suite *The Planets* by Holst or *Tarantulantics* by Gatiss; information about spiders; video: *L'Enfant et les Sortilèges*

Introducing the theme:
Pupils discuss what spiders look like, how they move, what they do and how people react to them. Watch spiders in action, live or on video. Discuss any stories which have spiders as important characters (e.g. Ananci, a common figure in African myths and legends).

Pupils suggest first ideas for interpreting these ideas in dance movement. Pupils watch the bat and dragonfly sections of *L'Enfant et les Sortilèges* to see how a professional choreographer has interpreted the actions of these creatures.

Developing theme and dance vocabulary:
Pupils learn some action phrases which might make useful starting points. Here are three examples:
Example 1, spider leg phrase: pupils start close to the floor. One leg moves, then another (perhaps an arm), then scurry close to the floor. Rhythm:

a leg _____, a leg _____, scurry and scurry and stop.

Example 2, spider travel phrase: step to the left and close right foot to left (= step join), look over left shoulder. Repeat. Bounce, bounce and shiver all over. Rhythm:

  &   1   &   2   3   4   5   6   7   8
step join, step join, bounce bounce shiver all over   -

Example 3, spider fall phrase: balance on one leg and reach forwards and upwards with both hands, transfer the weight on to two hands and one leg and gradually lower the body until lying on floor, very quickly tuck up the whole body on the side or the back, extend the limbs and spin, then tuck in the body and shoot to standing with well-spread limbs.

Pupils explore some of the possibilities of spider movement, e.g. from tightly tucked-in shape extend the limbs in all directions. Tuck in and repeat many times, using different parts of the body to support the action. Spin round in the tucked position before extending again. Practise these actions changing the speed at which they are performed. Accompany with drum rhythm.

Pupils explore some of the possibilities of travel in a spider-like way, e.g. travelling on hands and feet with tummies in the air, travelling sideways and backwards, climbing up the thread of a web, spinning round very quickly and swinging on the end of a thread. Give rhythm on the drum.

In pairs, pupils explore ways in which they could give an impression of having many legs, on the spot and in travel. Give rhythm on the drum, e.g.

1 & 2, 3 & 4, 5 & 6, 7 & 8, 1 & 2 & 3 & 4 & 5 & 6 & 7 (8)

Pairs of pupils make a short phrase for the spider antics section, e.g. balancing on a few legs with the others in funny shapes, tightrope walking, using threads from webs as trapezes, making terrifying shapes, feet having a merry dance. The phrase must have a clear beginning and end and must include stillness and a turn.

In small groups, pupils explore ways in which they could create a web image, e.g. in threes, make a long wide shape with hands and feet just touching, repeat keeping the wide shape but touching with parts of the body other than hands, or make a circle with pupils just making contact. Accompany with the cymbal. Pupils start in a small shape and grow into a web for as long as the sound lasts. Encourage pupils to use different parts of the body to support the action, to be very gentle in the contact and to think about the possible different shapes of webs. After exploring many different ways of making webs, pupils choose the three that work best and find ways of changing smoothly from to another.

Pupils hold one web shape and try to find different ways of looking out from the web without losing contact, as if looking for an insect to trap. Develop a short phrase of: look out, return to focus in, look out and end with focus in. Pupils stretch out each of their small group webs and try to touch other groups so that a whole class web is formed.

Developing the dance structure:
Pupils listen to the music and discuss ideas to be included in the dance, and how it should start and end. The following suggestions will need to be adapted to take account of the pupils' ideas. Take each section of the dance in turn, encourage pupils to choose the most appropriate ideas and improve the quality with which they are performed.

Pupils take up a starting position like a spider with its legs tucked in. They choose the best ways of 'waking up' the legs, e.g. stretch, wriggle and/or shake them, then travel just a little distance and end facing away from the audience in a spider shape. Encourage pupils to repeat exactly the ideas they choose, to make phrases clear, to have quicker and slower movements and to give the impression of having many legs. Remind pupils that their movements should show the quality with which spiders move. Some pupils enter later and use agile cartwheels, leaps and turns to join the others. Remind pupils to keep the spider-like quality.

Pupils practise the unison stretching and closing section, taking the timing from a pupil at the front. At the last moment, pupils turn and threaten the audience. Remind pupils to take the action right through to the ends of fingers and toes and to keep their faces hidden until the turn. After the turn, they spread their arms and legs, quiver all over and stare at the audience.

Pupils travel in a spider-like way to meet their partners for the antics section. They choose the best ideas and repeat with music many times. Remind pupils to have a clear beginning and end and that there must be a stillness and turn. Repeat the actions many times, with a teaching point on each repetition, e.g. 'Could you balance a little longer, or make the fall more spectacular? Does the action go right to the ends of the fingers and toes?' Pupils decide the order of

performance, two or three pairs working together. Guide the transition, encouraging pupils to watch for movement clues so that they know when to start their phrases. At the end of this section, all spin wildly and look for a fly. Tense muscles hard to maintain the stillness.

Pupils glide into web groups and improve these by making points of contact gentle, with smooth changes between one web shape and the next. Encourage pupils to change levels. Clarify the section looking in/out of webs by checking that pupils are looking in the same direction and are holding still on the look.

Discuss with pupils how the dance will end, e.g. by making one large class web and catching a few insects. Practise the whole dance many times to develop skill and confidence in performance. Give one or two teaching points each time, e.g. keep the spider-like quality, keep well spread out, move gently into the webs without rushing. Discuss with pupils what they might wear for a performance of this dance.

Unit 3, lesson 12

Theme: 'Tarantulantics'; appraisal

Purpose: PoS a, c

Resources: As for lessons 7–11 plus video camera and playback facilities

Pupils practise the dance as developed in the previous lessons. Give teaching points as necessary. Pupils change into costume for a dress rehearsal. Pupils perform the dance and it is recorded on video.

Pupils watch the video. Pupils talk about the dance as a whole. Use ideas such as the following to lead the

discussion: 'Are there any really effective parts? Where are these and why do they work? For any one group, describe the web section. Describe any two contrasting sections. Are there any particularly good 'spider' images? What makes you say this? Are there any parts you would wish to improve? How might you do this?'

Unit 4, lessons 1–6

Theme: 'The Quest'; selecting and refining movement to communicate the dance idea

Purpose: PoS a, c

Activity bank: Activities: 1, 2, 3, 4, 5, 23, 25, 26, 27, 28, 29

Resources: Tambourine; music: sections of *The Firebird* by Stravinsky, or sections of *Legend* by Clannad; video: *The Firebird*, choreography by Glen Tetley (see p. 21)

Introducing the theme:
Pupils discuss with the teacher the specific storyline for their dance (see Activity 26), including naming the characters (i.e. 'heroes' and 'trapped comrades'), agreeing on the 'barriers' to be overcome and on the nature of the 'enchanted forest'.

Pupils practise using chance methods to determine the dance content. For example, they choose one card from

the 'action' category (see Activity 26) and explore many different ways of showing this is movement. Then they select from these the one they like best. They practise this and try to remember and repeat it. Pupils then repeat this process, choosing cards from the other categories. Encourage pupils to try out many ideas by suggesting that they try using different body parts, qualities, directions and levels (as given by repeated selections of chance cards). Help pupils improve the quality with which they perform the actions (see Activity 5).

Assist pupils to develop individual 'hero' characters. Use chance methods to determine the movement content. Pupils choose one card from each of the categories 'body part', and 'quality' and two cards from the 'action' category (see Activity 26). For example, a pupil may have: shoulders, low level, quick, travel and spin. Pupils explore many different ways in which these ingredients could be joined to form a short phrase. Provide an accompaniment to help pupils establish the beginning and end of the phrase.

Pupils select from their explorations movements which best show the kind of 'heroes' the class agreed upon earlier. They should link the movements together to make a phrase which becomes the theme of their 'hero'. This theme should have a starting and ending position which shows the stance of the chosen 'hero'; the middle of the piece should show what the 'hero' is like and how it moves (see Activity 23). Encourage pupils to make the transitions between movements fluent, to involve the whole body and to have some contrast in the phrase. Practise the phrases with the chosen music.

Pupils practise the phrase as if travelling through an 'enchanted forest'. Ask pupils to show how they have to adapt their phrase as if avoiding objects or going under and over obstacles. Remind pupils about the kind of 'hero' the class decided upon, and ask pupils to check that their movements show this. Practise the phrase with the chosen music.

In small groups, pupils explore many different ways of making a 'barrier' (e.g. groups of pupils forming a wall, closed circle, maze or spoke-like shape; see Activity 28). Encourage pupils to use different parts of the body for support, to make contact with each other using different body parts, to make different body shapes within the 'barrier', to grow into the 'barrier' slowly and smoothly, or suddenly and precisely. Help pupils to improve their 'barrier' (e.g. by reminding pupils to keep the body tension between them, to have a really secure base, to focus outwards towards the imaginary attacker, to make sure there are no gaps in the 'barrier'). Practise making the 'barrier' shapes with the chosen music.

Developing theme and dance vocabulary:
Pupils join in groups of five or six and give their group of 'heroes' a collective name (e.g. 'Strider'). Pupils, as a group, choose some movement which will become the 'logo' for their group (e.g. a jumping upright turn, or three stamps with the right foot). All members of the group practise their own 'hero' phrase with the addition of the group 'logo'. Practise this with the chosen music.

Each group works out how the members can travel together. Their pathway is determined by selecting a card from the 'pathway' category (see Activity 26). The group may pause during the travel but must use the group 'logo'. Encourage pupils to think about how the group can keep together, how well their pathway matches that on the card, whether there are quicker and slower movements and how the group gives the impression of avoiding obstacles.

Each group works, with teacher guidance, on each of the following ways of overcoming the 'barrier': firstly, begging, pleading or negotiating; secondly, demonstrating such power that the 'barrier' breaks down; thirdly, using magic or clever tricks.

Pupils explore within their groups movement ideas for begging, pleading and negotiating. For example, ask each pupil to take a shape which suggests begging, then to find other shapes while retaining the begging idea. Pupils add travel, a turn or a jump before making the shape and retreat afterwards. Group members could do this one after the other or the whole group could move at the same time. Ask pupils to think about whether the negotiation takes place over a long time or is over in a flash.

In their groups, pupils select from these ideas those they think will best enable them to be successful in overcoming the 'barrier'. Provide an appropriate length of music to accompany this. Remind pupils to use some of the ideas from their individual 'heroes' and to use the group 'logo'. Encourage pupils to include contrast in their phrase, to have a beginning and end when everyone is still, to include variety in the use of body, quality and space, and to make their phrase so convincing that the 'barrier' will be overcome.

Pupils explore within their groups movement ideas for showing power. For example, suggest that they do together a rhythmic stamping; each group member in turn could leap and land in a menacing shape which is complemented by subsequent group members; the group could grow into an enormous threatening shape and advance. Pupils in their groups then select the most effective ideas (as outlined above for begging, pleading and negotiating) and practise these with the appropriate music.

Pupils explore within their groups movement ideas for magic movements or clever tricks. For example, ask pupils to show a 'speciality' movement such as spinning round on one leg many times in succession, balancing on the hands or jumping high into the air, landing on the feet and then spinning round close to the floor. Ask pupils to travel with an intricate floor pattern (e.g. using different parts of the feet on the floor, making an interesting rhythm, crossing and uncrossing the feet). Ask pupils to go straight from one movement to another with very different quality (e.g. doing a slow pressing action followed by a jittery action). Pupils in their groups then select ideas as outlined above and practise these with the appropriate music.

Developing the dance structure:
All pupils start on the edge of the dancing area and use the individual 'hero' phrase they made earlier, as if travelling through an 'enchanted forest'. Remind pupils to show how they avoid obstacles as they travel. At the end of the appropriate section of the music, pupils

should have arrived in the groups in which they worked previously. Encourage pupils to repeat pathways exactly, to make movements that create the impression of travelling through an 'enchanted forest' and to make every movement larger than in everyday life.

Pupils then work in their groups. On the spot, they perform together the group 'logo' and then travel together using the pathway and movements they worked on previously. Some alterations may be needed to ensure there is sufficient space for all groups (e.g. groups start at different times, some groups pause while others pass by). Remind pupils to repeat their chosen movements as accurately as they can. Help pupils to refine their movement by asking them, for example, to make quick movements even quicker and fluent ones more continuous, to make some actions go right through to the ends of fingers and toes and to make sure that all group members are looking in the appropriate direction. Practise several times with the music. Link individual travel with the group travel and practise several times with the music.

Use one of the methods given in Activity 27 to determine in which order the 'barriers' will appear, then again to determine the order in which groups will try to

overcome the 'barriers'. Each group in turn links its 'begging', 'power' and 'magic' phrases in the order determined (see Activity 27). Help pupils to refine these phrases. Then organise the first 'barrier' into position so that the first group can perform its 'overcoming' phrases. As the group performs the last phrases the 'barrier' collapses and the group travels through it. This is repeated for each group in turn. Help pupils to refine and improve the movements by suggesting ways in which the body, quality and space could be improved. After the last 'barrier' has been overcome the 'comrades' trapped by the barrier are released and all the pupils join in a dance of celebration.

Pupils perform the whole dance several times and then it is recorded on video. Pupils watch the video of their own performance. Ask them, for example, to describe the shapes of the 'barriers', to say how successful they thought the movements of the small groups were in conveying the ideas, and how they might improve their own performance.

Pupils watch the video of *The Firebird*. Ask pupils to tell the story of *The Firebird* and to compare it with the story of their own dance. See Activity 29 for ideas to help focus pupils' attention.

Unit 4, lessons 7–12

Theme: Carnival

Purpose: PoS a, b, c

Activity bank: Activities 1, 2, 3, 4, 5, 23, 30, 31, 32, 33, 34

Resources: Tambourine; music: selection from Kings of Calypso; video 'Caribbean Music Village' (see p. 21); film: 'Carnival' (see p. 21); pictures of carnivals.

Introducing the theme:
Note that throughout this example the message, 'Glitter not litter' has been taken as the basis. The process would be the same for other messages.

Pupils watch the video, look at the pictures and become familiar with the characteristic features of a Caribbean carnival. They also discuss examples of carnival which occur in this country (e.g. Liverpool or Notting Hill, London). Pupils discuss ideas which might underlie the 'message' of their carnival presentation. Groups of pupils might decide to present different messages. They explore some of the dance ideas they might use to communicate this message. Help them focus their thinking as outlined in Activity 23.

Pupils learn the procession phrase (see Activity 31). Help pupils to do this better by accenting the beat on a tambourine and by encouraging them to make the movement in the torso fluid, to keep the knees bent and the feet flat on the ground, and to keep the whole action well grounded on the floor. At the same time the

rhythm of the action should be vital and alive. Pupils practise this many times so that they can all perform it at the same time and so that they can make it travel in a procession round the room.

Pupils explore ways of showing 'litter' in dance. Encourage them to try taking the shapes of different kinds of litter with the weight on different body supports, travelling as if blown by the wind, changing the speed and fluency of the movement as if the wind stops and blows again, changing the level and direction of the action and spinning and whirling as if caught up in a tornado.

Pupils select from this the actions which for them best convey litter on a windy day. This phrase must include the following ingredients in any order: leap, roll and spin. Accompany this initially with the tambourine, then with the chosen piece of music.

Pupils discuss the costumes that might be appropriate and check that they think they could still perform their phrases wearing them.

Developing theme and dance vocabulary:
Pupils work in small groups to develop a group 'litter' phrase (Activity 32, Section 3). This must include the following sections in any order: travelling as if being

blown down a narrow street, being turned inside out, being blown high into the air and settling again, spinning as if in a tornado. Encourage pupils to explore many possible ideas and then to select and refine those which they think work best. Pupils practise this many times with the chosen music.

Pupils work in pairs on Section 4 of the dance, sweeping up the litter. One pupil takes the character of the 'litter', the other of the 'sweeper'. For example, sweepers might enter with a phrase of 'leap and leap and leap and land, two sweeping actions as if with broom, turn around as if swinging broom and pause as if leaning on broom'. As the sweeper moves towards the litter, the litter rolls

away but then spins round to land on the feet. The phrase can then be repeated with the litter menacing the sweeper. At the end of this section, all the litter is swept into the middle of the floor. Pupils explore many different ideas, select the best and practise with the chosen music.

Pupils learn and practise the celebration dance (see Activity 31). Help them to improve their performance (see Activity 5).

Developing the dance structure:
Pupils start outside the dancing space and process into and around it (Activity 32, Section 1) so that they end in a circle. Encourage pupils to make the step pattern accurate, to make a clear floor pattern (the whole class following that set by those who entered first) and to capture the lively festive mood of the occasion.

Pupils practise Section 2 (see Activity 32), where the litter 'kings' and 'queens' emerge. Encourage pupils to check that the shapes they are making look like litter. Those pupils not in the centre group should keep very still in their litter shapes. Encourage those in the centre to keep in time with the music and each other to give the impression that they are being blown in the wind. After two repeats of the phrase all pupils join in. Encourage them to improve their performance (see Activity 5).

Pupils practise linking Sections 1 and 2.

Pupils work on the link between Section 2 and Section 1b (see Activity 32). The litter 'kings' and 'queens' begin the change from the litter section at a selected point in the music; all pupils join in again and process round the room.

Pupils practise Section 3 (see Activity 32). Organise the groups so that the whole dancing space is being used and the groups are not working too close to each other. Encourage pupils to improve their performance (see Activity 5), to listen to the music so that each group begins at the right time and to watch for when other groups begin and end.

Pupils practise linking Sections 1, 2, 1b and 3. Encourage pupils to think ahead so that they are ready

for the next section as well as concentrating on the section they are performing.

Pupils add a repeat of Section 1b to the end of Section 3. The last group to have moved leads the procession round the room. Towards the end of this section half the pupils go off the dancing space so that they can return later as the 'sweepers'.

Pupils practise Section 4 (see Activity 32). Organise pupils so that those remaining on the floor are each in a space and their partner is able to travel towards them. Help pupils to improve their work in pairs and remind them to try to show their different characters in their movements.

Pupils link sections 1, 2, 1b, 3, 1b and 4.

Pupils work on the final celebration (Activity 32, Section 5), which follows sweeping the litter into a pile.

Pupils practise the whole dance many times. Encourage them to improve their performance and to make the links between sections smooth. Pupils will need particular encouragement to repeat movements exactly, especially in respect of pathway.

Pupils rehearse and perform the dance in costume and it is recorded on video.

Pupils watch the video of their performance and are helped to describe and interpret it (see Activity 33). Encourage pupils to make connections between the idea and what was actually happening in the dance, to look at their own performance and to suggest ways in which it could have been improved, and to give reasons for saying whether their dance is like that of a Caribbean carnival.

FLOORPLAN

Study this floorplan for 'Ragtime for Robbers':

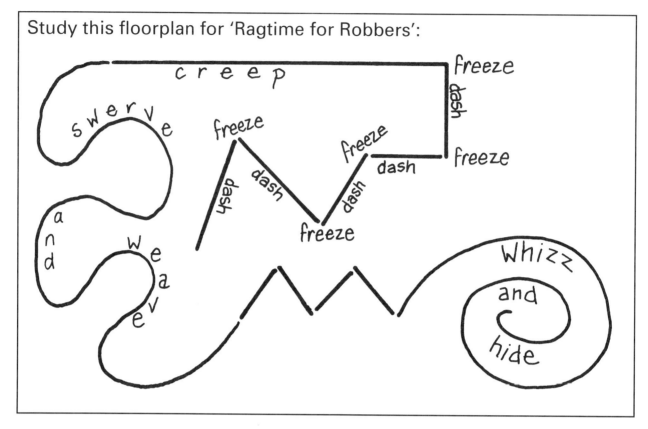

GYMNASTICS

ABOUT GYMNASTICS

Gymnastics is an activity in which the focus is entirely on the body. Participation in gymnastic movement is about control and mastery of the body in a variety of challenging situations. As such, gymnastics as an area of activity of the school curriculum offers a different set of challenges and a potentially different set of benefits than does the area of games, for example. One can be forgiven for thinking that the skill base for performance gymnastics is quite specialised and beyond the reach of many of our school pupils. Clearly not all children have the potential or the inclination to become skilful gymnasts. However, the skill base is only one element of the discipline of gymnastics and it is important to note at this point that the place for coaching skills to performance level is essentially outside the classroom, in extra curricular clubs and activities.

Gymnastic activity, if approached correctly, is of benefit to all pupils. It offers the opportunity to develop general body management and control by improving balance, co-ordination and the range of mobility of the body. The focus of work in schools is essentially about exploring and extending the range of movement possibilities within one's own limitations. Hence gymnastics contributes to the development of creativity in young people. In addition, attention to quality of movement is intrinsic to all gymnastics. There are expectations in terms of precision and control of movements. Hence gymnastics offers an aesthetic experience through movement and the opportunity to develop aesthetic awareness. Finally, gymnastics offers unique opportunities for pupils to develop important social skills through learning to work co-operatively and safely with one another in a challenging environment.

The next section details the National Curriculum requirements as they relate to gymnastics and should serve to reinforce the potential value of this activity for all pupils. The section headed 'Teaching gymnastics at Key Stage 2' attempts to shed light on the way in which the National Curriculum requirements might be delivered and hence illustrate ways in which those potential values can be achieved. Included in this section is one model lesson, which illustrates the underlying principles involved in teaching gymnastics in the PE National Curriculum, e.g. safety considerations, working with others and cross-curricular links. Finally, a series of lesson plans are presented in units of work which aim to cover a range of movement material and demonstrate the way in which this material can be organised and progressed through over a series of weeks.

NATIONAL CURRICULUM REQUIREMENTS AT KEY STAGE 2

The programmes of study (general) which apply to gymnastics are as follows:

Physical education should involve pupils in the continuous process of planning, performing and evaluating. This applies to all areas of activity. The greatest emphasis should be placed on the actual performance aspect of the subject. The following requirements apply to the teaching of physical education across all key stages.

1. To promote physical activity and healthy lifestyles, pupils should be taught:
   a to be physically active;
   b to adopt the best possible posture and the appropriate use of the body;
   c to engage in activities that develop cardiovascular health, flexibility, muscular strength and endurance.

2. To develop positive attitudes, pupils should be taught:
   b how to cope with success and limitations in performance;
   c to try hard to consolidate their performances;

3. To ensure safe practice, pupils should be taught:
   a to respond readily to instructions;
   b to recognise and follow relevant rules, laws, codes, etiquette and safety procedures for different activities or events, in practice and during competition;
   c about the safety risks of wearing inappropriate clothing, footwear and jewellery, and why particular clothing, footwear and protection are worn for different acivities;
   d how to lift, carry, place and use equipment safely;
   e to warm up for and recover from exercise.

The Programmes of Study (activity specific) for gymnastics are as follows:

Pupils should be taught six areas of activity. During each year of the key stage pupils should be taught Games, Gymnastic Activities and Dance. At points during the key stage pupils should be taught Athletic Activities, Outdoor and Adventurous Activities, and Swimming unless they have already completed the programme of study for Swimming during Key Stage 1. If aspects of the Swimming programme have been taught during Key Stage 1, pupils should be taught Key Stage 2 Swimming programme starting at the appropriate point.

Throughout the key stage, pupils should be taught:

■ how to sustain energetic activity over appropriate periods of time in a range of physical activities.

■ the short-term effects of exercise on the body.

AREAS OF ACTIVITY

2. Gymnastic activities

a different means of turning, rolling, swinging, jumping, climbing, balancing and travelling on hands and feet, and how to adapt, practise and refine these actions, both on the floor and using apparatus;

b to emphasise changes of shape, speed and direction through gymnastic actions;

c to practice, refine and repeat a longer series of actions making increasingly complex movement sequences, both on the floor and using apparatus.

TEACHING GYMNASTICS AT KEY STAGE 2 ▶

The National Curriculum documentation embodies all that needs to be done in order to deliver effective gymnastics in schools.

The sum of the end of key stage descriptions is the attainment target for PE, which consists of three strands (planning, performing and evaluating). In all that we do in PE we should be encouraging pupils to plan their work, to evaluate their own work and that of others and to perform their work. Performance is absolutely central to PE and, for the main part, it would be expected that pupils demonstrate the planning and evaluating through the practical performance of the activity. This is not always possible or desirable, however, and when one considers the need to develop knowledge, skill and understanding through all the activities, implications for teaching styles and methods of assessment begin to arise.

In addition to making planning, performing and evaluating elements of all activities, the non-statutory guidance draws attention to a number of other considerations which should run through all that we do in PE. These include differentiating teaching and learning to reach a wide range of abilities, safety considerations, health-related exercise, cross-curricular links and working with others. Whilst it may seem a tall order, there is no doubt that gymnastics can be structured and delivered in a way which accommodates all of these elements.

The material content and teaching styles

The programme of study for gymnastics clearly sets out a range of movement material to be covered in this key stage, including ways of rolling, jumping, swinging, balancing and taking weight on hands. Interestingly, the statements do not list a set of skills to be mastered, but instead use terms such as explore, select, adapt, refine and develop the range within these movement areas. This clearly has implications for the way in which material is presented and developed.

Good teachers know that a range of teaching styles are demanded throughout any lesson in order to keep motivation and effect learning. There will be times in gymnastics when it is necessary to teach in a fairly directed way in order to teach a specific skill. However if other ends are to be met, there is clearly the need for a more open-ended style of teaching to be included in a good deal of gymnastics work in schools. If pupils are to be allowed to select, then some way of setting tasks is necessary. This is not to say that core skills are not taught, but simply that the method of approach needs to be different. Nor is it to say that the lesson has no structure; indeed if task setting and differentiation of tasks are to work then a great deal of structure is necessary.

Teaching through themes

For the purposes of organisation of material, all the movement material to be covered in this key stage can be grouped into two broad movement themes. These two themes are 'Ways of travelling' and 'Moving into and out of balance'.

Ways of travelling can generally be classified as jumping, rolling, sliding and stepping actions. Balancing dealt with in isolation tends to be rather static and can therefore be better covered as ways into and out of balance, which forms a progression from the theme on travelling. Swinging actions and taking weight on hands do not seem to be included specifically in either of these themes; however, taking weight on hands will inevitably be involved in both themes and swinging can be dealt with effectively as a way of setting the body in motion for a variety of ways of travelling.

The programme of study tells us that we should encourage work on both floor and apparatus, on linking of moves into more complex sequences, on the range or variety of moves within the material and on the quality of movement. Attention to quality is intrinsic to gymnastics work, but is quite difficult to develop when working with pupils who have a wide range of abilities.

Attention to quality of movement can be guided by emphasis on aspects of movement, such as the body shape or the speed of the movement. A model for structuring gymnastics work is shown below. If all of these elements are included throughout a unit of work, pupils ought to progress effectively.

A formula for teaching gymnastics.

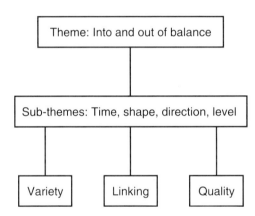

Differentiating for a range of abilities

Given the specialised nature of gymnastics as an activity, some pupils will never be successful in terms of skill competence. We have a responsibility to enable all pupils to participate and to succeed in some way. The simple way to achieve this is to try to teach as much of the programme as possible through task setting. When set skills are being dealt with, try to have in mind a number of variations which can make the skill easier or more difficult.

In the case of pupils with physical disabilities try to focus on the ability rather than the disability. Many can do more than we may imagine and given the right atmosphere and setting there is no doubt that physical activity has social, physical and psychological benefits for all. Listen to the pupil; he/she is the best person to judge what he/she can and can't do. Encourage and do your best to adapt activities where necessary to allow participation. These pupils are differently abled and in gymnastics some will come up with quite unique answers to tasks set.

Safety considerations

There are safety considerations in all PE activities, but perhaps more obviously in the area of gymnastics than in other areas.

Whatever age group or material you are teaching you will always have some pupils who cannot achieve a specific skill and you will probably have some who have already mastered it. Again, the pupil is generally the best judge of what they are capable of attempting, but we as teachers ought to be sure that we are not putting pupils at risk. Certain skills, such as forward and backward rolls, take the pupil right over the head and unless the learner is at the right stage of development and able enough, they should not be encouraged to try this. Other skills are potentially risky owing to the possibility of over-rotation, e.g. the handstand, and, whilst there are very effective ways of making the area safe, this would largely be beyond the bounds of an unqualified coach with a whole class group to cope with. Therefore, only teach set skills to the whole group when you feel it is appropriate because a good number of them are close to achieving the skill. This is not to say that you should not help individuals as they attempt a particular skill to fulfill a task. Again, try to have alternatives which will accommodate the least able and the most able in the group.

Use of equipment and space will vary greatly depending on the facilities within the school. In general, a great deal can be done in any hall of a reasonable size. Mats are necessary for certain work, but by no means for all floorwork, and the most versatile piece of apparatus is a bench or form. Any fixed apparatus, such as wall bars and beams, is a bonus and is useful for hanging and swinging work, as is a moveable frame which is often found in primary schools. It is important to note that equipment should be used as a progression from floorwork and should be set up accordingly to allow progression of the task. It is your role to check the condition of the space you intend to work in as well as the condition of the equipment. Part of our role as teachers is to make children aware of the safety of themselves and others and one way that this can be achieved is by training pupils to get out, work on and put away apparatus safely. This is time-consuming at first and relies on your effective authority and discipline but once the pupils have established a routine, they should work efficiently together.

Below is a suggested routine for getting out and putting away apparatus.

Getting out apparatus:
Divide pupils into groups. Pupils sit in groups in designated space in the gym.
If all groups are getting out a bench, a mat and a box top, all groups can be told together what they are to get and that they are to place it approximately where they are sitting. Alternatively if each group has a different piece of apparatus you will need to go to each group in turn and say what they are to get out. No group is to commence getting equipment until all have been told.
All equipment is to be carried between two or more pupils and placed in a space. Use the correct lifting technique with heavy pieces (see the diagram on the next page).
When equipment is out, pupils should sit on the mat and wait.
Try to stand in a position where all pupils are in sight.
Check apparatus and spacing.

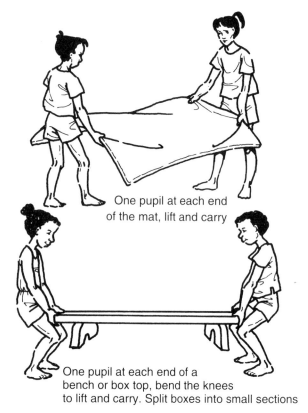

One pupil at each end of the mat, lift and carry

One pupil at each end of a bench or box top, bend the knees to lift and carry. Split boxes into small sections

Putting apparatus away:
Stop work and sit by apparatus.
Put away boxes first, then benches, then mats.
Sit in a space quietly when cleared.

Material should progress within the lesson and across a number of lessons. Again the National Curriculum states that we should help pupils to understand effects of exercise and ways of preparing for exercise. The lesson should always begin with an introductory session of activities which will warm up the pupils and introduce the movement material. This should progress to some floorwork, with or without mats, and at some point the work done on the floor will be transferred on to low or high apparatus. With the short lessons in some schools, it is not always possible to do floorwork followed by apparatus work. If the intention is to go on to the apparatus after the introduction, then the material in the introduction should include some of the moves to be taken on to apparatus, e.g. taking weight on to hands.

Cross-curricular links

There are opportunities in gymnastics to make cross-curricular links with other subjects. For example, shape and surface area could be linked to Mathematics. Where linking is possible it should be used in order to enhance learning, but it should never be contrived.

Health-related exercise

We have a responsibility for not only promoting health through exercise but also for developing the pupils' understanding of what is involved in health-related exercise. The implications here are that we need at some point to talk to pupils about why we warm up, for example.

Working with others

There is enormous potential for promoting favourable attitudes in pupils working together through gymnastics. This may be simply through getting out apparatus together, sharing space and equipment, or actually working with a partner or a group. There are examples of reciprocal teaching in the units of work which follow. This teaching style involves pupils using evaluative skills, but also demands that they communicate in a positive way with one another. Much of the time in gymnastics should be spent encouraging pupils to watch one another's work, analyse what they see and possibly share ideas and give feedback.

Assessment in gymnastics

You will by now be aware that there are no levels of attainment in the statutory orders for PE. Whilst the document has given us a process model for teaching PE, it also leaves us with a number of issues with regard to assessment of the subject which are yet to be resolved. One of the major problems facing teachers is the fact that some of the terms mentioned, for example 'understanding' and 'evaluative skills', are actually quite difficult to measure in the practical area.

A second area of contention is that the type of evidence which needs to be recorded for each key stage is as yet unclear. It would however seem to be necessary and valuable to record some evidence in order to provide feedback for pupils and parents and to aid the teachers themselves in future planning.

Assessment should be on-going throughout the units of work. The opportunity to observe or even record certain achievements can be accommodated through designing the lesson structure and the teaching style appropriately. For example, in lesson 4 of unit 3, part of the session is given over to reciprocal teaching, where the pupils try to help one another to master skills. This type of teaching style has clear implications for helping pupils to evaluate movement work, but also can perhaps provide the opportunity for the teacher to observe how effectively pupils work together or how well they understand what is being done. Later, in lessons 11 and 13 of unit 3 and lessons 6 and 7 of unit 4, photocopiable Workcards are used to help pupils to practise and refine work covered, or to link moves effectively. The use of these, or similar, cards can provide either written evidence from the pupils of what they can do, or at least an opportunity for the teacher to observe at what level the pupils are working and to make some simple record. The way in which cards are designed and used can vary greatly and considerations of the levels of literacy of the pupils must not be ignored here. The Workcards included may give some food for thought. If you as the teacher structure your teaching and bring pupils through a series of progressions effectively, you should be able to comment on the end of key stage statements quite effectively at various stages throughout the units of work. An ongoing profile of some description would appear to be the most effective way of recording learning and progress.

The activity bank and the units of work
The activity bank is designed to illustrate many of the moves which you will be aiming to help pupils to produce. It is set out in a way which should help you to distinguish the relative degree of difficulty of the movement material.

The lesson plans which follow are divided into four units of work, each consisting of twelve lessons. Units 1 and 2 cover the two movement themes mentioned previously and are designed for work with pupils in Years 3 and 4. Units 3 and 4 also cover work in both movement themes and are designed for work with Years 5 and 6. The lessons are set out to give progression throughout a series of lessons. Units 2 and 4, on the theme of 'into and and out of balance', are based on the assumption that some work has already been done on 'ways of travelling' (units 1 and 3).

References to the activity bank are provided at the start of each lesson plan. The intended purpose of the lesson, in terms of meeting the requirements of the programme of study (general), is also given.

The model lesson
The following model lesson, from unit 4, gives details of the organisation of material and the intended outcomes. The coding at the side refers to pupils evaluating (EV) planning (PL) and working with others (WWO).

Model lesson: unit 4, lesson 3

Theme: Moving into and out of balance; rolling into balance; pike seat, shoulder stand

Purpose: PoS a, b, c

Activity bank: Activities 5a, 5b, 5c, 5d

Resources: Mats

Activity	Organisation	Teaching points
Introduction:		
Travel round running.	Individually in space.	Work on quality by attention to pace.
Slow to walking.		Guide timing and action.
Freeze on command and stretch away in a balance.		Pull away from base.
Gradually tuck to a ball, lower to floor and travel by rolling.		Use of voice to get sustained movement.
Development:		
Repeat run, walk, balance tuck, roll. Freeze from roll and pull to balance.	Individually in a space.	Pull as many parts off the floor as possible.
Repeat in your own time.		Point toes.
Find ways of balancing from roll.		Be quiet, concentrate. (PL)
Show ideas and share by looking at other pupils' ideas.		Control roll, make it as slow as possible.
	You choose pupils with good moves. Quickly look at three or four ideas. (WWO)	
Get out mats.	In twos, sitting in a space. Move mats as instructed. Lift and carry the mat one at either end. Place where sitting. (WWO)	Sit in twos, space out. Move to mats, lift and carry. Put mat down where you were. Sit on mats until told what to do.
Sideways roll to pike seat. Pike seat to shoulder stand. Watch partner and help or extend skill. (WWO)	Working two to a mat.	Feed in ideas from others or from you. (PL)

43

Activity	Organisation	Teaching points
Practise ideas of into and out of pike seat and shoulder stand from roll.	Practice in own time.	Encourage quality, pointing toes, linking. (EV)
Show phrases.	One on each mat at a time, i.e. half group watching.	Focus pupils watching. (WWO)
Put away mats.		Give general feedback as each group finish. (EV)
Conclusion: Shoulder stand from pike seat.	Individually in a space.	Give clear instruction.
Rock forward to feet, without using hands on floor.	All pupils working together.	Encourage tucking legs tight as rocking through, with feet close to seat.
Repeat in own time.		Encourage looking forward, keeping shoulders low, reaching forward.(EV)
		Allow time for practice.
		Repeat key points.

GYMNASTICS ACTIVITY BANK

Activity 1: Jumping actions

A jumping action is one where the body is entirely off the ground and in the air for a moment.

In all jumping actions:

1 Use arm swing to assist elevation.
2 Ensure the head and chest are up.
3 Ensure good body line, point fingers and toes.
4 Bend knees and ankles to receive weight on landing.
5 Focus forward on landing to keep hips low and prevent forward rotation.

1a: Jump two feet to two feet

1b: Jump one foot to the other foot – a leap

1c: Jump one foot to the same foot – a hop

1d: Jump one foot to two feet – the hurdle step

1e: Jump two feet to one foot

44

Jumping actions can be developed by changing body shape in the air, changing direction in the air or by incorporating apparatus. In all of these actions it is important to:

- prepare by making an arm swing
- make a shape when in the air
- straighten out before landing.

1f: Two feet to two feet – a star jump

1g: Two feet to two feet – a tuck jump

1h: Two feet to two feet – a pike jump

1i: One foot to the other foot – a turning jump

1j: Jumping one foot to the other with leg design – a split kick (left) or a stag leap (right)

1k: Jumping two feet to two feet on to and off a bench

1l: Jumping one foot to two feet on to the bench

1m: Jumping two feet to two feet along the bench

1n: Jumping one foot to the other – leaping along the bench

1o: Jumping two feet to two feet over the bench

1p: Jumping two feet to two feet – star jump over the bench

1q: Jumping two feet to two feet – tuck jump over the bench

1r: Jumping one foot to the other – leaping over the bench

Jumping actions can be on to different body parts. In all of these actions, arm swing is very important as it gives momentum.

1s: Jumping from feet to hands – the bunny jump

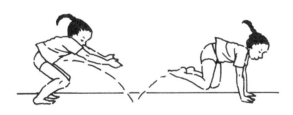

1t: Taking the bunny jump on to the bench or the box top

1u: Jumping on to bottom on a box top

1v: Jumping on to tummy on a box top

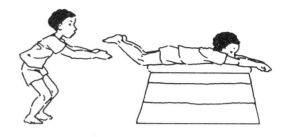

1w: Jumping into a rolling action on the box top

Activity 2: Stepping actions

A stepping action is one where different parts of the body come to the floor in turn, one after another. In these actions:

1 Concentrate on body line and tension.
2 Reach for the floor with the next body part.

2a: Crawling tummy down

2b: Crawling tummy up

2c: Rotating from tummy up to tummy down

2d: Cartwheeling

Stepping actions can be developed by changing body shape.

2e: A stepping action with legs straight

2f: A stepping action with legs straddled

2g: A stepping action with body tucked

These actions can be further developed by taking them across or along apparatus.

2h: Crawling along or over a bench

2i: Stepping with straddled legs along, over or around a bench

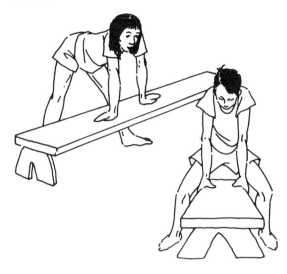

2j: Cartwheeling over or along a bench

2k: A donkey kick

Activity 3: Rolling actions

A rolling action is one which takes the body over large surfaces and where there is continual contact with the floor. In all rolling actions:

1 Concentrate on body shape; if tucked, keep tight; if stretched, stretch fully.
2 Stress key points for each action as outlined.

3a: A pencil roll

3b: An egg roll

3c: A side roll

3d: A circle roll

3e: A forward roll

3f: A backward roll

Rolling actions can be developed by taking them on to, off, along or into contact with apparatus.

3g: A side roll along a bench

3h: A side roll on to or over a bench

3i: A side roll to go from or to contact with a bench

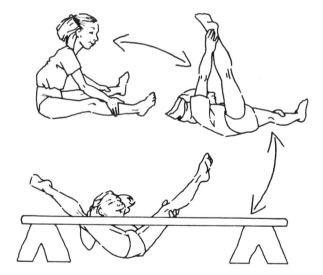

3j: A forward roll to come on to a bench

3k: A backward roll to come on to a bench

Activity 4: Sliding actions

A sliding action is one where the body remains supported on the same body part and there is continual contact with the ground.

In all sliding actions:

1 Stress body line and tension.
2 Ensure attention to body shape; if tucked, ensure body is fully tucked; if stretched, ensure it is fully stretched.

4a: Sliding on back

4b: Sliding on front

4c: Sliding on side

4d: Sliding on bottom

Sliding actions can be developed by changing body shape and by linking with apparatus.

4e: Sliding on back in tucked shape

4f: Sliding in a V shape with legs straddled

4g: Sliding along a bench on bottom

4h: Sliding off a box on front

4i: Sliding off a box on bottom

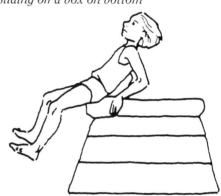

Activity 5: Balances

A balance is when the body is held still and good body line and body tension is maintained. In all balances:

1 Stress pulling away from the point of balance.

2 Stress the importance of body line – point toes and fingers, keep head up.

3 Stress the importance of body tension – pull everything together.

5a: Examples of simple balances on body patches

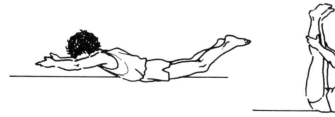

5b: Examples of more complex balances on body patches

5c: Examples of simple balances on body points

5d: Examples of more complex balances on body points

5e: Examples of more balances gained through a change of shape – usually leg design

5f: Examples of balances on large apparatus

Wall bars   Low beam or frame

5g: Examples of simple balances in contact with a partner

All balances can be developed in a number of ways:

1 The entry may be changed, i.e. the balance may be achieved from a different starting position.
2 The exit from the balance may be changed.
3 The body design in the balance may be changed.
4 The balance may be taken on to apparatus.

Examples of balances with different entries and exits and examples of further balances on apparatus can be seen on Workcards 7–12 (pp.82–84).

LESSON PLANS FOR YEARS 3 AND 4

Unit 1, lesson 1

Theme: Ways of travelling; jumping, rolling and sliding actions

Purpose: PoS a, c

Activity bank: Activities 1a, 3a, 3b, 4a

Resources: None

Introduction:
Pupils standing individually in a space. Run in and out of one another on command. No talking; move lightly on the feet. On command, speed up and slow down the running. Each time the stop command is given, everyone should be in a space. Slow to walking with back straight and toes pointed in front.

Development:
In a space, find another way of travelling on your feet. Pupils will skip, hop, jump. Find a way of travelling using feet only and keeping the feet together. This will focus on jumping actions. Practise a two feet to two feet jump, on the spot then on the move.
Link to a count of four: step 2, 3, 4 and jump, 2, 3, 4.
In a space, find a different way of travelling with the feet together. This time you may use other body parts. Pupils will use sliding, rolling, bunny jumping actions. Practice your way of travelling to a count of four. Look at some of the ideas from the group. All try some ideas and change your way of travelling if you wish.
Link to a count of four: step, 2, 3, 4, jump, 2, 3, 4 and travel, 2, 3, 4. Repeat. All perform this for teacher.

Conclusion:
In a space, all practise together a straight two feet to two feet jump. Land and crouch slowly to the floor to a sitting position with legs straight out in front of you. Turn over the legs in a rolling action towards the door. Stand and line up.

Unit 1, lesson 2

Theme: Ways of travelling; jumping, rolling and sliding actions

Purpose: PoS a, c

Activity bank: Activities 1a, 1c, 3a, 3b, 4a, 4b

Resources: None

Introduction:
Pupils work in a space individually. Practise the way of travelling used at the end of last lesson. All together, sit with legs straight out in front of you, feet together and turn across your legs in a rolling action. From the sitting position, find another way of travelling, still keeping feet together. Pupils will do a sliding action.

Development
Practice the roll and the slide. Can you do both of these moves with more of your body on the floor? This will give a pencil roll and slide on the back.
Link: from sitting, roll sideways, 2, 3, 4 and slide towards feet, slide towards head.

Link to previous lesson's work. Step, 2, 3, 4, jump, 2, 3, 4, lower to floor and roll, 2, 3, 4 and slide, 2, 3, 4.
All perform this movement phrase for teacher.

Conclusion:
Lie on tummy, slide towards head, slide towards feet, Curl into a ball and roll sideways.

Stretch out again and lie on tummy, relax, breath deeply like a 'sleeping lion'. When you are touched you are going to wake up, stretch and creep quietly to the door.

Unit 1, lesson 3

Theme: Ways of travelling; linking jumping to rolling to sliding

Purpose: PoS a, c

Activity bank: Activities 1a, 1b, 1c, 1d, 3a, 3b, 4a, 4b, 4c

Resources: Mats

Introduction:
Running in and out of one another, on command jump into the air as high as you can, and jump, and jump. Repeat several times. Change the way you jump each time.

In a space, practise a way of jumping from one foot, and then a way of jumping from two feet.

Development:
Join up with a partner. Each show your partner your ways of jumping. Partner then practises your ways of jumping. Choose two ways of jumping which you can both do and which look good. What makes a jump look good?
In turn, link your jumps together to a count of four. First person jumps one foot to same foot (a hop) 1, 2, 3, 4 and partner follows.
Link up with another pair and sit in groups of four. When you are told, go and get a mat. With one person to each corner, lift and carry it to a space. Set the mat down and sit on it.

Work with your partner travelling round the gym. When you come to a mat find a way of travelling across it using some of the sliding or rolling moves practised before. In between the mats, do your jumping sequence.
Give time for practise and then structure the movements with the pupils. Begin away from a mat, one partner leading the other following. Jump, 1, 2, 3, 4, partner follows. Repeat, if necessary, to bring you to a mat. Choose a way of travelling across the mat, partner follows. Repeat to next mat.
All perform this movement phrase for teacher.
Put away mats.

Conclusion:
Individually in a space, do a straight jump from two feet to two feet. Crouch down to the floor but stay on the feet. Hold this position, then put the hands on the floor and walk the hands out until you are lying on the floor on your tummy. Slide forwards, then walk back up to the crouch and then stand. Walk quietly to the door.

Unit 1, lesson 4 ▷

Theme: Ways of travelling; adapting moves to apparatus

Purpose: PoS a, b, c

Activity bank: Activities 1a, 1b, 1c, 3a, 3b, 3e, 4a, 4b, 4c

Resources: Mats and benches

Introduction:
With your partner from the last lesson, practise the last set of moves you did at the end of the lesson.

Development:
Join with another pair to get out apparatus. In your fours, first get out a mat and place it in a space when told to do so. Next get out a bench and place it in a space near to the mat. Sit on the mat.
Working with your partner, two pairs to one mat and one bench, begin away from the mat and travel to the mat using the jumping sequence from the last lesson. Travel across the mat using ideas from the last lesson.

Think about the change from jumping to low travel across mat. Try some different ways of linking so that all of the moves look smooth and attractive.
Find a way of travelling along the bench. Use some of the ideas you used on the floor, e.g. sliding, rolling or jumping. Link together the jumping sequence, low travel and bench travel.
All perform this movement phrase for teacher.
Put away apparatus.

Conclusion:
Work with your partner in a space on the floor. One person make a bridge for the other one to go under.

Change over and try again. Stand and walk quietly to the door.

Unit 1, lesson 5 ▷

Theme: Ways of travelling; moving under a partner

Purpose: PoS a

Activity bank: Activities 3a, 3b, 3c, 4a, 4b, 4c, 5c, 5d

Resources: Mats

Introduction:
Start by running around the room. On command, jump, 2, 3, 4 and crouch to slide down to tummy. Repeat.

With your partner, practise one of the ideas from the last lesson, where one person makes a bridge for the other to go under.

Development:
In fours, get out one mat and place it in a space, then return to get a second mat and place that in a space.
Work two to a mat. Begin away from the mat and perform a jumping sequence to come to the mat. One person starts and their partner follows. When the first person has jumped on to the mat, they make a bridge for their partner to go under when they have jumped on to

the mat. Find a way of both rolling along the mat and getting to feet to repeat. Think about links, e.g. how to get down into the bridge position and out into the roll, or down to go under the bridge and out into the roll.
Perform the movement phrase, jump to bridge to roll away, with half the group working at a time. The other half watch and look for good ideas.
Put away mats.

Conclusion:
Sitting in a space on the floor, turn to make a bridge tummy down. Turn to make a bridge tummy up. Turn

to make a bridge side up. Make a bridge standing. Straighten up and walk quietly to the door.

Unit 1, lesson 6

Theme: Ways of travelling; extending range of moves, smooth links

Purpose: PoS a, c

Activity bank: Activities 1a, 1b, 1c, 1f, 3a, 3b, 4a, 4b, 4c, 5c, 4d

Resources: Mats

Introduction:
Travel round the room by sliding or rolling. On command, stop and get into a bridge position, then continue travelling. Repeat, showing different bridge positions each time.

Development:
Get out mats in groups of four, one mat between two. Working individually on the mats try some of these ideas:
from sliding on tummy, push to make a bridge, tummy down. Lift one foot off the floor and stretch.
from pencil rolling, push to make a bridge, tummy down. Lift one foot off the floor and stretch.
from pencil rolling, push to make a bridge, tummy up. Lift one foot off the floor and stretch.
from sliding on back, push to make a bridge, tummy up. Lift one foot off the floor and stretch.
from sliding on side, push to make a bridge, side up. Lift one arm or foot off the floor and stretch.
from jumping two feet to two feet, make a standing bridge.
With partner, work out ways of sliding under the bridge and rolling under the bridge. Try a side tucked roll (egg roll) under the bridge.
Link jumping to making a bridge (partner goes under) to rolling and making a second bridge (partner goes under).
All perform your best ideas for teacher.
Put away mats.

Conclusion:
Sitting in a space on the floor, roll sideways across the legs, stretch to a pencil roll, tuck to an egg roll, stretch to a tummy slide and turn to a back slide. Stand and walk quietly to the door.

Unit 1, lesson 7

Theme: Way of travelling; adapting to apparatus

Purpose: PoS a, b, c

Activity bank: Activities 1a, 1b, 1c, 3a, 3b, 3c, 3d, 3e, 4a, 4b, 4c, 5c, 5d

Resources: Mats and benches

Introduction:
Running in and out of one another, stop on command and crouch to slide to front, roll to side and get back to feet, then jump, 2, 3, 4 and make a bridge.

Development:
In groups of four, get out one mat and one bench and place them in a space.
Work with your partner, two pairs to a bench.
Find ways of making a bridge in contact with the bench. One makes the bridge and their partner goes underneath. Try several ways and share your ideas with the rest of the group.
Encourage the pupils to try: bridge tummy down with hands on the bench; bridge tummy down with feet on bench; standing bridge with feet on bench.
Choose one way of making a bridge and going under and then find a way of both rolling away from the bench.
All perform for teacher: make a bridge on the bench, partner goes under and both roll away.
Put away apparatus.

Conclusion:
In a space, sit with legs straddled, then get to feet without bending knees. Repeat. Travel to door with legs straddled.

Unit 1, lesson 8 ▷

Theme: Ways of travelling; sequencing on apparatus

Purpose: PoS a, c

Activity bank: Activities 1a, 1b, 1c, 1d, 1f, 3a, 3b, 4a, 4b, 4c, 5c, 5d

Resources: Mats and benches

Introduction:
Travelling round the room, on command jump two feet to two feet. Repeat travel, but this time hop then skip, then jump one foot to the other (leaping).

Join with partner and recap on jumping phrase where one jumps, 2, 3, 4 and the other follows. Change jump and repeat.

Development:
In groups of four, get out two mats and one bench and place them in a space.
Working with a partner, begin away from the mat and perform a jumping phrase to bring you to the mat. Travel along the mat to come to the bench. One person makes a bridge on the bench, the other goes under then both roll away.

Repeat and practise.
Work on the links so that they are smooth.
All perform for teacher: jumping phrase to mat, travel to bench, make a bridge, partner goes under and both roll away.
Put away apparatus.

Conclusion:
In a space, sit with legs straddled. Push to a side star and

tuck to an egg roll. Repeat. Stand and walk quietly to the door.

Unit 1, lesson 9 ▷

Theme: Ways of travelling; over and under partner

Purpose: PoS a, b, c

Activity bank: Activities 1a, 1b, 1c, 1d, 1f, 3a, 3b, 4a, 4b, 4c, 4d, 5c, 5d

Resources: Mats

Introduction:
Travel round the room doing bunny jumps.
Stand with legs straddled and then travel with legs straddled.

Travel with legs straddled and make it turn. Find another way of travelling with legs straddled, using hands as well as feet. Can you make this travel turn?

Development:
In groups of four, get out two mats and one bench. Arrange the apparatus so that there is a pathway around the gym.
Recap on the sequence from the last lesson: jumping phrase to mat, travel to bench, make a bridge, partner goes through and both roll away. Practise and repeat, but this time the jumping phrase takes you to another bench.

Find ways of travelling along the bench and on to and off the bench with straddled legs. Choose one of these ways and link the whole sequence: jump to travel to make a bridge to roll to straddle travel and hold. Repeat from starting position.
All perform their best way of travelling along or on and off the bench with straddled legs for teacher.
Put away apparatus.

Conclusion:
Work in a space with a partner. One makes a shape on the floor and the other jumps over it. Change over and

try to do a different jump. Repeat several times. Stand and walk quietly to the door.

Unit 1, lesson 10

Theme: Ways of travelling; over and under partner

Purpose: PoS a, c

Activity bank: Activities 1a, 1b, 1c, 1d, 1f, 3a, 3b, 4a, 4b, 4c, 4d, 5c, 5d

Resources: Mats

Introduction:
Running round the space, on command freeze. Jumping two feet to two feet, on command freeze making a bridge with your legs. Travel by rolling, on command freeze.

Development:
Work in groups of three. Number each member of the group 1, 2 or 3.
Travel by jumping. On command Number 1 freezes and makes a bridge with the legs. Numbers 2 and 3 travel by rolling and free Number 1 by rolling under their legs.
All travel by sliding. On command Numbers 2 and 3 freeze and make a bridge and Number 1 frees them by sliding under the bridge.
In groups of four get out one mat and place it in a space, then return for a second mat.

Work in pairs, numbered 1 and 2. Number 1 makes a bridge for the other to go under, then Number 2 makes a shape for partner to go over.
Link jumping to making bridge to rolling out to travelling over shape made by partner.
Perform this phrase for teacher.
Perform this phrase for the other half of the group. The pupils watching look for smooth links between under and over movements.
Put away mats.

Conclusion:
Work in a space with a partner. Number 1 makes a bridge tummy down, Number 2 travels under by sliding and Number 1 travels along as 2 goes under. Change over and repeat.
Stand and walk quietly to the door.

Unit 1, lesson 11

Theme: Ways of travelling; sequencing in pairs on apparatus

Purpose: PoS a, b, c

Activity bank: Activities 1a, 1b, 1c, 1d, 1f, 3a, 3b, 4a, 4b, 4c, 5c, 5d

Resources: Mats and benches

Introduction:
Running round the space, on command freeze. Jumping two feet to two feet, on command freeze making a bridge with your legs. Travel by rolling, on command freeze.

Work in pairs, numbered 1 and 2. All travel by sliding. On command Number 2 freezes and makes a shape for Number 1 to go over. Repeat, with Number 1 freezing and Number 2 going over the shape.

Development:
In groups of four, get out two mats and one bench. Arrange the apparatus in a pathway round the room. With a partner, put together a sequence with a jumping phrase, an over and under phrase and a rolling phrase.

Guide individual pairs. Encourage use of the floor, mats and benches. Allow time for practise.
Perform your sequence (or as much of the sequence as you have practised).

Conclusion:
Lie on your back in a space on the floor beside your partner. When you are touched by the teacher, you and your partner show some way of travelling over and under, then line up at the door.

Unit 1, lesson 12

Theme: Ways of travelling; Sequencing in pairs on apparatus

Purpose: PoS a, b, c

Activity bank: Activities 1a, 1b, 1c, 1d, 1f, 3a, 3b, 4a, 4b, 4c, 5c, 5d

Resources: Mats and benches

Introduction:
Move around the room by rolling. On command, show a bridge, lower into a sliding action and on command show a shape for a partner to travel over.

Development:
In groups of four, get out two mats and one bench and place them in a space.
In pairs, practise the sequence from the previous lesson. Half the group shows their sequences. The other pupils watch one pair at a time to see whether they have answered the task: jumping phrase, travel under, travel over and rolling phrase.
Ask for comments about which moves look good and why.
Change roles and repeat.
Put away apparatus.

Conclusion:
Stand in a space, step to stand with legs straddled, walk hands down to lie on front. Like 'sleeping lions', relax and breath deeply. When touched, creep to the door.

Unit 2, lesson 1

Theme: Moving into and out of balance; Introduce idea of balance, how to balance gymnastically

Purpose: PoS a, b, c

Activity bank: Activities 3a, 3b, 3c, 4a, 4b, 4c, 5a, 5b

Resources: None

Introduction:
Travel round the room by running and on command freeze, hold position and stretch away from the floor, then continue travelling.
Travel using hands and feet, slow the travel down and on command, freeze and stretch away from the floor, then continue travelling.
Travel by sliding and on command freeze and stretch away from the floor, then continue travelling. This time on 'freeze', can you lift a foot or leg or hand off the floor.

Development:
From a sitting position, all travel by sliding on bottom and legs. On command, freeze and balance on bottom. Can you take hands off the floor?
From a sitting position, roll across legs. On command, balance on bottom, hold still for count of three, then continue roll. Find another roll where you can hold still somewhere in the roll. Find a slide where you can hold still within the slide.
Link, slide to balance, roll to balance, repeat. Stress pulling up and away from base to hold balance.
Perform repeated phrase for teacher.

Conclusion:
Stand with two feet together. Lift one foot off the floor, keep the lifted leg straight and point the toe. Can you hold this still with the foot out to the front? and to the back? and the side? What can you do with your arms to help?

Unit 2, lesson 2

Theme: Moving into and out of balance; introducing some balances

Purpose: PoS a, b, c

Activity bank: Activities 3a, 3b, 3c, 4a, 4b, 4c, 5a, 5b

Resources: None

Introduction:
Travel in and out of one another using any way of travelling that you think is 'gymnastics'. (Suggest bunny jumps, jumping, rolling, sliding etc.) On command, freeze and stretch away from balance.

Development:
All travel by rolling sideways from sitting, turning over legs. On command, turn on to bottom and freeze. Show straight legs with hands off floor if you can. Repeat and practise.
Walk round the room pointing toes. On command freeze and hold a one foot balance. Put the other leg out to the side, to the front, to the back and see where you can hold it still.

All travel by sliding on tummy. On command, pull up into a balance with two hands and one knee or one foot down. Stretch away from the floor.
Link: walk to one foot balance, slowly crouch to floor and move into roll to bottom balance, stretch to tummy and push to one knee or foot and two hands balance. Practise with the teacher counting out the timing. Perform phrase for teacher.

Conclusion:
In a space, sit with legs straight, feet and knees together. Lift to tuck or pike seat. Turn to hands and knees balance. Push to one knee or foot and two hands balance. Turn back to sitting and wait to be told to move to the door.

Unit 2, lesson 3

Theme: Moving into and out of balance; star-shape balances

Purpose: PoS a, b, c

Activity bank: Activities 3a, 3b, 3c, 4a, 4b, 4c, 5a, 5b

Resources: None

Introduction:
Travel round the room by walking. On command freeze and stretch. Pupils should have legs and arms stretched in a star shape. Repeat. Keeping the arms and legs stretched out, can you get the hands on the floor?

Development:
Show a star shape close to the floor. Show a star shape far away from the floor. Find another way of making a star shape. Look at other people's ideas and share ideas within the group. Look for star tummy down, star tummy up, star on side, star on one foot and star jump. Choose a star shape that you can balance in. Find a way of travelling into that balance, hold the star and find a way of travelling out of that star shape. Change the way of travelling; the way of travelling into the balance must be different from the way of travelling out.
Link: travel into star, out of star and back into star and hold.
Perform this phrase for teacher.

Conclusion:
Sitting with the legs straight out in front of you, lift to a pike or tuck seat, return to sitting and move into the star shape you had before. Repeat.

59

Unit 2, lesson 4

Theme: Moving into and out of balance; shoulder stand

Purpose: PoS a, c

Activity bank: Activities 3a, 3b, 3c, 4a, 4b, 4c, 5a, 5b

Resources: Mats

Introduction:
Travel round room using feet. On command, change to hands and feet. On command, freeze and stretch away from base. Repeat.

Travel by pencil roll. On command, stop on back and pull or push up into a balance with your feet above your head.

Development:
In groups of four, get out one mat and return for a second mat. Place them in a space and sit down with one pair on each mat.
In a space, from lying flat push to a shoulder stand. Hold still and stretch feet above head away from base. Try to straddle legs in the shoulder stand.

Link a balance on bottom to a balance on hands and feet or knees to a balance on shoulders or shoulders and back.
All perform this phrase for teacher.

Conclusion:
In a space, from standing crouch to squat and turn into shoulder stand. Try sideways, backwards and forwards. Repeat.

Put away mats.
Stand and walk quietly to the door.

Unit 2, lesson 5

Theme: Moving into and out of balance; distinguishing body 'points' and 'patches'

Purpose: PoS a, c

Activity bank: Activities 3a, 3b, 3c, 4a, 4b, 4c, 5a, 5b

Resources: Mats

Introduction:
Travel round by sliding and move into a balance on bottom, shoulders or tummy. These are body 'patches'. Travel on hands and feet and show a balance on two

hands and one foot or on two feet and one hand. These are body 'points'. Repeat.
Why do we call some body parts 'points' and others 'patches'?

Development:
Travel round using hands and feet. On command, freeze and show a balance on three points.
Travel round on bottom. On command, freeze and show a balance on two points or patches.
Travel on front and on command show a balance on two points or patches.
In groups of four, get out one mat and then return for a second mat.

Working individually, two to a mat, find ways of balancing on points. Try balances on three points, then two, then one.
Link movement into a balance on points to a balance on patches. Repeat this phrase.
Perform the phrase, with half the group working at a time. The others watch and look for the balances which look good. Why do some balance look better than others?

Conclusion:
Lie on your front and stretch to a star shape, then get to your feet without bending the legs. Stand upright, with

feet together, breath deeply and walk quietly to the door.

Unit 2, lesson 6

Theme: Moving into and out of balance; adapting balances to apparatus

Purpose: PoS a, c

Activity bank: Activities 3a, 3b, 3c, 3d, 3e, 4a, 4b, 4c, 5a, 5b

Resources: Benches or tressles and frames

Introduction:
Travel round the room by rolling. On command, balance on three points. Repeat several times, balancing on one patch, on two points, on two patches.

Development:
Link a balance on two or three points to a balance on one or two patches.
In groups of four, get out one bench and two mats.
Working on your own, find a way of putting one of your balances on to the bench or touching the bench in some way. Try to find another balance which touches the bench.
Link a balance on patches to a balance on points on, or touching, the bench.
Perform this phrase and repeat for teacher.
Put away apparatus.

Conclusion:
Sitting in a space with the legs straight out in front of you, tuck or pike to balance on bottom (patch). Rock to balance on the shoulders, pushing through to the feet. Stand and walk quietly to the door.

Unit 2, lesson 7

Theme: Moving into and out of balance; into and out of balance on apparatus

Purpose: PoS a, c

Activity bank: Activities 3a, 3b, 3c, 3d, 3f, 4a, 4b, 4c, 5a, 5b

Resources: Mats and benches/tressles

Introduction:
Travel by running and on command, freeze and pull away to balance on one foot (one point). Repeat.
Travel on hands and feet and on command, freeze to balance on three points. Repeat, this time balancing on two points.
Travel by rolling and freeze to balance on two patches. Repeat, balancing on one patch. Stress stretching away from the base to hold the balance still and make it look good.

Development:
In groups of four, get out two mats and one bench.
Working individually, find a way of travelling on feet into a balance on the apparatus.
Find a way of travelling on hands and feet into a balance on, or touching, the apparatus.
Find a way of travelling by rolling into a balance on, or touching, the apparatus.
Select two ways of travelling into different balances. Link the two together into travel and balance, travel and balance.
Present this phrase to teacher.
Put away apparatus.

Conclusion:
Extend the conclusion to the previous lesson: travel by sideways rolling across legs and hold in a pike seat balance, then push back into shoulder stand, pushing through to the feet. Stand and walk quietly to the door.

Unit 2, lesson 8

Theme: Moving into and out of balance; change of direction

Purpose: PoS a, b, c

Activity bank: Activities 3a, 3b, 3c, 3d, 3f, 4a, 4b, 4c, 4d, 4f, 4g, 4h, 5a, 5b

Resources: Mats and benches

Introduction:
Running in and out of one another, on command change direction.
On the spot, jump from two feet to two feet and turn on command to face a different direction.

Travel by rolling and on command change to travel in a different direction.

Development:
In groups of four, get out two mats and one bench. Set out the apparatus so that there are right angles between each mat and bench. The benches and mats should make a pathway round the room.
Working individually, begin at the end of a mat and travel towards a bench. Roll to balance, turn to get on to

the bench, travel along the bench and into a balance. Repeat this phrase.
Vary the phrase by changing the travel or the balance.
Practise travel to balance, turn and travel to balance.
Perform this phrase for teacher. Repeat, continuing along apparatus if possible.
Put away apparatus.

Conclusion:
Perform a pike or tuck seat balance and swivel to face a different direction. From this balance, push to a

shoulder stand and swivel to come down facing a different way. Stand and walk quietly to the door.

Unit 2, lesson 9

Theme: Moving into and out of balance; change of direction

Purpose: PoS a, c

Activity bank: Activities 3a, 3b, 3c, 3d, 3f, 3g, 4a, 4b, 4c, 4d, 4e, 4f, 4g, 4h, 5a, 5b

Resources: Mats and benches

Introduction:
Travel by sliding towards feet. Change to travel towards hands, to one side and to the other side.

Travel by rolling sideways towards a window, swivel to roll sideways towards the door.

Development:
In groups of four, get out two mats and benches.
Recap on the previous lesson. Roll to balance, turn and travel to balance, continue travelling, turn to get off the bench, onto and along another mat.
Return to starting position and practise moves. Teacher gives timing and direction.

Perform phrase of roll to balance, turn to travel and balance, turn to travel and hold finish.
Perform this phrase, with half the group working at a time. The other half should look for answering of the task and clear changes of direction.

Conclusion:
Stand with two feet together, stretch up and step to balance on one foot, tuck to balance in crouch on two

feet, roll to balance on seat or shoulders.
Stand and walk quietly to the door.

Unit 2, lesson 10

Theme: Moving into and out of balance; changing body shape in balance

Purpose: PoS a, b, c

Activity bank: Activities 3a, 3b, 3c, 3d, 3f, 3g, 4a, 4b, 4c, 4d, 4e, 4f, 4g, 4h, 5a, 5b

Resources: Mats, benches and low boxes

Introduction:
Walking round the room, on command freeze and balance on one foot, making a wide shape. Tuck slowly to crouch and roll. On command, freeze and balance in a long shape. Change way of rolling and balance in a wide shape this time.

Development:
In groups of four, get out two mats, one bench and one low box.
Working individually, link travel along the bench to a balance and travel over the box to a balance. Make one balance long and the other wide.

Look at some of the ideas from the group. Apparatus can help to stabilise and so allow for straddling the legs in a seat balance, shoulder stand, headstand etc.
Perform this phrase twice. Half the group perform, while the other half look for interesting ideas on shape in balance.

Conclusion:
Sitting back to back with a partner, lift into a tuck or pike seat and swivel round to face partner and touch feet in the air. Stand and walk quietly to the door.

Unit 2, lesson 11

Theme: Moving into and out of balance; shape and direction in relation to a partner

Purpose: PoS a, b, c   e2

Activity bank: Activities 1e, 3b, 3c, 3d, 3f, 3g, 4a, 4b, 4c, 4d, 4e, 4f, 4g, 4h, 5a, 5b

Resources: Mats

Introduction:
Work with a partner. One person leads by travelling on the feet, partner follows. Change travel, change leader, change direction.

Development:
In fours, get out one mat between two.
Working with a partner, choose one way of travelling into a balance that you can both perform.
Practise this move, working together so that both do the same thing at the same time.
Now change the balance so that one of you shows a wide shape while the other shows a long shape.

Choose another travel into balance and show the different shapes. Can you include a change of direction in your travel?
Link travel to balance, travel to balance and show change of shape and direction.
Perform this phrase and repeat it for teacher.
Put away mats.

Conclusion:
With partner, sit back to back and push to seat balance, shoulder stand or side star. One should show a long shape and the other a wide shape. Hold this still. Then stand and walk quietly to the door.

Unit 2, lesson 12

Theme: Moving into and out of balance; shapes in pairs on apparatus

Purpose: PoS a, b, c

Activity bank: Activities 3a, 3b, 3c, 3d, 3f, 3g, 4a, 4b, 4c, 4d, 4e, 4f, 4g, 4h, 5a, 5b

Resources: Mats, benches and low boxes

Introduction:
Travel round by rolling and freeze in a wide balance on command. Repeat, this time freezing in a long balance on command. Change travel to sliding and repeat.

Development:
Working with a partner, choose one way of travelling into a balance from the last lesson. Practise it, moving in time with one another and show the two different shapes in the balance.
In groups of four, get out two mats and one bench or low box.
With your partner, find ways of travelling over the bench into a balance, along the bench into a balance and on to the bench into a balance. Work on varying the shape of the balances.
Link travel to balance, travel to balance and show different shapes in the balances. Repeat the phrase.
Perform sequences with half the group working at a time. The other half watch and look for good shape in balance and smooth linking. They give feedback to the performers.
Change over and repeat.
Put apparatus away.

Conclusion:
In a sitting position, push to a side star balance, turn to a front support balance, walk hands towards feet to stand and step to a one foot balance. Stand and walk quietly to the door.

LESSON PLANS FOR YEARS 5 AND 6

Unit 3, lesson 1

Theme: Ways of travelling; jumping and stepping actions

Purpose: PoS a, c

Activity bank: Activities 1a, 1b, 1c, 1d, 1e, 1f, 2a, 2b, 2c, 2d

Resources: None

Introduction:
Work individually in a space, running in and out of one another. Use all the space, with no talking. Change speed, or direction, on command.

Running in and out of one another, on command jump, then continue running. Slow travel down to walking, with back straight, head up and toes pointed. Take this stepping way of travelling on to hands and feet.

Development:
Working individually in a space, choose any jumping action that you can do well and practise it. Concentrate on stretching away from the floor in the air and then bending knees and ankles to land quietly and safely. Can you hold your landing, i.e. not travel forward from it?
Travel by jogging and on command, jump, land and hold. Teacher counts the beat and talks the pupils through the phrase, e.g. travel, 1, 2, 3 and jump and land and hold.
From landing, take yourself into travelling by stepping using hands and feet. Repeat the phrase, first with teacher counting through, then in the pupil's own time.

Look at ways of travelling using hands and feet. Teacher should encourage pupils to move slowly, putting one part down after the other, concentrating on body line and pointing the toes.
Choose a different way of travelling using a stepping action. Can you turn whilst stepping? Share some ideas. All try starting from standing in straddle, bending to put the hands on the floor, walking the hands forward using little steps for 1, 2, 3, 4 and jumping to bring the feet in to follow. Practise this skill. Can you get the feet to land beside the hands? Practise your phrase of: travel and jump, land and hold, move into hands and feet travel and change into straddle walk.

Conclusion:
Working individually in a space, stand in a straddle position and find a way of getting into a straddle seat

without bending your knees. Repeat. Stand and walk quietly to the door.

Unit 3, lesson 2

Theme: Ways of travelling; jumping and stepping actions using low apparatus

Purpose: PoS a, b, c

Activity bank: Activities 1a, 1b, 1c, 1d, 1e, 1f, 1k 1l, 1m, 1o, 1p, 2d, 2e, 2h, 2i

Resources: Benches

Introduction:
Travel in and out of one another. On command, jump into the air, remembering how to land properly. Repeat several times, changing the jump each time.

Next time you jump, control the landing and take it into a hands and feet travel. All practise the straddle stepping skill from the end of the last lesson.

Development:
In a space, repeat the closing task from the previous lesson. How many ways can you find of getting from feet to seat in a straddle without bending the knees? Share some ideas, e.g. reaching through the legs to take the weight on the hands, walking the hands forwards and rotating sideways, straddle forward roll.
In twos, get a bench out and place it in a space, then sit by the bench.
Individually practise ways of jumping on to and off the

bench. Find ways of jumping along the bench. Link: jump on to, off, on to and along the bench.
Find a way of travelling along the bench with legs straddled. Use hands and feet if you can. Find another way.
Find a way of getting on to the bench with legs straddled.
Find a way of getting off the bench with legs straddled.
Find a way of getting from feet to seat on the bench with legs straddled.
Put away benches.

Conclusion:
Working individually in a space, stand in a crouch position with the hands on the floor in front of you and push from the legs to perform a 'donkey kick', i.e. take the weight on to the hands by lifting the hips above the hands. Do not tuck the head in. Look at the floor and keep the legs bent and the heels and the knees together. Those who can do this easily try it again, but with straddled legs. Can you feel a moment when the weight catches above the hands? Stand and shake the wrists out. Walk quietly to the door.

Unit 3, lesson 3

Theme: Ways of travelling; jumping and stepping actions, taking weight on hands on apparatus

Purpose: PoS a, c

Activity bank: Activities 1a, 1b, 1c, 1d, 1e, 1f, 1k, 1l, 1m, 1o, 1p, 2d, 2e, 2h, 2i, 2j

Resources: Benches and mats

Introduction:
Running in and out of one another, jump on command. Repeat several times. next time, control landing and go into either 'donkey kicks' or straddled legs lift.

Development:
In twos, get one bench and one mat. Place them in a space and sit on the mat.
Practise your jumping phrase from the last lesson. Jump onto and off, onto and along the bench. Stop your jumping phrase part way along the bench and check your landing. Take this into the 'donkey kicks' or the straddle lift. Try using hands and feet travel to take you along, off and back on to the bench.
Link your jumping phrase to your hands and feet travel. Look at the sequences, with half the group working at a time. Those watching should look for good linking of jumps to hands and feet travel.
Change roles and repeat.
Put away apparatus.

Conclusion:
Sit in a straddle seat position, lean forward and to one side and try to roll across your back. This is a circle roll. Teacher looks for someone who can perform this skill to show the group. Then all try again. This is the skill you are going to learn and link to your sequence next week. Stand and walk quietly to the door.

Unit 3, lesson 4

Theme: Ways of travelling; circle rolling and side rolling

Purpose: PoS a, b

Activity bank: Activities 3c, 3d

Resources: Mats; one copy each of Workcards 1 and 2 per pupil

Introduction:
Running in and out of one another, jump on command. Repeat several times, controlling the landings. On command, after the jump, step to a straddle stand and get to a straddle seat without bending the knees or closing the straddle. Use the rolling action you tried at the end of the last lesson.

Development:
In twos, get out a mat between two and sit on your mat. Practise the circle roll. Concentrate on body tension – you must hold the angle between the legs and the tummy. Use a demonstration and help individuals who are having difficulty.
Show the starting position for the side roll. Ask the pupils to find a way of rolling from that position. Ask the pupils to try to get back to the same position to finish the roll. Look for a pupil who can do the side roll; use a demonstration. It may be necessary to have all pupils facing in the same direction in order to orientate them. All try the roll together, then pupils practise on their own. Working in pairs, use Workcards 1 and 2 (see pp. 78 and 79) to help with practising the circle roll and side roll. Put mats away.

Conclusion:
Working individually in a space, show the starting position for either a side roll or a circle roll. Perform the roll, get to a straddle stand from the finishing position and then jump to bring the feet together. Walk quietly to the door.

Unit 3, lesson 5

Theme: Ways of travelling; jumping, stepping, rolling on to apparatus

1m, 1o, 1p, 2d, 2e, 2h, 2i, 2j, 3c, 3d, 3f, 3g, 3h, 3i

Purpose: PoS a, c

Resources: Mats and benches

Activity bank: Activities 1a, 1b, 1c, 1d, 1e, 1f, 1k, 1l,

Introduction:
Running in and out of one another, jumping on command. Take this into hands and feet travel, come to a straddle stand and lower to a straddle seat, then travel from this position.

Development:
In twos, get out one mat and one bench and sit down on the mat.
Practise the side roll or the circle roll on the mat. Work out a way of doing one or both of these rolls in contact with you bench. It may be along the bench, from the bench or to the bench.

Look at the ideas, with half the group working at a time. Working individually try some more ideas or practise one way.
Link jumping to hands and feet travel to rolling. Practise this and then show sequences, with half the group working at a time. Those watching should look for good ideas and smooth links.

Conclusion:
Stand in a space, with feet together. Swing your arms up and back, bending the knees as the back swing goes through. Swing 1, 2, 3, 4 and jump forward. Repeat.

Stand still and swing one leg back and forward, swing 1, 2, 3, 4 and jump forward. Try this again, but this time swing the leg through, bring the knee high and jump to two feet. Walk quietly to the door.

Unit 3, lesson 6

Theme: Ways of travelling; swinging to put body into motion on and from apparatus

Activity bank: Activities 1a, 1b, 1c, 1d, 1e, 1i, 3a, 3b, 3c, 3d

Purpose: PoS a

Resources: Mats and apparatus (see diagram)

Introduction:
Running in and out of one another, jump on command; repeat. Stand still and swing a part of your body which will take you into a jump. Try arms, try one leg, then the other. Try swinging sideways the across body to make you turn. Go into hands and feet travel. Can you use an arm or a leg to swing into a turn or roll? Look for ideas.

Development:
In groups of four, get out apparatus and set it out as shown below. Sit down by your apparatus when ready.

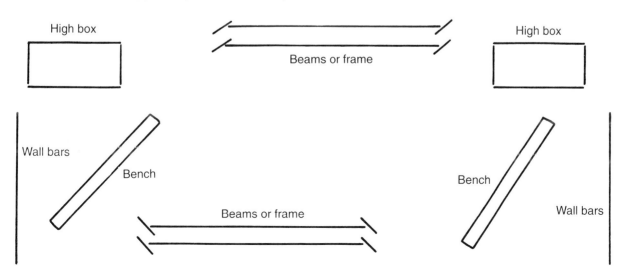

Using your section of apparatus, find ways of swinging to take you into motion. If you can hang from the apparatus, swing the lower body to take you away from the apparatus. If you can stand on the apparatus, swing to take you up from it and then land on the floor. On the floor, swing to make you turn.

Stop work and sit by your apparatus. When told to do so, move to the next piece. The task is as in the Introduction. When you have attempted the task on each different piece of apparatus, stop work and sit down by the apparatus.

Put away apparatus and sit in a space on the floor.

Conclusion:
Stand in a space, with feet together. Swing your arms up and back, bending the knees as the back swing goes through. Swing 1, 2, 3, 4 and jump forward. Repeat.

Stand still and swing one leg back and forward, swing 1, 2, 3, 4 and jump forward. Try this again, but this time swing the leg through, bring the knee high and jump to two feet. Walk quietly to the door.

Unit 3, lesson 7

Theme: Ways of travelling; swinging into travelling with speed change; the split kick

Purpose: PoS a, b

Activity bank: Activities 1a, 1b, 1c, 1d, 1e, 1f, 1g, 1h, 1i, 1j, 1k, 1l, 1m, 1n, 1o, 1p, 1q

Resources: Mats and apparatus (as lesson 6)

Introduction:
Travelling round the gym, swing into jumping on command. Swing into motion from stillness; travel on any body parts.

Development:
In groups of four, get out apparatus and set out as in previous lesson. Sit down by your apparatus when ready. Working individually, find a pathway round the apparatus that gives a jumping action, a stepping action and a rolling action linked together. Put swinging actions in where you can. Practise the sequence. Try to stress the swing by giving it strength and speed and by slowing down the movement after the swing.

Show the sequences, with half the group working at a time. Those watching should look for good swinging actions and contrasting speeds.

Put away apparatus and stand in space.

Conclusion:
Swing one leg forward and high. As it pulls you off the ground, follow through with the other leg and change legs in the air. Use the arms to help. This is a 'split kick'.

Step with the left foot, kick with the right, follow through with the left, land on the right and step through with the left. Walk quietly to the door.

Unit 3, lesson 8

Theme: Ways of travelling; stepping and jumping; the split kick, hurdle step and cartwheel

Purpose: PoS a, b, c

Activity bank: Activities 1d, 1t, 2d

Resources: Mats

Introduction:
Stepping round the room, lift the knees and point the toes. Skipping round the room, swing the arms and lift the knees, keep the head up. Go from step to hop and jump. Repeat.

Development:

In twos, get out one mat between two and sit on your mat.

Practise the split kick jump. Watch one another and try to help. Teacher feeds in teaching points, as previous lesson.

Move two steps away from your mat. Stand with the feet together, then step on to the left foot and hop, bringing the right knee through. Now do the same but hop and land on two feet. Step on the left, hop lifting the right knee and land on two feet. This is a hurdle step. Some pupils will find this difficult so practise it through quickly and then give a choice.

Practise linking two swinging jumps of your choice, e.g. a hurdle step (as above) followed by a split kick. Link the jumps closely, i.e. with only one or two steps in between. Practise any other action which takes you on to other body parts and has a swinging action in it. Look for pupils doing a bunny jump and using arm swing to get length. Look for pupils doing a cartwheel. Again, some pupils will have difficulty with these skills so you need to go through the actions and main teaching points quickly and allow variation of skill as soon as possible.

Bunny jump – start at edge of the mat in a crouch position, draw the arms back in preparation, look forward keeping the hips low, drive the arms through fast and reach forward and up, extend the hips, place hands on the mat and pull the legs into tuck. Practise getting as far along mat as possible.

Cartwheel – begin sideways on to the mat, generally with the mat to your left. Lift the left foot and reach step with the left foot then the left hand, the right hand and the right foot. Aim to go along the mat in a straight line. Count one and two and three and four as the hands and feet are placed. To bring the body round in a wheeling action, you need to push with the left leg and swing with the right leg, then reach with the right leg and push with the left hand, then the right hand.

To travel across your mat, do two jumping actions with swings linked to a travel which is lower and on other body parts, with a swinging action if you can.

Look at the whole group's work.

Conclusion:

Standing in a space, all try stepping on to the left foot, swinging the right leg through, lifting the knee in a hopping action and landing on two feet.

Tell the group that when they enter the gym for the next lesson they must practise one of the skills they learnt today – the split kick, the hurdle step, the cartwheel, the bunny jump, or all four linked. Walk quietly to the door.

Unit 3, lesson 9 ▷

Theme: Ways of travelling; swinging into travel, partner work on low apparatus

Purpose: PoS a, c

Activity bank: All activities

Resources: Mats and benches

Introduction:

Individually, run around the room; use the space and get yourself warm. When you feel ready, practise one or several of the skills you worked on in the last lesson.

Development:

In twos, work with a partner and link at least two different skills which involve swinging actions together. If you can do so, include the split kick or the hurdle step. Get out one bench between two.

Put your moves on to the apparatus. They may take you on to and off, along or over the apparatus.

The next section of this lesson is designed to help pupils begin to draw on what they learned previously in this unit of work.

In twos, either do the two moves with swinging actions together or one after the other, so that someone watching could tell you are working with a partner. From the second move, work on your own and show one way of rolling away from the apparatus, one way of rolling towards it and one way of turning along it. Choose moves which you can do well but which are the most difficult and skilful that you have mastered.

Conclusion:

With your partner, stand back to back and move away from one another using the first action you had on the apparatus. Then turn to face one another and lower to the floor; slide towards one another until you can hold hands. Can you pull one another to sitting? Repeat. Stand and walk quietly to the door.

Unit 3, lesson 10

Theme: Ways of travelling; partner work on apparatus

Purpose: PoS a, c

Activity bank: All activities

Resources: Mats and benches

Introduction:
Running in and out of one another, on command change travel to stepping, to hands to feet stepping, to rolling, to jumping. Repeat.

Development:
In twos, get out one mat and one bench. Sit down on the mat and think about the work you did in the previous lesson.
Recap on two swinging actions and then share ideas on rolling away from, to and along the apparatus. Link a sequence together so that both of you can work on the apparatus together. You need not necessarily both be doing the same moves or working in unison or relationship with one another.
Look at the sequences, with half the group working at a time. Those watching should remind themselves of all the moves they have tried and have learned over the past term. Next week they will be answering some tasks on the floor and apparatus linked to the work covered.

Conclusion:
Sit facing your partner and pull one another to your feet. Repeat.

Stand and walk quietly to the door.

Unit 3, lesson 11

Theme: Ways of travelling; Workcards to assess development of floorwork

Purpose: PoS a

Activity bank: See Workcards 3 and 4 (p.80)

Resources: Mats; one copy each of Workcards 3 and 4 (see p. 80) per pupil

Introduction:
Travel on the feet in any way you choose. Change to hands and feet and travel, change to rolling, change to jumping. Repeat.

Development:
In twos, get out one mat between two. Sit on your mat. Teacher issues Workcards. Tell the pupils that you are using these Workcards to allow them to show what they can do whilst working at an appropriate level. The cards should also give you some feedback on how far each individual has come.
Individually they should choose where they come into the series of tasks and at the end of the session you will be looking at how well they have mastered one of the tasks.
Allow time for practise and watch the work at the end of the session. If you need to use this session for some evidence of attainment for recording purposes, it may be possible to make a brief note of which task each pupil did or to video the session.

Conclusion:
Sit in a space on the floor and think of one of the moves you have just been performing which you know that you can take on to apparatus. Do the move on the floor.

Think of another move, and do that move on the floor. Next week you will work with similar Workcards which will ask you to take moves on to apparatus.
Stand and walk quietly to the door.

Unit 3, lesson 12

Theme: Ways of travelling; Workcards to assess adapting skills to apparatus

Purpose: PoS a

Activity bank: See Workcards 5 and 6 (p. 81)

Resources: Mats and benches; one copy each of Workcards 5 and 6 (see p. 81) per pupil

Introduction:
Travel on feet, travel on hands and feet, take weight on to hands, travel by rolling.

Development:
In twos, get out one mat and one bench. Sit down on the mat.
Teacher issues Workcards.
As in the previous lesson, explain the purpose of the Workcards and stress the focus on looking for good work which shows that the pupils have found ways of taking simple moves on to apparatus.
Allow time for practise, then look at the work and monitor it in some way depending on your needs.

Conclusion:
In a space, sit with the legs straight out in front of you and the toes pointed. Think about one way of travelling gymnastically that you can do now which you could not do before. Do that move and repeat it if you can. Walk quietly to the door.

Unit 4, lesson 1

Theme: Moving into and out of balance; step to balance, star shape, arabesque

Purpose: PoS a, b

Activity bank: Activities 5a, 5b, 5c, 5d

Resources: None

Introduction:
Running in and out of one another, use the space and slow down and speed up the run on command. Slow down and change to walking. Step with the head and the chest up and point the toes. On command, freeze. Hold your position still and then make it in to a gymnastic balance by pulling away from the point of balance. Continue to travel, and repeat.

Development
Travel by stepping using the feet only, then stop and pull away into an arabesque. Bring the arms forward, look along the lie of the hands, keep the head up and the back leg lifted. Try to achieve a horizontal position with the back and arms. Bend the supporting leg slightly to hold the balance.
Lower the arabesque to both hands and feet on the floor and turn over to move tummy up, then tummy down. On command, stop. In your own time, try stopping with tummy up, then with tummy down, then with side down. Can you lift an arm or a leg off the floor in any of these balances?
Link travel by stepping to an arabesque to travel by hands and feet to holding a balance on hands and feet. Can you make it a three point or a two point balance?
All try to travel from a press up position into a star shape.
All try to travel from a press up position to tummy up and hold a bridge and lift one leg off the floor. Can you make this a star shape? Do this with tummy down, lifting your head up.
Link one way of travelling by stepping and balance on command. Repeat. If you want to change the way of travel, you can do so.
Look at the whole group's work.

Conclusion:
In a space, in a front support position, lift one leg and show a good three point balance. Turn over to tummy up and show a three point balance. Stand and walk quietly to the door.

Unit 4, lesson 2 ▷

Theme: Moving into and out of balance; side star, arabesque, bridge

Purpose: PoS a, b, c

Activity bank: Activities 5a, 5b, 5c, 5d

Resources: Benches

Introduction:
Travel in and out of one another and change the way of travelling on command. Choose one way of travelling using hands and feet. Travel slowly and concentrate on good body shape. Stop on command and pull away into a balance. Hold still for three seconds and then continue to travel. Repeat several times.

Development:
In twos, get out a bench and place it in a space. Sit down on the floor by the bench.
Try to put one of the balances from the last lesson or the start of this lesson on to the bench. Can you do: an arabesque on the bench, a star shape on the bench, a press up position, a tummy up balance?
Begin away from your bench and travel to it using hands and feet travel. Can you make that take you on to the bench? Can you then hold it in a balance.
Practise travelling to and on to the bench, balancing and travelling away. Select a phrase of movement. Show the phrases, working half the group at a time. Pupils watching should look for good body shape in travel and in balance. Put benches away and sit in a space on the floor with the legs together and straight out in front of you.

Conclusion:
Put the hands on the floor beside the bottom and lift the legs off the floor to show a pike position. Lower the legs and repeat. Try to lift the legs while keeping them straight and together. Can you pull the hands away from the floor to reach for the feet so that you are balancing on only your bottom? Come back to sitting and turn over in a rolling action across your legs. When you come round to a seat pull up into a pike seat. Hold it for a moment and then repeat. Stand and walk quietly to the door.

Unit 4, lesson 3 ▷

Theme: Moving into and out of balance; rolling into balance; pike seat, shoulder stand

Purpose: PoS a, b, c

Activity bank: Activities 5a, 5b, 5c, 5d

Resources: Mats

Introduction:
Travel round the room by running. Gradually slow this down to a walking action; walk upright and point the toes. On command, freeze and stretch away into a balance. From the balance, gradually pull your body in so that you are tucking into a ball, lower to the floor and take the travelling into a rolling action and then rest.

Development:
Repeat the sequence of: run, walk, balance, tuck, roll. This time travel by a rolling action and on command freeze and show a balance position by pulling away from the base. Repeat, and stop the roll in your own time to show a different balance. Allow time to experiment. All show your ideas using your own timing. Share some ideas; teacher chooses some examples of good balances for everyone to try.
In twos, get out a mat and place it in a space. Sit down on the mat.
All try a sideways rolling action into a pike seat. Do this from a perfect pencil roll if you can. From a pike seat come to sitting and push gently back and reach up with your feet into a shoulder stand. All practise the shoulder stand position in turn. Look at your partner's balance: is it perfect? If not, can you tell them anything which will improve it? If it is perfect, how can this balance be made more difficult?
Answers to this question might be to straddle the legs or have the arms flat along the floor rather than supporting the back. Remind pupils that the more they can stretch away, the better the balance and the fewer body parts on the floor, the more complex the balance.
In your own time, practise moving into and out of the pike seat and the shoulder stand from rolling. Some pupils may be able to roll forwards into either or both of these balances.
Link travel using hands and feet to balance, roll to balance.
Show these phrases, all working together.
Put away mats and sit in a space.

Conclusion:
Sit in a space on the floor and get into a shoulder stand either by rocking back or by rolling into it; hold it still and straight. On command, rock forward and come through to standing on the feet without placing the hands on the floor to push you up. Repeat; keep the shoulders low and reach forward with the arms. Walk quietly to the door.

Unit 4, lesson 4 ▷

Theme: Moving into and out of balance; shoulder stand using apparatus

Purpose: PoS a, b, c

Activity bank: Activities 5a, 5b, 5c, 5d, 5e, 5f

Resources: Benches or low box tops, mats

Introduction:
Travel in and out of one another by running. On command, jump and continue to travel. Repeat several times and change the way of jumping each time. Travel by hands and feet and balance on command. Stretch away from the floor, then slowly tuck and move as smoothly as you can into a shoulder stand. Repeat.

Development:
In twos, get out a bench, or a low box top, and a mat and sit down on the mat.
Practise ways of balancing in a shoulder stand or a pike seat in contact with your bench. Can you turn sideways into either balance? Can you turn backwards or forwards into them?
Practise moving into a shoulder stand and a pike seat in contact with, or on, the apparatus. Can you move from one into the other?
Recap on ways of travelling along the apparatus using hands and feet and stopping in a balance. Link hands and feet travel to balance, roll to balance.
Look at these phrases with half the group working at a time. This work will be extended next week so pupils watching should look for ideas that they have not tried. Put away apparatus and stand in a space.

Conclusion:
Jump from two feet to two feet, land and stretch out into an arabesque or star shape. Try jumping from two feet to land on one foot and stretch to an arabesque. Repeat. Walk quietly to the door.

Unit 4, lesson 5 ▷

Theme: Moving into and out of balance; working on larger apparatus

Purpose: PoS a, b, c

Activity bank: Activities 5a, 5b, 5c, 5d, 5e, 5f

Resources: Fixed apparatus, e.g. wall bars or frames, benches, low box tops, mats

Introduction:
Move in and out of one another by running. On command, jump. Repeat and change your way of jumping. Slow travel down to a walk if it helps you to control the movement. Practise jumping to a balance.

Development:
In groups of four, get out two pieces of apparatus and one mat. Set out the apparatus as shown on the following page. Sit down on your mat.

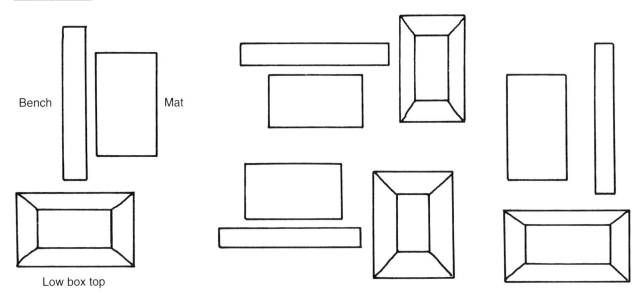

Bench   Mat

Low box top

From your mat, jump on to a low piece of apparatus, hold the position and pull into a balance. Practise one way or more different ways.

Show a shoulder stand on the mat with part of your body touching the apparatus. Find a way of getting into that shoulder stand smoothly. Can you roll into it? Can you do a shoulder stand or a pike seat on your apparatus? How can you get into this position smoothly?

Recap on ways of travelling using hands and feet along, on to and off the bench. Where can you hold a balance? Try ways of travelling along or up and down the wall bars using hands and feet. Can you balance anywhere? Select one way of jumping to balance, one way of rolling to balance and one way of stepping to balance. Look at these ideas, half the group working at a time. The pupils watching should look for ideas they had not thought of. Put away apparatus and stand with a partner.

Conclusion:
Stand back to back, two steps apart. Each do a turning jump to face the other, then one of you lean in and show an arabesque using your partner for support. Change over and repeat. Walk quietly to the door.

Unit 4, lesson 6 ▷

Theme: Moving into and out of balance; extending the range of moves on apparatus

Purpose: PoS a, c

Activity bank: Activities 5a, 5b, 5c, 5d, 5e, 5f

Resources: Large apparatus, e.g. frames, wall bars and box tops; benches, mats; one copy each of Workcards 7–13 (see pp. 82–85) per pupil

Introduction:
Travel round by running and on command, jump and pull to balance. Then lower to the floor to roll, balance and move into hands and feet travel.

Development:
In groups of four, get out the apparatus and set it out as in the previous lesson.
Using Workcards 7–13 try out ideas on different parts of the apparatus.

Link jump to balance, hands and feet travel to balance, roll to balance. The sequence can be in any order.
Put away apparatus and sit in a space.

Conclusion:
Lie flat on the floor on your back. Get to your feet without bending your legs. Try again. Walk quietly to the door.

Unit 4, lesson 7

Theme: Moving into and out of balance; extending the range of moves on apparatus; varying body shape

Purpose: PoS a, b

Activity bank: Activities 5a, 5b, 5c, 5d, 5e, 5f

Resources: Large apparatus, e.g. frames, wall bars and box tops; benches, mats; one copy each of Workcards 7–13 (see pp. 82–85) per pupil

Introduction:
Travel round by jumping. Change direction on command. Jump 1, 2, 3, 4 and balance. Repeat. Travel by using hands and feet with the legs straddled and balance on command. Travel by rolling with the legs straight and balance on command.

Development:
In groups of four, get out the apparatus you used in the last lesson and set it out as before. Then sit down on your mat.
Move on to a different section of apparatus, i.e. change places with another group.
Use Workcards 7–13 to develop a range of ways of moving on the apparatus, as in the previous lesson.
Link the different ways into a sequence.
Show the sequences, with half the group working at a time.
Put away apparatus and sit down in a space.

Conclusion:
Show a wide shape balance. Show a long balance. Stand and walk quietly to the door.

Unit 4, lesson 8

Theme: Moving into and out of balance; extending the range of moves on apparatus; varying body shape

Purpose: PoS a, b

Activity bank: Activities 5a, 5b, 5c, 5d, 5e, 5f

Resources: Large apparatus

Introduction:
Travel round the room in a wide shape and balance in a wide shape.
Travel in a long shape and balance in a long shape, then make the balance wide.
Travel in a folded or piked shape and balance in a piked shape.

Development:
In groups, get out the apparatus and sit down on your mat.
Build a sequence of travel and balance and show wide, piked and long shapes. Use ideas from the previous lessons.
Show your sequences, with one person working on each section of the apparatus. When Number 1 has finished Number 2 should start and so on. The pupils watching should look for good body shape, balances held still and smooth linking.
Put away apparatus and stand in a space.

Conclusion:
Lean forward into a pike balance. Can you get to a hands and feet balance from here? Can you get to a pike seat? Stand and walk to the door.

Unit 4, lesson 9

Theme: Moving into and out of balance; extending the range of moves on apparatus; varying body shape (continued)

Purpose: PoS a, b, c

Activity bank: Activities 5a, 5b, 5c, 5d, 5e, 5f

Resources: Large apparatus

Introduction:
Travel in a long shape and balance in a wide shape. Travel wide and balance piked. Travel piked and hold. Repeat.

Development:
Repeat the apparatus work from the previous lesson. The sequence produced should be the culmination of a concentrated block of work on apparatus.
Show the sequences, one pupil working on each piece of apparatus at a time. Try to give some feedback on what has been produced.

You may be able to use the product to assess the pupils' progress. This could be done by video-taping the sequences at the end or by getting the pupils to write out for homework what their sequence was, or what they found difficult etc.
Put away the apparatus and sit in a space facing a partner.

Conclusion:
In time with your partner, turn on to your tummy by pulling the legs round the side of your body so that you are facing your partner. Do the reverse to come back to sitting. What shape are you going to and from? Go from folded sitting position to a long shape on the tummy. Repeat and make the shapes clear. Stand and walk to the door.

Unit 4, lesson 10

Theme: Moving into and out of balance; partner work; timing moves with a partner

Purpose: PoS a, c

Activity bank: Activities 5a, 5b, 5c, 5d, 5g

Resources: Mats

Introduction:
Travel in and out of one another by running. On command, stop and show a balance. Reach towards someone who is near to you. Travel towards that person. Stop when you can touch them and balance. Repeat.

Development:
Join up with a partner and number yourselves 1 and 2. Number 1 travels round the gym and Number 2 follows. On command, freeze and see whether you can reach to touch one another in a balance. Repeat, changing the way of travelling. Repeat with Number 2 leading. Change the way of travelling again.
In twos, get out a mat and place it in a space. Begin at opposite ends of the mat. Choose a way of travelling on hands and feet that you can do from opposite one another to bring you into a balance in the middle of the mat. You should both do the same moves and the same balance. Can you touch one another in your balances? Try this again, this time using a roll into balance. Link hands and feet to balance, travel away, roll to balance and hold.
Show these phrases of movement, with the whole group working at once. Emphasise that you are looking for good timing of the moves within pairs.
Put away mats and sit on the floor facing your partner.

Conclusion:
Spin on to the tummy, arch and touch hands or link arms. Spin on the seat and do a pike seat with touching feet. Repeat. Stand and walk quietly to the door.

Unit 4, lesson 11

Theme: Moving into and out of balance; extending the range of moves with a partner on low apparatus

Purpose: PoS a, c

Activity bank: Activities 5a, 5b, 5c, 5d, 5e, 5g

Resources: Mats and benches

Introduction:
Travel round the room running in and out of one another. On command, jump and balance. Join up with a partner and travel round the room together. Jump and balance on command. Practise one jump and balance that you can match. Repeat several times.

Development:
In twos, get out a bench and a mat and place them in a space. Sit down on your mat.
With your partner, try out ideas for jumping on to the bench and balancing so that you are matching one another. Can you come into contact with one another (perhaps touching hands or arms)?
Find a way of getting down close to the bench and travelling off the bench using hands and feet travel. Work out the spacing so that you move away from your partner, i.e. you go off the bench on opposite sides.

Link jump on to bench, balance on bench, hands and feet travel away from bench.
Try out different ideas for rolling towards one another from opposite sides of the bench to come to a balance on the bench. Can you touch?
Link jump onto bench, balance on bench, hands and feet travel away from bench, roll to bench and balance on bench.
Watch other pairs. Try to get new ideas which you can use when you continue this work in the next lesson.
Put away apparatus and sit in a space with your partner.

Conclusion:
Sitting back to back, pull the legs up into a pike seat, then lower and spin on to tummy to face each other. Arch while on the tummy and join hands. Repeat. Stand and walk quietly to the door.

Unit 4, lesson 12

Theme: Moving into and out of balance; extending the range of moves on low apparatus with a partner; linking into a sequence

Purpose: PoS a, c

Activity bank: Activities 5a, 5b, 5c, 5d, 5e, 5g

Resources: Mats and benches

Introduction:
Travel round the room by skipping. On command, jump to a star shape, travel in a star shape. On command, balance in a star shape, then travel using hands and feet to meet your partner and balance in a star shape in contact with one another. Repeat.

Development:
In twos, get out a bench and a mat and sit down on the mat.
Continue the work from the previous lesson. Link a sequence which has jump to balance, hands and feet travel to balance. You should meet your partner and move away. If you already have this worked out you can try to vary the speed of the moves so that some are very fast and others are slow. There should be clear contrasts in the sequence.
Show the sequences, with two or three pairs working at a time. As previously, you may wish to make a record of the product for assessment purposes. Try to give some feedback on what has been produced.
Put away apparatus and sit in a space.

Conclusion:
Lie flat on your back and when teacher says 'Tight', go as stiff as a board and hold. Relax and repeat. When teacher says 'Star' make a star shape and then make it tight. Can you hold that shape and tension and get to your feet? Can you make it travel to the door? Stand and file out.

THE CIRCLE ROLL

Teacher: Watch your partner do the circle roll.

What is he/she doing well?

Can it be improved? If so, can you help?

Look at the picture and compare.

- Does the starting position look right?
- Are the legs straight?
- Does he/she keep the chest close to the knees?

Change over and repeat.

THE SIDE ROLL

Teacher: Watch your partner do the side roll.

What is he/she doing well?

Can it be improved? If so, can you help?

Look at the picture and compare.

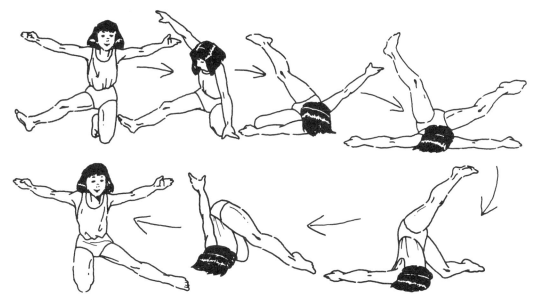

- Does the starting position look right?
- Does he/she tuck to roll?
- Does he/she open out to finish?

Change over and repeat.

FLOORWORK – LEVEL 1

Which of these can you do?

Rotate over in a straight position

A jump from two feet to two feet

A leap

A pencil roll

A turning jump

A side roll

A circle roll

Link three moves together.

FLOORWORK – LEVEL 2 W4

Which of these can you do?

A tuck jump

A cartwheel

A forward roll

A backward roll

Can you change leg design in any of the rolls?
Link three moves together.

APPARATUS WORK – LEVEL 1

Where on the apparatus can you do each of these?

1 A jump

2 A roll

3 A hands and feet travel

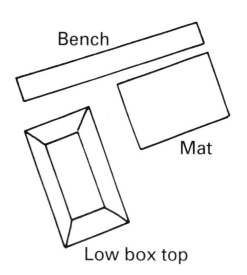

Bench

Mat

Low box top

Link three moves together.

APPARATUS WORK – LEVEL 2

Where on the apparatus can you do each of these?

1 A jumping action

2 A hands and feet travel

3 A roll

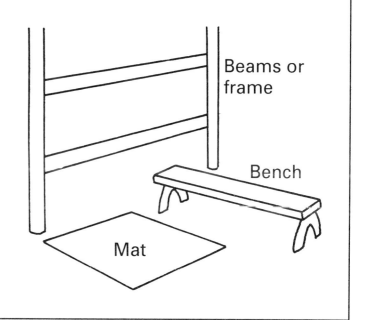

Beams or frame

Bench

Mat

Link three moves together.

BALANCES ON APPARATUS – SHOULDER STAND

Can you do a shoulder stand on or against each of these?

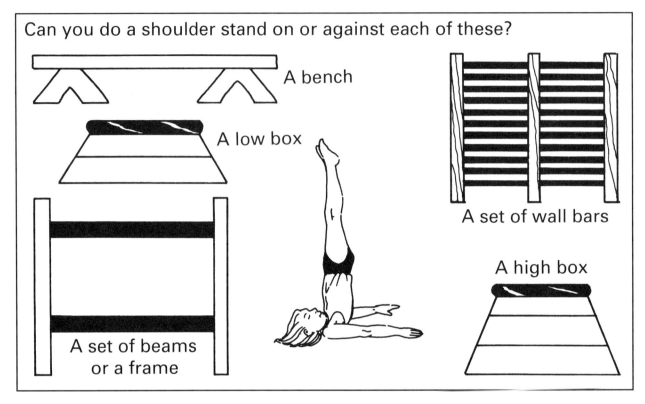

A bench

A low box

A set of wall bars

A high box

A set of beams or a frame

BALANCES ON APPARATUS – PIKE SEAT

Can you do a pike seat on or against each of these?

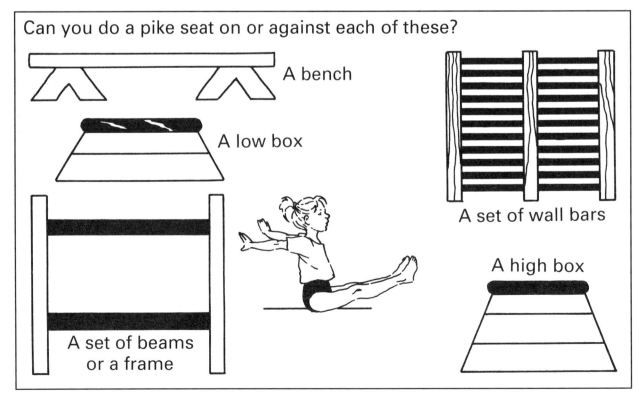

A bench

A low box

A set of wall bars

A high box

A set of beams or a frame

BALANCES ON APPARATUS – STAR BALANCE

Can you do a star balance on or against each of these?

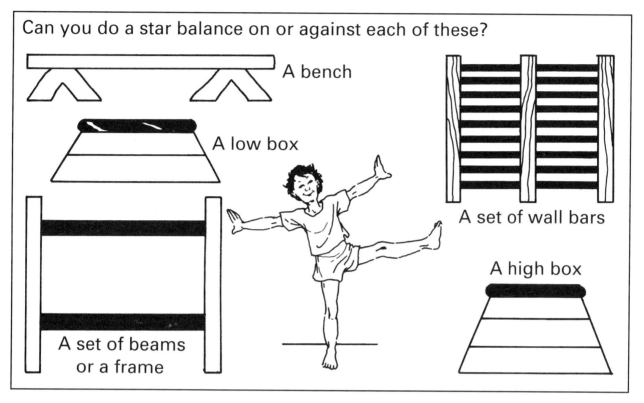

A bench

A low box

A set of wall bars

A high box

A set of beams
or a frame

BALANCES ON APPARATUS – HEADSTAND

Can you do a headstand on or against each of these?

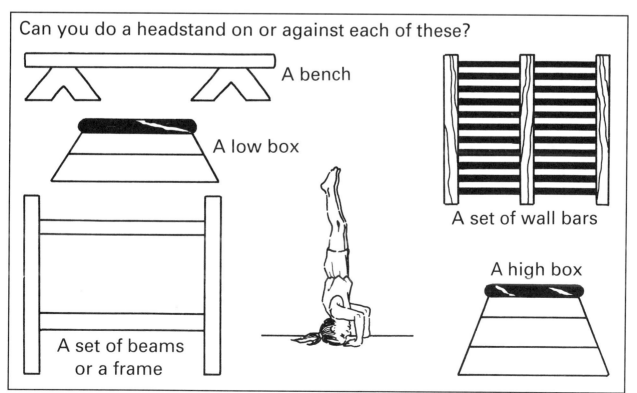

A bench

A low box

A set of wall bars

A high box

A set of beams
or a frame

BALANCES ON APPARATUS – HANDSTAND

Can you do a handstand on or against each of these?

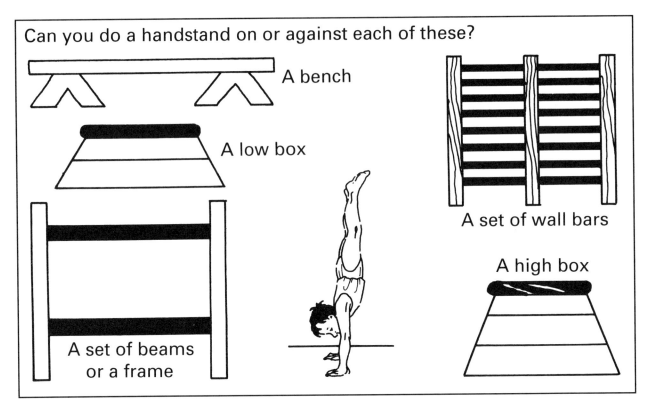

A bench

A low box

A set of wall bars

A set of beams or a frame

A high box

BALANCE ENTRIES FOR FORWARD ROLL

Forward roll

Can you get into a forward roll from each of these?

An arabesque   A kneeling position   A pike position   A handstand

Can you do these entries from apparatus? or on to apparatus?

BALANCE ENTRIES FOR HANDSTAND

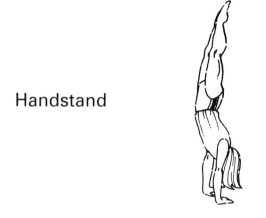

Handstand

Can you get into a handstand from each of these?

An arabesque   A kneeling position   A headstand   A straddle stand

Can you do any of these entries on or against apparatus?

GAMES

Games in the National Curriculum provide a range of stimulating and exciting educational opportunities. The key features of playing games are the development of motor skills, hand–eye co-ordination and strategies linked to playing games. Games produce a high degree of physical activity and skills as well as providing children with the opportunity to develop their social skills and mental alertness.

Teachers who use this book will come from a range of backgrounds and experiences. The lesson plans for games are designed to present two sets of units of work, one for years 3 and 4 and one for years 5 and 6. Although, for the purposes of this book, the units have been divided into the two age bands, they can be used by either. It is important therefore that the maturational level of pupils both in terms of skill and personal development is considered by the teacher. From the material provided, teachers can choose an appropriate starting point that will allow the pupils to succeed and at the same time will provide a challenge for them.

At Key Stage 1 the emphasis in games was on individual motor control leading to co-operation with other pupils. At Key Stage 2, whilst the opportunity for pupils to develop their skill level is still a key feature of the programmes of study, the emphasis is on the application of these skills in a game situation. The games that pupils play at this stage are many and varied; they may be games made up by the teacher or the pupils, they may be adaptations of standard games, using smaller teams or sides. It is important to remember that, although the units are linked to traditional games, the large-sided 'adult' games seen on TV are not encouraged. Small games are far more effective as they provide all pupils with the opportunity to apply the skills they have developed.

The major assumption that is made in all of the lesson plans is that games should preferably be played outside on a tarmac area or, when appropriate, on a grass area. Firstly, from a safety point of view, when using games equipment, open space is required to ensure that pupils are not in danger from the activities

of others. Secondly, skill development can only occur when there is space for children to practise and explore their own capabilities within the tasks set. An important organisational aspect of the units of work is that many of the activities and games are played within grid areas. Although it is advantageous in the long term to mark these grids permanently on the playing area, if this is not possible, markers may be used to define the grids.

Being able to communicate effectively is essential in controlling safe activity in large outdoor areas; therefore appropriate use should be made of whistle and voice. When there are many small games occurring within the playing area, it is important that the teacher is in a position to be able to see all of the pupils in order to observe and present feedback to each of the groups.

One of the important developmental aspects of teaching games is the transition from individual work to partner work. It is important to point out that pupils should experience a number of attempts in each role. Five attempts is considered to be suitable to provide children with an opportunity for success without allowing the activity to become too repetitious.

Progressive activity is a feature of all the units of work through the constituent lessons. Constant reinforcement is an essential part of motor development, therefore many activities are repeated in more than one lesson. There are three units of work for years 3 and 4 and three for years 5 and 6. Units 1 and 4 address invasion games, Units 2 and 5 address net/wall games and Units 3 and 6 address striking/fielding games. There are some activities that are repeated within the units of work and in some cases the activities used within, for example, a rounders lesson, may be adapted to a cricket lesson along a similar theme.

The bank of activities for games contains descriptions, accompanied by illustrations, of the key activities included in the units of work. The bank therefore aims to provide the teacher with key points for introducing and developing skills within a unit of work.

NATIONAL CURRICULUM REQUIREMENTS AT KEY STAGE 2

General programmes of study that are addressed within the units of work for games are as follows:

1. To promote physical activity and healthy lifestyles, pupils should be taught:
   a to be physically active;
   c to engage in activities that develop cardiovascular health, flexibility, muscular strength and endurance.
2. To develop positive attitudes, pupils should be taught:
   a to observe the conventions of fair play, honest competition and good sporting behaviour as individual participants, team members and spectators;
   b how to cope with success and limitations in performance;
   c to try hard to consolidate their performances;
   d to be mindful of others and the environment.
3. To ensure safe practice, pupils should be taught:
   a to respond readily to instructions;
   b to recognise and follow relevant rules, laws, codes, etiquette and safety procedures for different activities or events, in practice and during competition.

The programme of study or games are as follows:

1. Games

Pupils should be taught:

a to understand and play small-sided games and simplified versions of recognised competitive team and individual games, covering the following types – invasion, *eg mini-soccer, netball*, striking/fielding, *eg rounders, small-sided cricket*, net/wall, *eg short tennis;*
b common skills and principles, including attack and defence, in invasion, striking/fielding, net/wall and target games;
c to improve the skills of sending, receiving, striking and travelling with a ball in the above games.

TEACHING GAMES AT KEY STAGE 2

The programmes of study (activity specific) for games should provide pupils with a broad and balanced experience within the key stage.

The sum of the end of key stage descriptions is the attainment target for PE, which consists of three strands (planning, performing and evaluating). Throughout the lesson plans these three processes are addressed as well as the strands of health, safety and working with others. A model lesson is given in this section highlighting how these processes and strands are incorporated into lesson planning. It is hoped that the model lesson will provide an example which can be used to help you to expand on the lessons in each unit.

Games are divided into three main categories: invasion games, net/wall games and striking/fielding games. Invasion games include netball, football, hockey and rugby. Here there are two teams; each team defends one half of the pitch/court preventing the opposition from scoring into their goal/net whilst at the same time aiming to gain possession and score a goal into their opponent's goal/net. Net/wall games include those games where the court is divided by a net or a wall, e.g. tennis and volleyball. Striking and fielding games, e.g.

rounders and cricket, can be described as those games involving two teams, one side batting and one side fielding. The batting side aims to score as many runs/points as possible whilst the fielding team attempts to prevent them scoring runs by fielding the ball and trying to get the batting team out.

Within Key Stage 1, although pupils do not play these games in the common form, they are taught skills and strategies that provide a solid foundation for future years. However, at Key Stage 2, pupils are able to extend the skills and tactics from Key Stage 1, applying them to the different groups of games. The units of work within this section are based around invasion, net/wall and striking/fielding games.

The first programme of study for games is 'Pupils should be taught to understand and play small-sided games and simplified versions of recognised competitive team and individual games, covering the following types: invasion (e.g. mini-soccer, netball;) striking/fielding (e.g. rounders, small-sided cricket); net/wall (e.g. short tennis).' Within the units of work presented in this section, the conclusion of each lesson involves the playing of a game. The game is generally determined by the teacher, and is a modified version of the common form of the game played by adults. It is vital that the numbers involved in each team are small; this way the skills that the children have been encouraged to develop can be frequently applied to the same situation.

The second programme of study is 'Pupils should be taught common skills and principles, including attack and defence, and invasion, striking/fielding, net/wall and target games.' This is a direct progression from the first PoS. It is addressed throughout all units of work. The aim is to provide pupils with the opportunity to apply the skills related to each game, as well as helping them in their understanding that within the groups of games there are skills and principles that are linked. For example, the methods of attack and defence in foorball and hockey are similar.

The third programme of study is 'Pupils should be taught to improve the skills of sending, receiving, striking and travelling with a ball in the above games. This is a development of the second programme of study at key stage 1. The three skills of travelling, sending and receiving are the basis on which all games are built. At key stage 2, pupils will be expected to work on larger groups and develop these skills under pressure.'

In order that games in the National Curriculum can be delivered successfully to pupils at Key Stage 2, the following equipment list is considered to be a minimum requirement:

Bean bags
Hoops
Quoits
Ropes
Cones
Multi-markers
Large balls – plastic footballs
          – plastic covered foam balls
          – rugby balls (size 3/4)
Medium balls
Small balls – air flow
          – plastic-covered sponge balls
Skittles
Canes
Coloured bands/braids.

The majority of activities, however, can be carried out using the equipment available in the school, although the opportunities for children to practice and explore individually may be limited.

The model lesson

A model lesson is provided to illustrate planning (PL), evaluating (EV) and safety (!) issues. These kind of considerations need to be built into all your work in this area of PE.

Model lesson: unit 3, lesson 2   ▷

Theme: Striking/fielding; cricket

Purpose: PoS a, c

Activity bank: Activity 25 Washing baskets, Activity 26 Batter striking the ball, Activity 57 Underarm bowling

Resources: Cones, large balls, large cricket bat shapes, washing basket, quantity of bean bags

---

Introduction:

Activity 25: Washing baskets	In small groups of 6–8. Put each group in a space within the playing area.	Player sending the bean bags should be thinking where the most appropriate places are to send them before they are collected by the other members of the group.
		The player in the middle can send one bean bag at a time ensuring that they do not hit any other member of the group. (!)

Development:

In pairs.

A large ball and a cone between two.

The batter aims to protect the cone from being hit by the bowler.　(PL)

Bowler sends ball to batter who stands 3–4 metres away in front of the cone.

The batter uses feet and other parts to send the ball away.

Five attempts each then change roles.

Progression to using a large cricket bat instead of parts of the body.

Batter must let the bowler see the wicket (cone).

Bowler aims to hit the wicket whilst batter must protect it.

Bowler must allow the ball to bounce before batter hits it.

How can the bowler make it more difficult for the batter to hit the ball?　(EV)

Conclusion:

Play a small sided game in fours: bowler, batter and two fielders

Five attempts as batter then change roles.

Batter gets a point every time the ball lands away from a fielder.

Encourage the batter to stand sideways on.

Pupils should consider the following:

what happens if the ball is hit in the air?　(EV)

can you direct the ball to a space away from the fielders?　(PL)

GAMES ACTIVITY BANK ▶

Activity 1: Touch ball

Six children per grid. One player is the 'runner'. The 'runner' has to be tagged by the others by touching them with the ball. The 'taggers' must remain in contact with the ball. Swap roles regularly.

Activity 2: Corner game

Four players to a grid. Each player stands on the corner of the grid (as shown below). The players are numbered 1, 2, 3 and 4. The ball starts with player number 1, they pass the ball to number 2, then they run to number 2's space and back to their own space before the ball comes round to them from number 4. Each player runs to the space to their left and back to their own space after they have sent the ball.

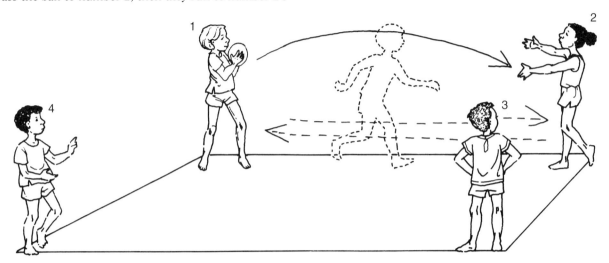

Activity 3: Numbers game

The whole group travels around a given area. On your command, a number is shouted out, e.g. 3. The pupils have to get into the stipulated group sizes as quickly as possible. Repeat a number of times.

Activity 4: Two-way rugby game

The attacking team start from their line. The aim is to pass the ball down to the opposite 'end' line with at least three passes. The defence aim to touch the ball before it is grounded. If they are successful, the attackers place the ball on the ground, the defence retreat 3 m and play continues. The ball must be sent backwards by the attacking team. After three tackles the attacking team give possession to the opposition.

A progression from the previous week would be to place two markers (e.g. cones) on each end line, approximately 3 m away from each other. If the attacking team place the ball down between the two markers they score 2 points; if the ball is placed outside the markers then they score 1 point.

Activity 5: Travelling with rugby ball

The ball is carried under either arm close to the body. Ensure that the ball is kept away from opponents.

Activity 6: Passing rugby ball (a) forwards
(b) backwards

Hold the ball with the hands underneath it.

Working with a partner, pass and catch the ball with two hands. Swing the ball across the body from the shoulders and pass the ball to partner's hips. When sending the ball backwards; turn shoulders towards partner.

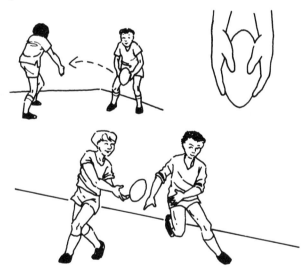

Activity 7: Travelling with ball using hands

Rolling the ball

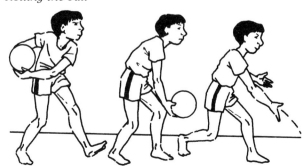

90

Dribbling the ball

Using either hand, shape the hand to the contours of the ball. Be flexible at the wrist. Avoid slapping the ball. Never use both hands together.

Activity 8: Sending ball with hands to partner

Stand sideways, feet apart, with the ball in the strongest hand, take weight on the back foot, transferring weight forwards. Push the right arm through, turning the right shoulder forward. Partner indicates where they want the ball and runs into that space in order to receive the ball.

Activity 9: Rolling ball into space/against wall

Roll the ball into a space or against a wall, step forward with the opposite foot and bend the knees getting low to the ground.

Activity 10: Bouncing ball

Bounce and then catch the ball. Begin stationary, lead to travelling. Catch the ball at the top of the bounce.

Progress to bouncing the ball further forward to challenge yourself.

Activity 11: Patting ball

Use the palm of the hand as a bat. Ensure that the hand remains flat and the fingers are together. Pat the ball into the air, allowing it to bounce off the hand back into the air.

Activity 12: Tracking the ball

As the ball travels towards the player, they move their whole body in order to get behind the ball and be able to catch/trap/stop the ball.

Activity 13: Sending ball into hoop

Bounce the ball into a hoop that is placed equi-distant between two players. Each player has to track the ball in order to receive it.

Activity 14: Tennis squash

Two players play this game. They both stand facing the wall. One player sends the ball against the wall so that it bounces off for the other player to receive. The receiving player then sends the ball, and so on.

The game is co-operative to begin with, leading to a competitive game where the players attempt to outwit their partners.

Activity 15: Rolling ball using bat
The player uses the bat to 'walk' the ball along the ground. The player must be close to the ground. The ball is controlled using the wrist. Start slowly, progress to travelling quickly.

SAFETY: Ensure that players watch out for other class members.

Activity 16: Sending ball using forehand
Player stands sideways on with opposite shoulder leading. Player moves whole body behind the path of the ball; allow one bounce then hit the ball. Swing the bat through to hit the ball, stepping onto the opposite leg. The shot is hit at arm's length.

Activity 17: Bouncing ball on ground with bat
Hit the ball just after the top of the bounce. Hit it at arm's length; watch the ball very closely. Keep the bat as flat as possible, flexing the wrist when hitting the ball. Use the other arm for balance.

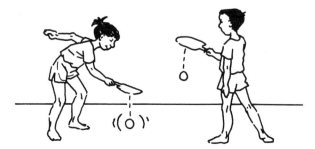

Activity 18: Hitting ball in air with bat
Watch the ball. Hit the ball at arm's length with palm upwards. The arm bends slightly at the elbow when hitting the ball. The ball hits the bat only once before going into the air. Progress to hitting the ball using both sides of the bat.

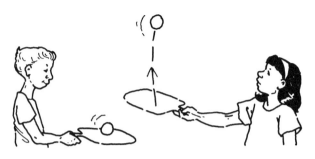

Activity 19: Sending ball using backhand
The player stands sideways on with the right shoulder forwards and steps on to the right foot as the shot is played. Swing the bat through to hit the ball, playing the ball at arm's length.

Activity 20: Tennis rounders
Team A are the batters. Team B throw the ball over for Team A members to hit. They take it in turns to hit the ball to team B, who are standing on the other side of the net. Team B aim to catch the ball. If they are successful they get 1 point; if not then team A gets 1 point.

Activity 21: Volleying the ball

The bat is held in front of the player's chest. A punching action is used, keeping the wrist firm. Both backhand and forehand volleying require a short backswing with the bat held in a vertical position. As the volley is made the player transfers their weight forward. The bat is punched forwards slightly across the body using a short follow-through. The volley is played with a bent arm.

Activity 22: Service (underarm)

The underarm service is the same skill as the forehand stroke, with the server bouncing the ball on their right side (if they are right-handed) then stepping into the ball to play a forehand.

Activity 23: Mini tennis game

This game is played in pairs using the court and a net made up of bean bags/multi markers/skittles and canes. Each player takes it in turns to serve the ball underarm, aiming to get the ball into their opponent's court. The first to score five points wins.

Activity 24: Fielding the ball

As the ball approaches along the ground, move the whole body so that it is behind the ball. Kneel sideways on one leg, with the fingers and hands together pointing down to the ground to receive the ball. Make a long barrier with the lower leg in the kneeling position in case the hands miss the ball.

Activity 25: Washing baskets

Work in groups of 6–8. One person (the 'thrower') aims to keep the basket empty of bean bags whilst the remaining members of the group ('fielders') aim to keep it full. The 'thrower' sends the bean bags, one at a time, to areas of the large grid unoccupied by 'fielders'.

SAFETY should be stressed at all times throughout this game.

Activity 26: Batter striking the ball

Batter stands sideways on; if they are right-handed, the left shoulder faces the bowler. As the bowler is about to release the ball, the batter swings the bat backwards, ensuring that it remains straight. As the batter strikes the ball, they place the opposite foot forwards in line with the bounce of the ball.

Activity 27: Chase the bean bag game 1

Work in groups of four. One player stands at the top end of the sector with six bean bags. They aim to throw the bean bags into spaces within the arc, without them being caught by the fielders. If the fielders are finding it easy, restrict them to taking one pace in any direction to catch the bean bags.

Activity 28: Chase the bean bag game 2

Start as in Activity 27. However, after the bean bags have been sent to different parts of the sector, the 'thrower' runs around the two cones. Meanwhile the fielders collect the bean bags and place them in a hoop in the centre of the sector. The thrower stops when all the bean bags are in the hoop. The thrower collects 1 point for every time they visit a cone, but loses 1 point for every bean bag caught by the fielding team.

Activity 29: Run and chase activity

Work in groups of three, with members A, B and C. The three players start in a straight line. C is in the middle with the ball, with A and B on either side. C rolls the ball in a straight line forward, A and B chase after it. The first person to field it throws the ball back to C. After three rolls, players change positions.

Activity 30: Triangle fielding activity

Work in groups of three, with members numbered 1, 2 and 3. The three players stand in a triangle shape. Using a medium/small ball, 1 starts with the ball and rolls it to either 2 or 3. Player 1 then swaps places with the person they have *not* sent the ball to. For example, if 1 sends the ball to 2, 1 and 3 then swap places. Then 2 has the ball and decides whether to send it to 1 or 3.

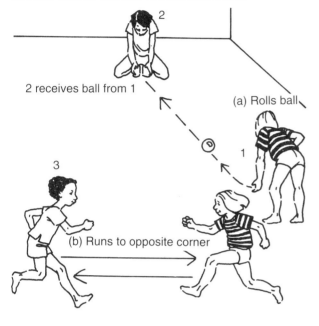

2 receives ball from 1

(a) Rolls ball

(b) Runs to opposite corner

Activity 31: Circle activity

Work in groups of 4 or 5. One player is in the middle of the circle made by the other players. The player in the middle is the wicket keeper, so is situated by the stumps (a cone can be used).

The wicket keeper rolls the ball to the edge of the circle for one of the fielders to run on to. The fielder receives the ball using the long barrier stop. They then quickly send the ball back to the wicket keeper. Whilst this is happening the remaining fielders are running around the edge of the large circle. Repeat a number of times so that all the fielders have an opportunity to field the ball.

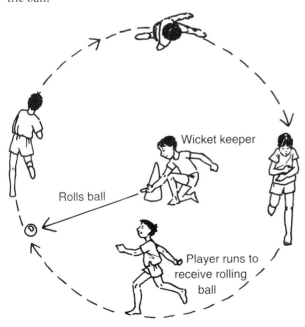

Wicket keeper

Rolls ball

Player runs to receive rolling ball

Activity 32: Mini game

Work in groups of four: two batters, one bowler and one wicket keeper/fielder. Use a medium/small ball depending on the pupils' ability levels. The batters work together. The bowler and the wicket keeper/fielder work together. They bowl six balls each underarm to the batters, then change roles. When the ball is hit, the batters have to decide if they can both run successfully to the opposite stumps (cone) before the fielders can get the ball to either cone.

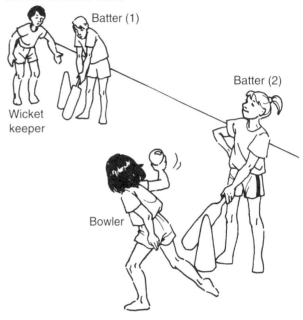

Batter (1)

Batter (2)

Wicket keeper

Bowler

Activity 33: Cricket pairs game

Work in pairs within groups of six:

Couple No. 1 are batters, Couple No. 2 are fielders, Couple No. 3 are the bowler and the wicket keeper.

Each bowler bowls six times and then swaps places with the wicket keeper. Each batting pair starts with 10 runs. They collect runs, but lose 1 run every time they are 'out', i.e. bowled, caught or run out or bat hits wicket (see diagram).

Couples rotate from No. 1 to No. 2 to No. 3.

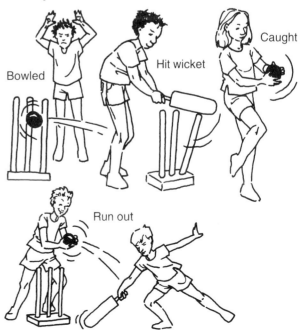

Bowled

Hit wicket

Caught

Run out

Activity 34: Tag game

Work in pairs. One person is 'on'. They chase after their partner and 'tag' them when they are close by. The other person is then the chaser. The game is repeated. This game should be played for about 3–4 minutes.

To vary this simple tag game, a bean bag may be carried by the 'chaser' and placed lightly on the shoulder of the partner when close by.

SAFETY: Children should be conscious of others as they move around the area at random. Also, if the game is played with a bean bag, the chaser should *place* the bean bag on the shoulder of their partner; the bean bag should *not* be thrown.

Activity 35: 3 v 1

Work in groups of four: one defender and a team of three attackers. The defender wears a bib/band. The team of three aim to get the ball over the opposite line to score 1 point.

They must have at least four passes before the ball can be taken over the line. If the defender touches the ball, he/she scores 1 point. Change over defender regularly.

Activity 36: Cat and mouse

Work in pairs. Each player tucks a coloured braid/band into their waistband, to hang down the back of their shorts or skirt. They face each other and, without making any physical contact, they each attempt to get the coloured band out of their partner's waistband. After each successful attempt, the band/braid is returned to the partner and the successful player gains 1 point. The game is repeated for about five minutes.

Activity 37: Trapping the ball with feet

The leg is placed forward to meet the ball, and the impact is controlled by relaxing and withdrawing the leg quickly. Weight should be over the stationary leg and balance should be achieved by using the arms. The foot should be turned out to meet the ball. Use either foot. Control the ball fully before passing it.

Activity 38: Sending the ball with feet

The side of the foot should contact the centre of the ball. Swing the kicking foot well back for power. The non-kicking foot should be level with the ball at the point of contact, while the arms are used for balance. The head should be well over the ball. Pupils should not lean back when kicking, ensuring a follow through in the direction of the pass.

Activity 39: Travel with ball using feet

Keep the ball close to the feet, do not lose control, ensure that the ball is tapped lightly. Move in and out of the other players, avoiding contact. Begin slowly and build up speed with confidence. The teacher should use a command for pupils to change speed, pathway and direction as well as changing from using the inside of the foot to the outside of the foot.

Activity 40: 3 v 3 football

One team has bibs/bands on. Set up two markers at each end for goals. The team which has possession of the ball is 'attacking'. They have to pass the ball at least three times before they are allowed to score between the markers.

Activity 41: 3 v 3 hockey

One team wears bibs/bands. Score by shooting between the cones. If the ball goes out of the grid, the opposition take a push in from the side.

The grid is large. There is a restriction on the shooting distance, e.g. the area within 7 m of the goals. The attacking team have to be in that area before shooting. Discourage the use of a goal keeper.

The attacking team can only push the ball; there is no hitting of the ball.

Activity 42: Running games

Here is a selection of running games for use in the introductory section of the lessons.

(a) Chain tag

One pupil is 'on'. They have to catch another member of the group. They then join hands and move around together in an attempt to catch another player. This is repeated until the line becomes four long; at this point the pupils divide into two chains of two and the game continues.

(b) Pinch the tail

Each pupil has a band/braid placed in the waistband of their skirt/shorts as a 'tail'. One pupil is 'on' and has to collect as many 'tails' as possible in the allotted time. A variation on this is for anyone who has their 'tail' taken to join the catcher and attempt to collect other tails.

(c) Numbers game

The pupils move around the area alone. The teacher shouts out a series of numbers, e.g. 3, 5, 7. The group then has to divide exactly into smaller groups of those numbers. Those who are not in the said groups collect a point. The aim is to collect as few points as possible.

(d) Object game

Place hoops/bean bags/multi markers/cones out around the playing area. The pupils move around them individually using the method of travel indicated by the teacher, e.g. running, hopping, jumping.

On command, pupils move to a designated place, e.g. yellow hoops, green cones, blue bean bags etc. The last pupil to arrive at the designated place collects a point. The aim is to collect as few points as possible.

Activity 43: Tackling with hockey stick

The tackler does not approach directly from the front but from an angle. The stick is held with the left hand high up the stick. The tackler steps forwards onto the left leg, jabbing at the ball with the stick.

SAFETY: Ensure that the tackler touches the ball only with control, so as not to hit any part of the other player's body.

Activity 44: Travelling with a hockey stick

The left hand should be at the top of the stick, with the right hand placed approximately 25 cm below the left. The ball should be tapped gently whilst remaining close to the head of the stick. The ball should be controlled just ahead of the right foot. The body should be bent slightly forwards with the knees bent. The head and shoulders should remain over the ball with the right hand being relaxed around the stick in order to allow the ball to change pathway.

Note: If pupils are playing with traditional hockey sticks, they should only use the flat side of the stick.

Activity 45: Stopping the ball with a hockey stick

The grip is the same as for travelling with the ball (see Activity 44). The stick is held vertically, with the stick held away from the body, in order to stop the ball. The pupil should move the whole body behind the ball, ensuring that the feet are away from the ball.

Activity 46: Passing the ball with a hockey stick

The ball should be pushed and not hit. The grip is similar to the dribble and the stop, although the right hand is now taken further down the stick. The feet should be placed apart with the left shoulder facing the direction of the pass. The stick begins behind the ball; hence there is no backswing. The force is applied through the push using the right hand. Body weight should be transferred from the back to the front foot on impact.

Activity 47: Catch volley

Send the ball high into the air and try to catch it just above the forehead. The pupil should move quickly underneath the falling ball and bend the knees, getting low to catch the ball above the forehead. Use the fingers to catch the ball, not the palms. The ball should remain in the fingers for a fraction of a second. The ball is then volleyed back using the fingers only.

Activity 48: Volley – in pairs

As in Activity 47, move quickly to get right underneath the dropping ball, adopting the same position using the bent knees. Return the ball immediately by flexing fingers and wrists, whilst straightening arms and legs on impact. Aim to volley the ball in front of the forehead, with the hands following the ball. The ball should be volleyed high in order that the partner is given the chance to get into place to return the ball.

Note: Pupils should play the ball with two hands at all times.

Activity 49: Dribbling the ball double-handed

Place two hands on the ball, pushing it into the ground. The ball should be returned to both hands. Begin this activity statically, progress to travelling around the playing area. The fingers should push the ball into the ground. Avoid using the palms and avoid slapping the ball.

Activity 50: Volleyball service

The ball is held in the left hand and flipped up into the path of the hitting hand. The ball is struck, preferably using the heel of the hand. Ensure that the hitting hand follows through in the same line that the ball is travelling. The body weight should be transferred from the back foot to the front foot on impact. The ball should be struck through the centre, keeping the head over the ball and watching it throughout the service.

Activity 51: Volleyball dig

One hand is placed on the other hand, with the fingers of the hand underneath clasped around the top hand. The forearms should be placed together, with the fleshy part of the arms (rather than the bony part) coming into contact with the ball.

The ball is played on the arms between the wrist and the forearms. The player should get under the ball as it falls, bending the knees with one leg in front of the other. The ball should be played back high. The arms should remain straight and together throughout, with elbows locked together to prevent arms bending. The player should be stationary when playing the dig.

Note: Arms must not be swung at the ball.

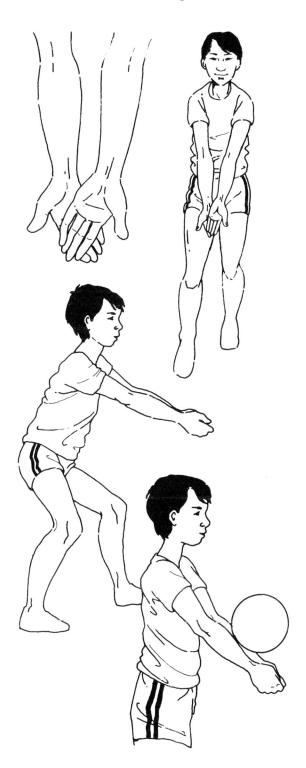

Activity 52: 3 v 3 dig game

Use a large court and a high net. Throw the ball to start the game. Dig the ball (see Activity 51) as many times on each side of the net as necessary before sending the ball over the net. A point is scored if the other side loses control of the ball.

Activity 53: 4 v 4 mini volleyball game

Use a large court and a high net. For each team, two players stand close to the net and two stand at the back of the court, as shown.

Start the game with an underarm service. The player at the back right-hand corner of the court serves the ball. The player serving continues to do so until the opposition win the point. The service then goes to the other side. Before serving, the opposition rotate clockwise one place. The person then at the back right-hand corner of the court proceeds to serve.

Activity 54: Passing the ball around the body

Take the ball with two hands. Choose a body part, e.g. the waist, and take the ball around that body part without allowing it to drop to the floor. At first, the ball will touch the body part as it travels around the body.

However, with confidence the player will be able to pass the ball around the body part without touching, passing it from one hand to the other.

Other body parts to use are: knees, right leg, head, left leg, hips, neck.

Activity 55: Hitting ball against a wall

Throw the ball against the wall to begin. Watch the returning ball carefully as it may come back quickly. Only one bounce is allowed. Step into the ball placing the opposite foot forward. Take the bat back as an early preparation for the stroke and allow a good backswing.

Activity 56: Bowler sends ball for batter to return

The bowler must ensure an accurate feed. The batter stands sideways on, with the left shoulder forwards and the batting arm lifted backwards in preparation to strike the ball. Movement of the feet is essential to add force to the hit. Keep the bat vertical when hitting the ball and follow-through after the ball has been hit.

Activity 57: Underarm bowling

The bowler stands sideways and the bowling arm swings backwards but is kept close to the body. They step on to the left foot as the arm swings forwards and the ball is released. A follow-through with the throwing arm is important. To begin with the ball is sent with a bounce just in front of the batter. To progress, the ball is sent through the air. The skilful bowler will be able to send the ball to the batter varying the speed, height and angle.

Activity 58: 4 v 2 rounders

The team of four consists of: two out fielders, a back stop and a bowler. There are two bases. The opposing team bats in pairs (one innings).

The fielders aim to stump either of the two bases that a batter is heading towards. 'Home base' can also be stumped. The batter can only score by getting around both bases and back to 'home base'. The batter can stop on any base.

Allow five bowls per innings and then rotate pairs.

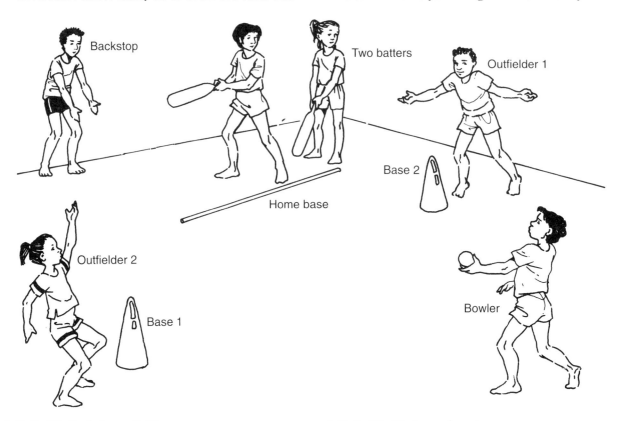

Activity 59: Backstop activities

Pupils can adopt the following positions when playing backstop or practising in this role. In the first instance, the bowler sends the ball to the backstop with the batter 'standing in', they then progress to the batter being 'active' and attempting to hit the ball as it is bowled. A first base player may then be added. When the batter misses the ball, the backstop sends the ball to the first base in an attempt to 'stump' the batter out.

Activity 60: Mini rounders game

This mini game is played in groups of three: a bowler, a batter and a fielder. Each player has five attempts at batting. The playing area is divided into sectors. The batter aims to get the ball into the designated sectors to score maximum points (1, 2 or 3 per sector). The fielder retrieves the ball and returns it to the bowler.

Activity 61: Danish rounders

A minimum of 6 v 6 players is required. The fielding team has a bowler, a backstop and 1st, 2nd, 3rd and 4th base. The ball is bowled and wherever it is sent to it has to be returned to 1st base, then to 2nd, 3rd and then 4th base. The batter has to run all the way round regardless of where the ball landed. The aim is for the ball and the batter to race each other around the posts. If the pupils are able, include a rule that if the ball is dropped it must be returned to 1st base. Each player has three attempts at batting before the fielding and batting teams change over.

LESSON PLANS FOR YEARS 3 AND 4

Unit 1, lesson 1

Theme: Invasion games; 'netball'

Purpose: PoS c

Activity bank: Activity 1: Touch ball, Activity 7: Travelling with ball using hands

Resources: Grids, large round balls

Introduction:
Play 'touch ball' (Activity 1).

Development:
Pupils travel with the ball using the hands, finding as many different ways as possible.
On command they should:
change method of travelling
change speed
change pathway
change direction.
Work in pairs, with one ball per pupil. Repeat the above, changing on command.
On the whistle, swap ball with partner.

Conclusion:
Work individually. Make up a game that involves travelling with the ball using the hands.
Work in pairs. Share your game with your partner. Play each other's games.

Unit 1, lesson 2

Theme: Invasion games; 'netball'

Purpose: PoS b, c

Activity bank: Activity 1: Touch ball, Activity 8: Sending ball with hands to partner

Resources: Grids, large balls, hoops

Introduction:
Play 'Touch ball' (Activity 1).

Development:
Work individually. Travel with the ball using hands.
Work in pairs. Send the ball to partner using hands.
Progress to travelling into a space to receive the ball from partner.

Conclusion:
Work with a partner, in a grid with a hoop at one end to score into. Play a co-operative game. Start together at the opposite end to the hoop. Pupils decide on the method of travelling and sending.

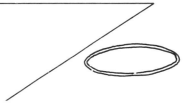

Unit 1, lesson 3

Theme: Invasion games; 'netball'

Purpose: PoS a, b

Activity bank: Activity 2: Corner game

Resources: Grids, large balls, bibs/bands

Introduction:
Play the 'Corner game' (Activity 2).

Development:
Work in groups of four to a grid: 3 v 1.
The attacking team (of three) aim to pass the ball to each other within the grid at least four times without the defender (individual player) touching the ball.

If the attacking team are successful they score 1 point; if the defender makes contact he/she scores 1 point.
Attackers are allowed to move with the ball.
Change roles regularly.
Count up the number of points after an allotted time.

Conclusion:
Continue with the above 3 v 1 game; however, now the attackers must remain stationary if they are holding the ball.
The group should be encouraged to think about the

following:
how is the ball sent?
how do the players travel with the ball?
how can the game be changed to make it more difficult for the attackers to score?

Unit 1, lesson 4

Theme: Invasion games; 'netball'

Purpose: PoS a, b, c

Activity bank: Activity 3: Numbers game

Resources: Grids, large balls, hoops or skittles, bibs/bands

Introduction:
Play the 'Numbers game' (Activity 3).

Development:
Work in groups of five to a grid: 3 v 2. One team wears bibs or bands.
Each team starts on an 'end' line. The attacking team aim to pass the ball to each other at least three times

before bouncing the ball over the opposite end line. The defenders attempt to intercept the ball using hands.
Take it in turns to be the attacking team.
The pupils are allowed to travel with the ball.

Conclusion:
Continue playing 3 v 2 as above, but the pupil in possession of the ball is not allowed to travel with the ball.
Each team has to aim to shoot into a hoop or between two skittles in order to score a goal.
The defending team are not allowed to stand in front of the goal in order to defend it.

There have to be at least three consecutive passes before the attacking team can score.
The group should be encouraged to think about the following:
how is the ball sent?
how do the players travel with the ball?
how can the game be changed to make it more difficult for the attackers to score?

Unit 1, lesson 5

Theme: Invasion games; 'rugby'

Purpose: PoS c

Activity bank: Activity 5: Travelling with a rugby ball,
Activity 6a: Passing rugby ball forwards

Resources: Rugby balls, grids, bibs/bands

Introduction:
Work individually. Travel around the grid with ball in hands:

change pathway,
change direction,
change speed.

Development:
Work in groups of four pupils to a grid: 3 v 1.
The team of three pass the ball around in an attempt to touch the other player with the ball.

Contact with the ball must be made.
Change roles regularly.

Conclusion:
Work in groups of four: 3 v 1.
The team of three pass the ball around the grid. To score they have to achieve four consecutive passes.
The individual player has to touch the ball to score a

point. When the ball is touched by the individual player, it is placed on the ground. The defender retreats and the attacking team continues passing the ball.
Change the defender regularly.

Unit 1, lesson 6

Theme: Invasion games; 'rugby'

Purpose: PoS b, c

Activity bank: Activity 6b: Passing rugby ball backwards

Resources: Rugby balls, grids, bibs/bands

Introduction:
Working individually, pupils each carry a ball around the grid. On command, pupils place their ball on the ground. Pupils keep running around the edge of the grid. On the second command they come into the grid and collect the nearest ball. They continue carrying the balls around the grid. Repeat.

(a) Players travel around the grid each carrying a rugby ball

(b) On the first command, players place the rugby balls on the floor

(c) Players run around the outside of the grid

(d) On the second command, the players come into the grid and pick up any ball

Development:
Work in pairs, with one ball per pair.
Play follow my leader: the leader carries the ball and the follower stays close behind.
On command the leader gives the ball to the follower, i.e. passes the ball back to them.

Repeat a number of times, progressing to the follower receiving the ball backwards from a distance.
Change roles regularly.

Conclusion:
Work in fours in a grid: 3 v 1.
The team of three aim in one direction. To score they have to touch the ball down over the end line.
A minimum number of three passes is required before the ball can be placed down over the line.

The ball must be sent at waist height.
The defender touches the ball to score a point. After interception the defender must retreat. The game is restarted by the attacking team sending the ball backwards.

Unit 1, lesson 7

Theme: Invasion games; 'rugby'

Purpose: PoS a, b

Activity bank: Activity 4: Two-way rugby game

Resources: Rugby balls, large grids, bibs/bands

Introduction:
Work in pairs, with one ball per pair.
Play follow my leader: the leader carries the ball and the follower stays close behind.
On command the leader gives the ball to the follower, i.e. passes the ball back to them.

Repeat a number of times, progressing to the follower receiving the ball backwards from a distance.
Change roles regularly.

Development/Conclusion:
Play a 3 v 3 or 4 v 4 two-way rugby game (Activity 4). The attacking team start from their line. The aim is to pass the ball down to the opposite end line with at least three passes. The defence aim to touch the ball before it is grounded. If they are successful, the attackers place the ball on the ground, the defence retreat 3 m and play continues. The ball must be sent backwards by the attacking team.

After three 'tackles' (i.e. the ball has been touched three times) the attacking team give possession to the opposition.
Encourage pupils to think about the following:
the best place to receive the ball,
where to stand to restart the game,
when to run with the ball and when to pass the ball.

Unit 1, lesson 8

Theme: Invasion games; 'rugby'

Purpose: PoS a, b

Activity bank: Activity 4: Two-way rugby game

Resources: Rugby balls, large grids, markers (e.g. cones), bibs/bands

Introduction:
8 per grid. Play a 4 v 4 rugby game.
One team has possession of the ball, they have to tick

the opposition with the ball in order to score a point.
Change roles frequently.

Development/Conclusion:
Play a 3 v 3 or 4 v 4 two-way rugby game (see Activity 4 and Lesson 7).
A progression from the previous week is that two markers are placed on each end line, approximately 3 m away from each other. If the attacking team place the ball down between the two markers they score 2 points; if the ball is placed outside the markers then they score 1 point.

Encourage pupils to think about the following:
the best place to receive the ball,
where to stand to restart the game,
when to run with the ball and when to pass the ball,
the best place to score maximum points,
the best way to defend the ball and to stop the attacking team from scoring.

Unit 2, lesson 1

Theme: Net games; 'short tennis'

Purpose: PoS c

Activity bank: Activity 9: Rolling ball, Activity 10: Bouncing ball, Activity 11: Patting ball, Activity 12: Tracking the ball

Resources: Large foam/soft balls, use of wall, bean bags/multi markers

Introduction:
Work individually with one large soft ball per pupil.
Travel around the area with the ball:

rolling it,
bouncing it,
patting it in the air.

Development:
Work individually with a large ball, using a wall.
Roll the ball against the wall and retrieve it.
Throw the ball against the wall and catch it.
Are pupils moving their feet in order to track the ball?

Ask pupils to consider the following:
what happens if you change the speed of the ball?
can you throw right and left handed?
can you catch right and left handed?

Conclusion:
Work in pairs, with one large soft ball per pair.
Set out three bean bags/multi markers equi-distant from each player.
Roll the ball to your partner through the spaces.
Bounce the ball to your partner through the spaces.
Play co-operatively. Progress to a competitive game.

Unit 2, lesson 2

Theme: Net games; 'Short tennis'

Purpose: PoS b, c

Activity bank: Activity 11: Patting ball, Activity 13: Sending ball into hoop

Resources: Large ball, use of wall, hoops

Introduction:
Work individually, with one large ball per pupil.
Send the large ball against the wall, e.g. by bouncing or rolling it.

Pupils challenge themselves:
can they hit a specified area/mark 15 times?
can they send the ball high/low and right/left?

Development:
Work in pairs, with one large ball per pair.
Place a hoop equi-distant between the two players.
The first player bounces the ball into the hoop for the other player to receive.
Playing co-operatively, see what happens when the ball is sent in the following ways:
hard,
gently,
with right hand/left hand.
Progress to working on a court with markers in the middle for a net.
Send the ball to partner with a bounce and catch to retrieve.
What happens when the ball is sent long/sent short?
What happens when the sides of the court only are used?
Progress to sending the ball to partner with a patting action.

Conclusion:
In pairs, make up a game using either patting the ball with the hand or bouncing and catching it.
Use a hoop or a 'net' in the middle of the court.

Is the game co-operative or competitive?
How do you score in the game?
What are the basic rules?

Unit 2, lesson 3

Theme: Net games; 'short tennis'

Activity bank: Activity 14: Tennis squash

Purpose: PoS b, c

Resources: Use of wall, bats, medium/small balls

Introduction:
Work in pairs, with players numbered 1 and 2. Each player has a bat, with one ball per pair.
Player 1 balances the ball on the bat whilst player 2

remains stationary. All the players numbered 1 move as fast as they can in and out of all the stationary players and each moves back to their partner on command.

Development:
Work individually, using a wall.
Send the ball against the wall. How many times can pupils hit it before they lose control?
Aim to beat that score.
Work in pairs using the wall.
Play 'tennis squash' (see Activity 14).
Pupils should consider the following:
which side is it easier to hit the ball on?
what happens if you hit the ball harder/softer?
which side does your partner find it most difficult to hit the ball on?

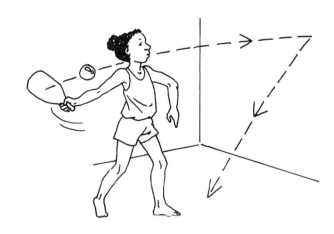

Conclusion:
Work in pairs, using the wall.
Make up and play a game.
Pupils should consider the following:

can other equipment be used?
what are the rules?
how is a point scored?

Unit 2, lesson 4

Theme: Net games; 'short tennis'

Purpose: PoS b, c

Activity bank: Activity 10: Bouncing ball, Activity 15: Rolling ball using bat, Activity 16: Sending ball using forehand

Resources: Bats, small/medium balls, bean bags/markers

Introduction:
Work individually using a bat and a medium/small ball.
Roll the ball along the ground with the bat.
Balance the ball on the bat and take the ball for a walk.

Bounce the ball on the floor while stationary, then lead on to bouncing the ball while travelling.
Hit the ball in the air with the bat while stationary, then lead on to doing this while travelling.

Development:
Work in pairs. Make a net out of markers.
One person feeds the ball to their partner's 'favoured' side (forehand). Partner returns the ball for the feeder to catch.

After five attempts, change roles.
Ideas for progression are:
make partner move for the ball,
send the ball long then send the ball short,
send the ball to the opposite side.

Conclusion:
Work in pairs. Each player has a bat.
Have a co-operative rally over the 'net'. Send the ball to partner's forehand.

How many times can the players hit the ball before losing control?
Can the pupils make the rally competitive?

Unit 2, lesson 5

Theme: Net games; 'short tennis'

Purpose: PoS b, c

Activity bank: Activity 16: Sending ball using forehand, Activity 19: Sending ball using backhand, Activity 20: Tennis rounders

Resources: Grids, bats and small balls, bean bags

Introduction:
Play some running and jumping games over the lines on

the playground; include in these games hopping and skipping.

Development:
Work in pairs (one feeder and one hitter) using a grid.
Use a 'net' made of bean bags.
Start on the baseline of the grid and send the ball to the opposite baseline using the forehand stroke.

Progress to backhand, with one person acting as feeder and the other as hitter.
Make up one or more practice(s) in pairs that involve(s) the forehand and backhand.

110

Conclusion:
In groups of 4–6 play 'tennis rounders' (Activity 20) using a large grid.
Team A are the batters. Team B throw the ball over for team A members to hit. They take it in turns to hit the ball to team B, who are standing on the other side of the net. Team B aim to catch the ball. If they are successful they get 1 point; if not then team A get 1 point.

Unit 2, lesson 6

Theme: Net games; 'short tennis'

Purpose: PoS a, b, c

Activity bank: Activity 20: Tennis rounders, Activity 21: Volleying the ball

Resources: Markers for a net, small balls, bats, hoops

Introduction:
Play 'tennis rounders' (see Activity 20).

Development:
Work in pairs, using a large grid with a 'net'.
The hitter has a bat and stands close to the net; the feeder stands close to the opposite baseline.
The feeder throws the ball underarm to the hitter who attempts to 'punch' the ball into a hoop just on the other side of the net.

After five attempts, change roles.
Move the positions so that the feeder stands on one baseline and the hitter on the other. The feeder sends the ball to the hitter, who returns the ball with a forehand/backhand. Then, moving to the net, the feeder returns the ball with a hit for the hitter to volley back.

Conclusion:
Work in pairs. Have a co-operative rally.
Can the players send the ball using a groundstroke/volley alternately?

How many times can they hit the ball without losing control?
Using the same principles, can the pupils lead this into a competitive game?

111

Unit 2, lesson 7

Theme: Net games; 'short tennis'

Purpose: PoS a, b, c

Activity bank: Activity 22: Service (underarm)

Resources: Large grids/courts, bats, small balls, hoops, markers

Introduction:
Practise individual throwing and catching activities with a small ball.

Development:
Divide the grid/court into quarters. Work in pairs. Pupils stand in the square diagonally opposite to their partner.
One pupil throws the ball underarm so that it bounces into the box that their partner is standing in. The partner catches the ball after one bounce and returns it using the same method.
Progress to throwing overarm.

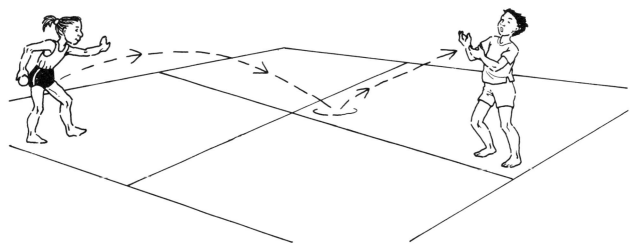

Repeat the above, but one player has a bat and serves the ball underarm for the other player to catch.
Repeat three times, then change roles.

To progress the player may be asked to aim their service into a hoop in the box diagonally opposite.

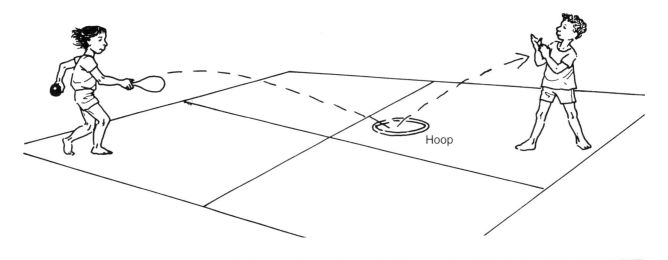

Hoop

Conclusion:
Work in pairs. Play a game that involves both players using a bat and beginning the game with an underarm service.

Unit 2, lesson 8

Theme: Net games; 'short tennis'

Purpose: PoS a, b, c

Activity bank: Activity 22: Service, Activity 23: Mini tennis game

Resources: Large grids/courts, bats, small balls, ropes, markers

Introduction:
Working individually, practise the service from Lesson 7 against a wall.

Development:
Work in pairs on a court, with a bat each and one ball between two.
Using ropes, divide the court into sections, as shown. Concentrating on the depth of the pass, play a 1 plus 1 (co-operative) game aiming to get the ball into the 'short' and 'long' areas.

Move the ropes to the sides of the court, as shown. Concentrate on shots sent to the side areas. Score 1 point if the ball lands in the roped areas.

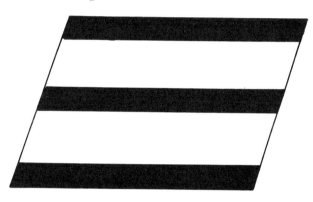

Conclusion:
Play a game in pairs using the court and a 'net'.
Take it in turns to serve.
Each player can only score while serving. The first to score five points wins.
Encourage pupils to think about the position that the ball is served to in order to beat the opponent, i.e. long or short, right or left.

Unit 3, lesson 1

Theme: Striking/fielding; cricket

Purpose: PoS c

Activity bank: Activity 9: Rolling ball, Activity 10: Bouncing ball, Activity 24: Fielding the ball

Resources: Large balls, cones

Introduction:
Work individually using a large ball each.
Roll the ball, chase after it and field it.
Roll the ball, chase after it, pass the ball and then field it.

Bounce the ball into a space, chase after it and retrieve it.
Throw the ball up high and catch it before it lands.

Development:
Work in pairs with a large ball and a cone per pair.
The bowler sends the ball to the batter who stands 3–4 m away in front of the cone, protecting it.
The batter may use any part of the body (hands, legs, feet) to send the ball away, ensuring that the bowler does not hit the wicket (cone).
After six attempts each, change roles.

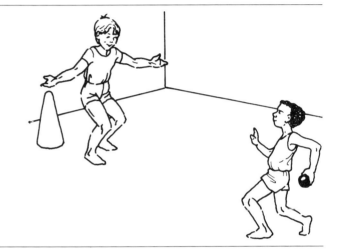

Conclusion:
Work in groups of four: one bowler, one batter and two fielders.
Play as above, but this time the batter is limited to using only their hand/arm.
Encourage the pupils to stand sideways on when 'batting'.

Unit 3, lesson 2

Theme: Striking/fielding; cricket

Purpose: PoS a, c

Activity bank: Activity 25: Washing baskets, Activity 26: Batter striking the ball, Activity 57: Underarm bowling

Resources: Cones, large balls, large cricket bat shapes, baskets

Introduction:
Play 'Washing baskets' (Activity 25).

Development:
Work in pairs, with a large ball and a cone between two. The bowler sends the ball to the batter who stands 3–4 m away in front of the cone, protecting it (see Lesson 1). The bowler aims to hit the wicket whilst the batter must protect it.
The batter uses parts of the body to send the ball away, ensuring that the bowler does not hit the wicket (cone). After six attempts, change roles.

Progress to using a large cricket bat instead of parts of the body.
The batter must let the bowler see the wicket (cone).
The bowler must allow the ball to bounce before the batter hits it.
Ask pupils:
how can the bowler make it more difficult for the batter to hit the ball?

Conclusion:
Work in groups of four: one bowler, one batter and two fielders.
One pupil has six attempts as the batter, then changes roles.
The batter gets a point every time the ball lands away from a fielder.
Encourage the batter to stand sideways on.
Pupils should consider the following:
what happens if the ball is hit in the air?
how can the batter direct the ball to a space away from the fielders?

Unit 3, lesson 3

Theme: Striking/fielding; cricket

Purpose: PoS c

Activity bank: Activity 27: Chase the bean bag game 1

Resources: Bean bags, sector made up of markers, different coloured cones, medium balls, cricket-shaped bats

Introduction:
Play 'Chase the bean bag game 1' (Activity 28).

Development:
Work in pairs, with a bat, a medium ball and three cones (different colours) per pair.
The batter stands in front of the wicket (a cone). The other two cones (of different colours) are placed at either side of the batter equi-distant from the batter and bowler.
The batter aims to send the ball to the cone of his/her own choice.
After six attempts, change roles.

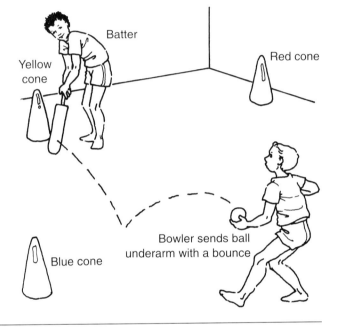

Batter

Red cone

Yellow cone

Bowler sends ball underarm with a bounce

Blue cone

Conclusion:
Work in groups of four. Play as above, but with fielders to retrieve the ball.
This time the bowler shouts out clearly and in good time the colour of the cone that they want the batter to hit the ball to.

The batter gets 2 points for hitting the ball in the direction of the specified cone and 1 point if the ball is hit in any other direction.
After six attempts, change roles.

Unit 3, lesson 4

Theme: Striking/fielding; cricket

Purpose: PoS c

Activity bank: Activity 28: Chase the bean bag game 2

Resources: Small/medium balls, cricket bat shapes, different coloured cones, hoops, bean bags, sector made up of markers

Introduction:
Play 'Chase the bean bag game 2' (Activity 28).

Development:
Work in pairs, with one ball, a bat and four cones per pair.
Set up the cones and play as in Lesson 3, but this time the batter has three cones to hit: one to the right, one to the left and one directly in front (as shown).
The batter makes the choice of where to send the ball to.
Encourage the batter to move their feet in the direction they are hitting the ball.
As before, change roles after six attempts.

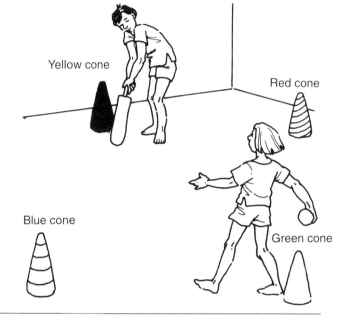

Yellow cone

Red cone

Blue cone

Green cone

Conclusion:
Work in groups of four, with a batter, a bowler and two fielders.
The group uses a medium or small ball depending on their ability to strike the ball.

The bowler calls out the cone the batter has to hit the ball towards.
The batter gets 2 points for a correct aim and 1 point for a hit in any other direction.
After six attempts, change roles.

Unit 3, lesson 5

Theme: Striking/fielding; cricket

Purpose: PoS a, b

Activity bank: Activity 29: Run and chase activity, Activity 32: Mini game, Activity 57: Underarm bowling

Resources: Small balls, bats, cones

Introduction:
Use the 'Run and chase activity' (Activity 29).

Development:
Play 'Mini game' (see Activity 32 for details).

Conclusion:
As above, but make it into a competitive situation.
The batters start with 10 runs, if they are 'out', i.e. either they are 'run out' or the bowler hits their wicket,

they lose 1 run. However, they add to their total the number of runs they collect.
Note: only count the runs made by the batter who actually hits the ball.

Unit 3, lesson 6 ▷

Theme: Striking/fielding; cricket

Purpose: PoS c, b

Activity bank: Activity 30: Triangle fielding activity

Resources: Cones, small balls, bats, markers

Introduction:
Use the 'Triangle fielding activity' (see Activity 30).

Development:
Work in groups of three: one batter, one bowler and one fielder. Set out the cones as shown.
The batter aims to get the ball into the sector (if right handed to their left, and vice versa). They score 1, 2 or 3 points depending on the area they hit the ball into.

The fielder retrieves the ball sending it back to the bowler.
Each player has six attempts at batting. Total the number of points each scores.
Change roles and repeat, attempting to beat individual scores.

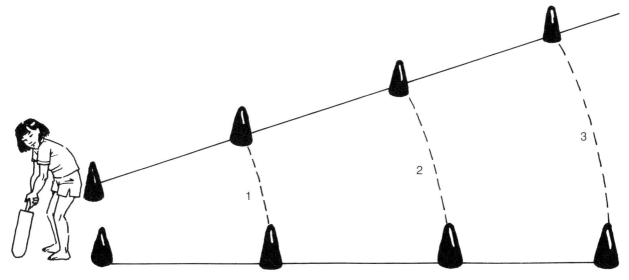

Conclusion:
Make up and play a game in groups of three that involves hitting a ball in certain directions or over certain distances.

Show your game to another group. Try out each others' games.

Unit 3, lesson 7 ▷

Theme: Striking/fielding; cricket

Purpose: PoS a, c

Activity bank: Activity 31: Circle activity, Activity 32: Mini game

Resources: Cones, small balls, bats

Introduction:
Use the 'Circle activity' (see Activity 31).

Development/Conclusion:
Working in groups of four, pupils should make up practices that involve each member of the group and improve their skill at:
bowling the ball

fielding the ball.
Play the 'Mini game' (see Activity 32).
Did the practices the pupils made up and played improve their games?

Unit 3, lesson 8

Theme: Striking/fielding; cricket

Purpose: PoS a, b

Activity bank: Activity 30: Triangle fielding activity,
Activity 33: Cricket pairs game,
Activity 57: Underarm bowling

Resources: Cones, small balls, bats

Introduction:
Use the 'Triangle fielding activity' (see Activity 30), using an underarm throw instead of a roll.

Progress to throwing the ball overarm, making the triangle shape larger.

Development/Conclusion:
Play the 'Cricket pairs game' (see Activity 33 for details). Encourage pupils to think about the following:
where is it best to stand if you are fielding?
where is the best place to hit the ball if you are batting?

is it better to keep the ball near the ground or to hit it in the air?
if you are bowling the ball, how can you make it difficult for the batter to hit it without sending the ball too wide?

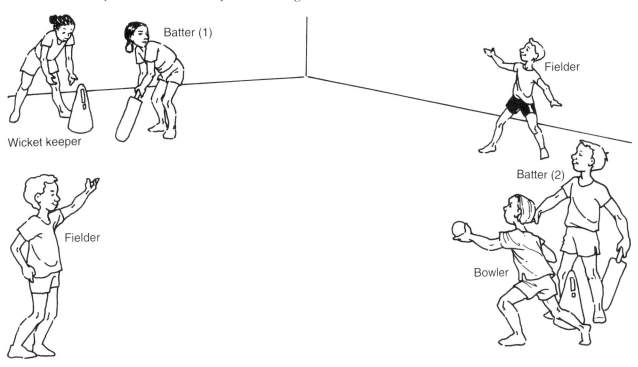

Wicket keeper

Batter (1)

Fielder

Fielder

Batter (2)

Bowler

LESSON PLANS FOR YEARS 5 AND 6

Unit 4, lesson 1

Theme: Invasion games; football

Purpose: PoS c

Activity bank: Activity 34: Tag game

Resources: Large ball, grids, bands/bibs

Introduction:
Play the 'Tag game' (Activity 34).

Development:
Work in groups of eight per grid, with a ball each. Travel with the ball using the feet. On the whistle, the pupils must control the ball with their feet.
Repeat a number of times.
Encourage pupils to change speed, pathway and direction, either on your command or at their own choice.
Work in pairs with a ball each.
Both players travel with the ball at their feet, one player behind the other. Play follow-my-leader. Travel in the same pathway, direction and at the same speed.
Change leader and repeat a number of times.
Progress to a competitive situation, where the leader aims to lose the follower whilst keeping the ball close to their feet.
Repeat, using one ball between two. The leader has the ball and the follower keeps close by. On command, the leader sends the ball to the follower who is in a space to receive it.
Change roles and repeat.

Conclusion:
Work in pairs in a grid with one ball between two.
Play a competitive game, 1 v 1.
The players start at opposite ends of the grid. One player has the ball. The player with the ball aims to get it past the other player and over the line his opponent is defending.

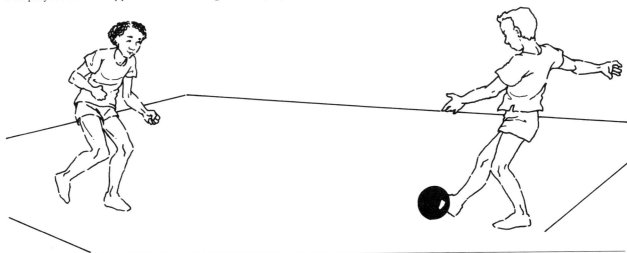

Unit 4, lesson 2

Theme: Invasion games; football

Purpose: PoS b, c

Activity bank: Activity 35: 3 v 1 game, Activity 42: Running games

Resources: Large balls, grids, bands

Introduction:
Play some running games (see Activity 42 for ideas). Work individually, in pairs and in small groups.

Development:
Work in pairs, with eight people to a grid. Each pair is labelled No. 1 and No. 2. There is one ball per pair. Each No. 2 is inside the grid with the ball and each No. 1 is just outside the grid. No. 2 travels around the grid with the ball at their feet, changing pathway etc. On command, they look for their No. 1 and send the ball to them using their feet. They then swap places and the activity continues.

Repeat the above, but instead of No. 1 remaining still on the outside of the grid, they keep moving around the grid so that No. 2 has to look up before sending the ball.

Conclusion:
Play a '3 v 1 game' (see Activity 35 for details).

121

Unit 4, lesson 3 ▷

Theme: Invasion games; football

Purpose: PoS a, b, c

Activity bank: Activity 37: Trapping the ball with feet, Activity 40: 3v3 football, Activity 42: running games

Resources: Large balls, grids, bands, cones

Introduction:
Play some running games (see Activity 42 for ideas).

Development:
Work in pairs, with one ball per pair.
Travel around the space. On command, the player with the ball sends it to their partner.
Ask pupils to think of different ways of stopping the ball with their feet.
Work in groups of four in a grid. Number each player.

Players move around the grid either dribbling the ball or moving into a space. When a number is shouted out, that player has to move into a space in order to receive the ball.
Encourage pupils to concentrate on stopping the ball dead as it is sent.

Conclusion:
Play '3 v 3 football' (see Activity 40).
Ask pupils to think about the following:

where is the best place to receive the ball?
can you find ways of communicating to your team that you want the ball?

Unit 4, lesson 4 ▷

Theme: Invasion games; football

Purpose: PoS a, b, c

Activity bank: Activity 37: trapping the ball using feet, Activity 38: Sending the ball using feet, Activity 40: 3 v 3 football

Resources: Large balls, grids, bands/bibs, cones

Introduction:
Work in grids, with 6–8 people per grid. They travel around the grid, each with a ball at their feet. On command, the ball is stopped dead. The pupils leave the balls and continue running around the edge of the grid.

On the second command, they then come back into the grid and retrieve a ball that is close to them.
Repeat a number of times. For an alternative activity, take one of the balls away and see who is left without a ball.

Development:
Work in groups of four in a grid: 3 v 1.
The team of three, using at least four passes, have to dribble the ball over the opposite line without the defender touching the ball.
Pupils should consider the following:
how do you communicate with your team players?
where is the best place to move to in order to receive the ball?

Change roles regularly.
Add a goal/goals and elongate the grid (encourage pupils to pass and move forward).
Ask pupils:
how does this change the way that the team move into a space?

Conclusion:
Play '3 v 3 football' (see Activity 40).
Add the following rules:
two touch game
no goalkeeper

can only shoot from 2 m away from the goals
defending team cannot block the goals.

Unit 4, lesson 5

Theme: Invasion games; hockey

Purpose: PoS c

Activity bank: Activity 36: 'Cat and mouse' game, Activity 44: Travelling with a hockey stick, Activity 45: Stopping the ball with a hockey stick, Activity 46: Passing the ball with a hockey stick

Resources: Bands/bibs, unihockey sticks, small balls, grids

Introduction:
Play the 'Cat and mouse' game (see Activity 36).

Development:
Work individually with a hockey stick and ball each.
Travel with the ball close to the stick head.
Change pathway, direction, speed, stop/start on command.

Work in pairs in a grid: 1 v 1.
Each player starts on an end line. The player with the ball attempts to cross the grid and pass the other player whilst still keeping possession of the ball.

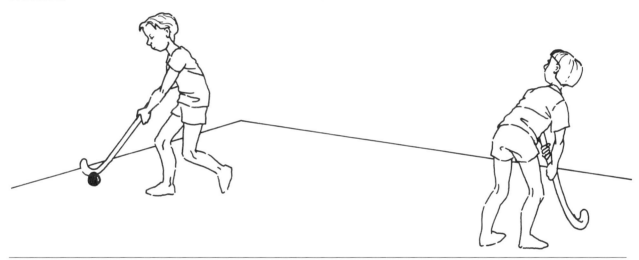

Conclusion:
Make the grids larger than above and work in groups of four. There are three players: 2 v 1. The fourth group member focuses on evaluating the small game.
The attacking team aim to get from one end of the grid to the other without the defender intercepting the ball.
If the defender touches the ball, he/she scores 1 point.

The attacking player without the ball should be encouraged to think about the best position to be in to support their team mate.
The on-looker referees the game with simple rules and evaluates how the attackers perform in relation to supporting each other.
Change roles and repeat.

123

Unit 4, lesson 6

Theme: Invasion games; hockey

Purpose: PoS a, b

Activity bank: Activity 41: 3 v 3 hockey, Activity 44: Travelling with a hockey stick, Activity 45: Stopping the ball with a hockey stick, Activity 46: Passing the ball with a hockey stick

Resources: Grids, unihockey sticks, small balls, bibs/bands

Introduction:
Working in groups of three, play the 2 v 1 game from the Conclusion of Lesson 5.

Development/Conclusion:
Play a 3 v 3 hockey game in a larger grid. One team wears bibs.
Attacking team aim to get the ball over the opposite line with at least three passes before they do so.
The attacking team start on the baseline. They may travel with and/or send the ball using the stick.

The ball can only be intercepted, no tackling is allowed. Concentrate again on support play, finding the best place to be in order to take the ball in a space.

If the defence intercept the ball (no tackling allowed), the game stops. The roles change (i.e. the intercepting team become the attacking team). The new attackers move to the base line and the game starts again.

Unit 4, lesson 7

Theme: Invasion games; hockey

Purpose: PoS a, b

Activity bank: Activity 41: 3 v 3 hockey, Activity 43: Tackling with hockey sticks

Resources: Bibs, unihockey sticks, small balls, cones, grids

Introduction:
Work in groups of four.
Make up and participate in a practice that involves the whole group and concentrate on travelling with the ball.
Work in pairs. Sandwich the ball between the sticks, as shown.
Can the pupils lift the ball off the floor whilst keeping the sticks close together?
Can they take the ball up and down to the ground a number of times before losing control?

Development:
Work in pairs in a grid: 1 v 1.
Start together in the middle of the grid with the ball sandwiched between the two sticks.
Aim to get the ball over the other player's stick and over the line that they are defending (see the diagram on the next page).

Start on opposite sides of the grid. One player starts with the ball. They travel across the grid towards the other player's line. The other player attempts to stop them passing over the line by tackling the ball (not the stick or the player).

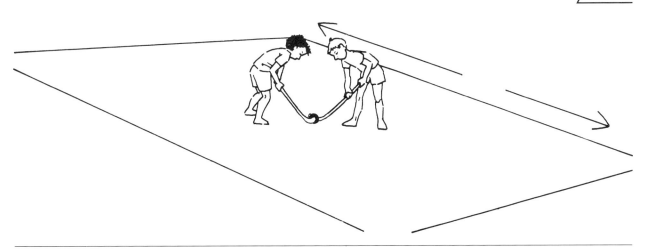

Conclusion:
Play '3 v 3 hockey' (see Activity 41). Two cones are set up along each baseline for goals. Play a two-way game. One team wear bibs.
Start in the middle of the grid. To start, play the ball back to another member of the team.

Encourage teams to adopt the following triangular formation:
Direction of shooting
⟶   A

     A

      A

Unit 4, lesson 8

Theme: Invasion games; hockey

Purpose: PoS a, b

Activity bank: Activity 41: 3 v 3 hockey

Resources: Large grids, small balls, unihockey sticks, cones, bibs

Introduction:
Work in groups of three. Make up and participate in a

practice that will help you to send the ball more accurately.

Development/Conclusion:
Play '3 v 3 hockey' (see Activity 41).

Bring in the positional play from Lesson 7.

Unit 5, lesson 1

Theme: Net games; volleyball

Purpose: PoS a

Activity bank: Activity 47: Catch volley

Resources: Soft balls/volleyballs, markers for net

Introduction:
Work individually, with one ball per pupil.
Throw the ball high and catch it.

Throw and catch the ball whilst moving around. Move forwards/backwards/sideways.
Throw the ball and catch it after a bounce.

Development:
Work individually, with one ball per pupil.
Volley the ball and catch it. How many times can you do this?

Move around the area using the catch volley.
Catch volley against the wall.

Conclusion:
Work in pairs, with one ball per pair.
Each pair finds a space within the playing area.

Using the catch volley, see how many times the pupils can keep the ball in the air without losing control.
Aim to beat the best score.

Unit 5, lesson 2

Theme: Net games; volleyball

Purpose: PoS c

Activity bank: Activity 47: Catch volley, Activity 48: Volley – in pairs

Resources: Soft balls/volleyballs, markers for net

Introduction:
Work individually, with one ball per pupil.
Keep the ball up in the air using any part of the body above the waist.

How many different ways can pupils find?
How many times can they repeat this in 30 seconds?
Share ideas with a partner.

Development:
Work individually, with one ball per pupil.
Play the ball to yourself using the catch volley from Lesson 1.
Work in pairs, with one ball per pair.
Using the catch volley, send the ball to partner. Play the ball to yourself before sending to partner if necessary.

How many times can the players keep the ball in the air without losing control?
Progress to the volley, without catching the ball.
One player feeds the ball, with a high throw, to the other who returns the ball with a volley for the feeder to catch.
Repeat five times, then change roles.

Conclusion:
Make up and play a co-operative game using the volley and/or the catch volley.

Use a restricted area if necessary.
Introduce one rule.

Unit 5, lesson 3

Theme: Net games; volleyball

Purpose: PoS b, c

Activity bank: Activity 48: Volley – in pairs, Activity 49: Dribbling the ball double-handed

Resources: Soft balls/volleyballs, markers for net, skipping ropes

Introduction:
Work individually, with one ball per pupil.

Travel around the playing area using the double-handed dribble (see Activity 49).

Development:
Work individually, with one ball per pupil. Send the ball high, volley it, allow it to bounce, then volley it again.
Work in pairs. Set up a court and place markers across the middle for a net.
Volley the ball over the net to partner.
Repeat, trying to travel to the side whilst continuing with the volley.
Progress to increasing the distance.
Work in groups of four, three playing and one observing.
Volley the ball to each other in a triangular formation.
Return to using the catch volley if the volley is difficult.

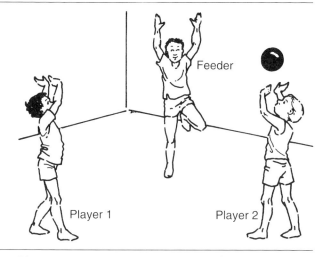

Feeder

Player 1   Player 2

Conclusion:
Work in fours: 2 v 2.
Use a higher net than before (skipping ropes suspended from the sides of the playing area could be used). Use a court.

Play a co-operative 2 v 2 game using the volley only.
Start the game by throwing the ball over the net to the opposition. Each team may play the ball as many times as they like before sending the ball over the net.
(Use the catch volley if necessary.)

Unit 5, lesson 4

Theme: Net games; volleyball

Purpose: PoS a, c

Activity bank: Activity 51: Volleyball dig

Resources: Soft balls/volleyballs, markers for net, skipping ropes

Introduction:
Work individually, with one ball per pupil.
Volley the ball in the playing area, moving around if possible.

Volley the ball standing, on knees, return to standing.
Volley the ball whilst turning a full circle, then turn the opposite way.

Development:
Work in pairs, with one ball per pair.
The feeder lobs the ball (i.e. throws it high) to their partner who returns the ball with a dig (see Activity 51).
Repeat five times, then change roles.
Lob the ball to the side of the player, who returns it with

a dig (allowing it to bounce if necessary).
The feeder lobs the ball in front of and over the other player's head to encourage foot movement before they return the ball with a dig.
Volley and dig the ball alternately in pairs.

Conclusion:
Use a court and a higher net.
Make up a game using the volley and the dig.

Start the game by throwing the ball over the net.
How many times is each player allowed to play the ball before returning it over the net?

Unit 5, lesson 5

Theme: Net games; volleyball

Purpose: PoS a, b, c

Activity bank: Activity 51: Volleyball dig, Activity 52: 3 v 3 dig game, Activity 54: Passing ball around the body

Resources: Soft balls/ volleyballs, markers for net, skipping ropes

Introduction:
Work individually, with one ball per pupil.
Pass the ball around the head, waist, knees and other parts of the body (see Activity 54).

Lead on to travelling around the playing area whilst passing the ball around the body.
Teacher shouts out body parts.

Development:
Work in groups of three, with one feeder and two players.
The feeder sends the ball to each player (calling their name out).
The feeder lobs the ball up for the player called out to return with a dig. That player then returns to their place.
Repeat five times, then change roles.
Progress to having two feeders (each with a ball) and one player returning.
The feeders take it in turn to lob the ball for the returning player to dig.
Repeat five times, then change roles.

Conclusion:
Play a 3 v 3 game (see Activity 52).

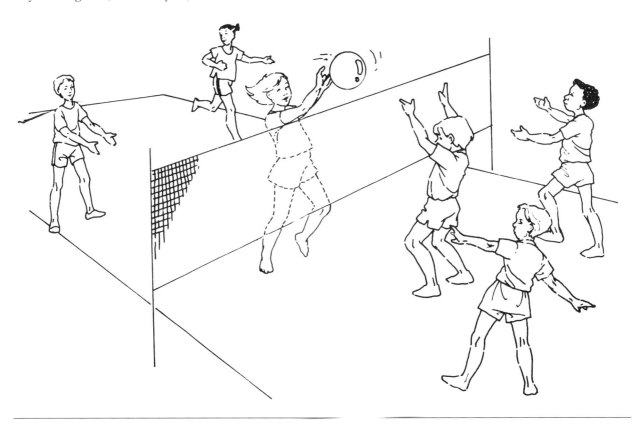

Unit 5, lesson 6

Theme: Net games; volleyball

Purpose: PoS a, b, c

Activity bank: Activity 51: Volleyball dig, Activity 52: 3 v 3 dig game

Resources: Soft balls/volleyballs, markers for net, hoops, skipping ropes

---

Introduction:
Work individually, with one ball per pupil.
Dig ball to self, allow ball to bounce at first, then progress to working without a bounce.

Can the pupils move around whilst digging the ball?

Development:
Work in groups of three, with one ball per group.
Pupils make up and participate in a practice that helps them to improve:

volleying
digging.
Use a net, a court, hoops etc. to assist with the practice.

Conclusion:
Play a 3 v 3 dig game (see Activity 52).
Play in a triangular formation.

As a progression, the ball is only allowed to be played three times on one side before it has to be sent over to the other side.

Unit 5, lesson 7

Theme: Net games; volleyball

Purpose: PoS a, b, c

Activity bank: Activity 50: Volleyball service, Activity
52: 3 v 3 dig game

Resources: Soft balls/volleyballs, markers for net, hoops, skipping ropes

Introduction:
Work individually, with one ball per pupil.
Volley ball to self, allow it to bounce at first, progressing
to working without a bounce.

Progress to travelling around the playing area volleying
the ball to self.

Development:
Work in pairs on the court. Use a low net.
One player serves the ball to the other player to be
caught on the opposite side of the court.
If necessary, allow the ball to bounce before striking it.
Stand further back and send the service with more force.
After five attempts, change roles.

Set up hoops in various positions. Each is given a
different number of points. Each player has five
attempts to score the maximum number of points by
serving into the hoops.

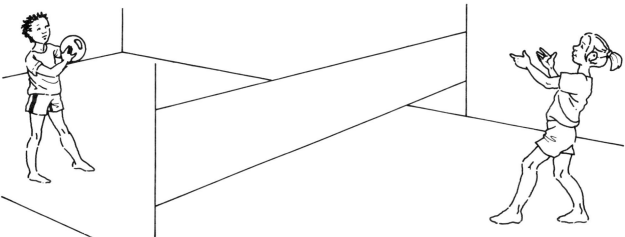

Conclusion:
Play a 3 v 3 dig game (see Activity 52).

Start the game by serving over the high net with an
underarm service.

Unit 5, lesson 8

Theme: Net games; volleyball

Purpose: PoS a, b, c

Activity bank: Activity 50: Volleyball service, Activity
53: 4 v 4 mini volleyball game

Resources: Soft balls/volleyballs, markers for net, skipping ropes

Introduction:
Practise serving in pairs (see Activity 50).

Aim to serve into a hoop in front of the player.

Development:
Work in groups of four: 2 v 2.
Use a high net, without a designated court.

Play the ball three times on each side before sending the
ball over the net.
Start the game using an underarm service.

Conclusion:
Play a 4 v 4 mini volleyball game (see Activity 53).

Unit 6, lesson 1

Theme: Striking/fielding; rounders

Purpose: PoS c

Activity bank: Activity 55: Hitting ball against a wall, Activity 56: Bowler sends ball for batter to return

Resources: Padder bats, medium balls, cones

Introduction:
Work individually with one bat and one ball per pupil. Bounce the ball and hit it against the wall (see Activity 55).

Development:
Work in pairs: one batter and one bowler. Set a cone at either side of the bowler (see diagram). The bowler sends the ball to the batter, with a bounce.

Work in pairs. The bowler sends the ball, with a bounce, for the batter to return (see Activity 56). Play co-operatively. After five attempts, change roles.

The batter directs the ball to either cone (of their choice). Change roles after five attempts.

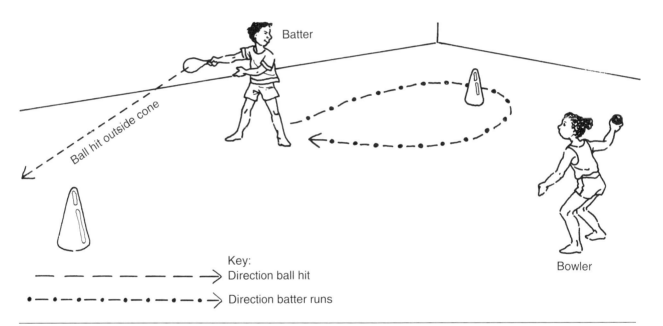

Key:
— — — — —→ Direction ball hit
•—•—•—•—•—•→ Direction batter runs

Batter
Ball hit outside cone
Bowler

Conclusion:
Work in pairs: 1 v 1. Set out the cones and play as above, but this time the batter aims to hit the ball outside one of the cones, then tries to run around the other cone before the bowler can retrieve the ball and stump the batting space.

If the ball is hit between the cones then there is no run. The batter must run if the ball is hit outside the cones. After five attempts, change roles.

Unit 6, lesson 2

Theme: Striking/fielding; rounders

Purpose: PoS a, c

Activity bank: Activity 56: Bowler sends ball for batter to return, Activity 57: Underarm bowling

Resources: Padder bats, medium balls, cones

Introduction:
Work in pairs, with one bat and one ball between per pair.
The batter and the bowler co-operate.
The batter aims to hit the ball into a sector marked out by cones (see diagram).

The batter can score 1, 2, or 3 points depending on the area of the sector that the ball lands in.
After five attempts, change roles.

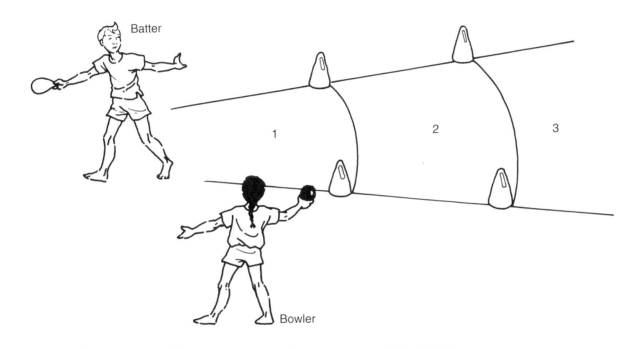

Development:
Work in pairs, one batter and one bowler.
Two cones, of different colours, are set at either side of the bowler (as shown).

The bowler shouts out the colour of one of the cones and then sends the ball to the batter with a bounce. The batter directs the ball to the coloured cone that the bowler has shouted out.

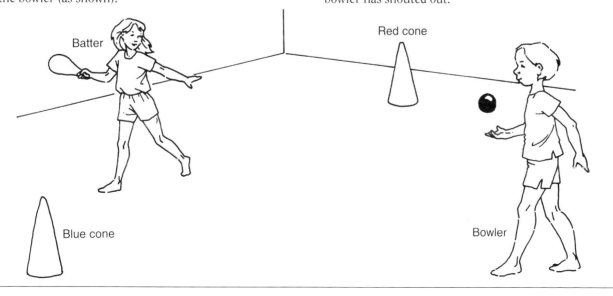

Conclusion:
Work in groups of three: 2 v 1 (two batters and one bowler).
Set out the cones as shown in the diagram.
The batter hits the ball anywhere between the cones.
The batter runs to cone A (1 point), stops or carries on to cone B (2 points) depending on where the ball has landed.

The batter must run if the ball is hit between the cones.
The bowler can stump the batter out at the cone they are approaching.
The bowler must get back into the bowling position before bowling again.
Take turns to bat and bowl.

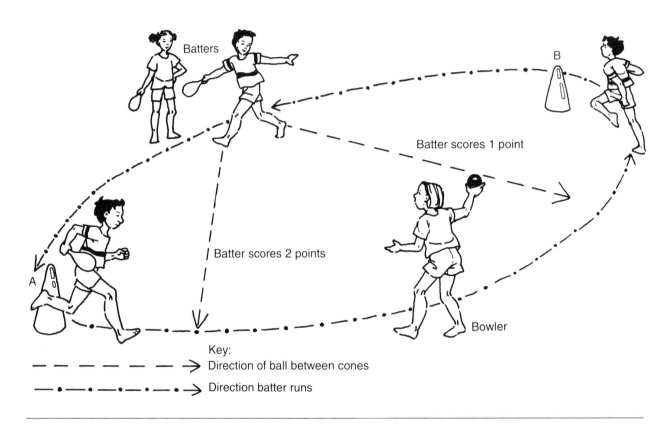

Batters

Batter scores 1 point

Batter scores 2 points

Bowler

A

B

Key:
— — — — — — —> Direction of ball between cones
— • — • — • — • —> Direction batter runs

Unit 6, lesson 3

Theme: Striking/fielding; rounders

Purpose: PoS a, b, c

Activity bank: Activity 57: Underarm bowling

Resources: Bats, tennis balls, cones, hoops

Introduction:
Work in pairs, with one ball and one bat per pair.
One pupil bowls the ball underarm, without a bounce, to their partner, who aims to hit the ball back to the first pupil (see Activity 57).

Development:
Repeat the above, but competitively.

Have five attempts each.
How many times can you catch your partner out?

Conclusion:
Work in groups of four: 2 v 2 (two batters and one bowler and one fielder).
Set out the cones and play as in Lesson 2 Conclusion, but this time the bowler has a fielder to help in trying to stump out the batters.
How can the bowler make it more difficult for the batters?

Unit 6, lesson 4

Theme: Striking fielding; rounders

Purpose: PoS a, b

Activity bank: Activity 24: Fielding the ball, Activity 25: Washing baskets

Resources: Bean bags, bats, balls, cones, baskets, markers

Introduction:
Play 'Washing baskets' (see Activity 25).

Development:
Work in groups of four: a bowler, a batter and two fielders.
The layout is shown in the diagram.
The batter and bowler co-operate.
The batter has five attempts, then everyone changes role.

The batter scores points according to the sector that the ball lands in (see diagram).
The fielders aim to stop the ball before it goes through the 'cone line'.
Encourage fielders to think about their positioning, aiming to stop the batters from scoring points.

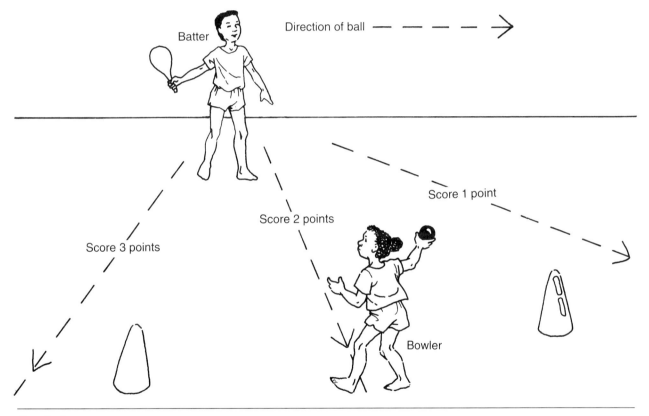

Batter

Direction of ball — — — — →

Score 1 point

Score 2 points

Score 3 points

Bowler

Conclusion:
Play as above, but this time competitively.

Unit 6, lesson 5

Theme: Striking/fielding; rounders

Purpose: PoS a, b

Activity bank: Activity 58: 4 v 2 rounders

Resources: Small balls, markers/cones, bats

Introduction:
Work in pairs, with one ball per pupil.
Each player places two markers, one to their right and one to their left.

Each player rolls their ball, aiming to hit either of their opponent's markers. The opponent tries to prevent this. Play co-operatively, then lead on to playing competitively.

Development/Conclusion:
Play '4 v 2 rounders' (see Activity 58).

Encourage pupils to think about their positions when they are off the bases.

Unit 6, lesson 6

Theme: Striking/fielding; rounders

Purpose: PoS a, b, c

Activity bank: Activity 58: 4 v 2 rounders, Activity 59: Backstop activities

Resources: Bats, balls, cones

Introduction:
Work in groups of three, with one ball per group.
Stand in a triangle. How many passes can the group make in 30 seconds?

Repeat a number of times aiming to beat the record.

Development:
Work in groups of three: bowler, backstop and batter.
The bowler aims to play the ball to the backstop. The batter stands in but does not hit the ball.
The backstop aims to take the ball before the bounce.
Progress to the batter taking the hit (co-operatively).
The backstop aims to catch the ball before it lands and returns it to the bowler, who moves to first base.
The batter aims to run to first base before the bowler stumps it.
Repeat a number of times, then change roles.

Conclusion:
Work in groups of six. Play '4 v 2 rounders' (see Activity 58).

This time the batter can only hit within a marked sector (see diagram).

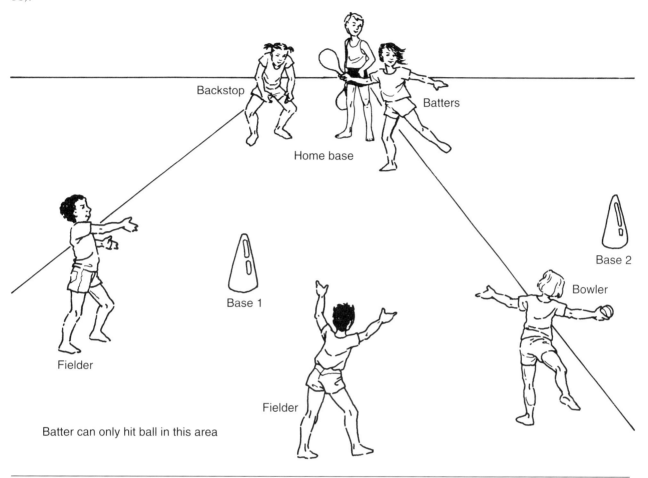

Backstop

Batters

Home base

Base 1

Base 2

Bowler

Fielder

Fielder

Batter can only hit ball in this area

Unit 6, lesson 7 ▷

Theme: Striking/fielding; rounders

Purpose: PoS a, b, c

Activity bank: Activity 60: Mini rounders

Resources: Bats, balls, cones/bases

Introduction:
Play 'Mini rounders' (see Activity 60).

Development/Conclusion:
Work in groups of nine: three batters v six fielders (i.e. bowler, backstop and four fielders).
There are three bases (see the diagram on the next page). The batters must run even if they miss the ball. They can stop on any base.
The fielders can stump the batters out or catch them out.

Encourage the four out-fielders to consider their positioning:
which position is essential?
when a fielder throws a ball, can the other fielders work together to 'cover' the ball?
A point is scored if a batter makes it round all the bases in one go.

Backstop   Batters

Home base

Base 3

Bowler

Base 1

Fielder 4

Base 2

Fielder 1

Fielder 2

Fielder 3

Unit 6, lesson 8 ▷

Theme: Striking/fielding; rounders

Purpose: PoS a, b, c

Activity bank: Activity 25: Washing baskets, Activity 61: Danish rounders

Resources: Washing baskets, medium balls, bats, small balls, cones/bases

Introduction:
Play 'Washing baskets' (Activity 25) with medium balls.

Development/Conclusion:
Work in groups of nine: 6 v 3 (as in Lesson 7).
Play as in Lesson 7, but this time the aim is for the ball to be sent round the bases in sequence and to get to the third base before the batter.

ATHLETICS

ABOUT ATHLETICS ▶

Athletic activities at Key Stage 2 provide a range of athletic challenges for children in the form of running, jumping and throwing. Such activities extend the learning that occurred in Key Stage 1, and also overlap in part with activities covered in other areas, such as games and gymnastics. The challenges in athletic activities are, however, different in focus and involve the principles of *citius, altius, fortius* (faster, higher, further). Key Stage 2 athletic activities will be presented in such a way as to provide a safe and stimulating learning environment for the children to be 'individually challenged' through the media of running, jumping and throwing.

Individual motor development, through developing co-ordination and skill at this age and stage, is essential for future participation. However, children will learn to succeed at their own level, and individual development should be given at least as much encouragement as competition between children. Extending children to perform at a more advanced level should be left to extra-curricular activity, or to local athletic clubs, where specialised facilities, equipment and coaching can be utilised.

Children should be encouraged to record some of their achievements, as some of these will be suitable for work in maths and science, providing valuable cross-curricular links. Such measurements as distance jumped, time taken for a certain run and distance thrown will be particularly useful 'live data'. Athletic activities are also a useful place to consider the effects of exercise on the body. The general requirements of the National Curriculum ask children to know about safe and effective exercise, and to understand the long and short term effects of exercise on the body. These issues are also related to the 'processes of life' section of the science curriculum.

Athletics at this level should normally take place outside on dry, non-slip surfaces. Fields or playgrounds may also be marked out to assist in the organisation of activities. Very little specialised throwing or jumping equipment is required for teaching the material included in this section. A range of balls, quoits, bean bags, canes with corks on the end (to avoid splitting), skittles, tape measures, stopwatches, pieces of elastic etc. will be adequate. Painted targets on playground walls, or floor areas marked out for specialist activities, may also help in the organisation of activities. Specialised equipment requires specific safety procedures which are not covered in this section as it is assumed that most schools will not have access to such equipment.

During jumping lessons, landing areas should be able to absorb impact. Some of the lessons in the units of work which follow concentrate on jumping for the whole lesson. It is important that children have adequate time to rest between jumps. If the landing areas are hard, then the amount of jumping during lesson time should be limited, and it may be worthwhile combining some of the jumping activities with others such as throwing, in the same lesson. Throwing activities should also be carefully organised, and care should be taken that implements are thrown into a space not occupied by other groups.

The units of work aim to develop challenging and enjoyable whole body activities, that require progressive improvement in co-ordination and motor control at this important stage of motor development. Such challenges, if delivered in a structured and progressive manner, will enable the teacher to help children attain the end of key stage National Curriculum requirements.

NATIONAL CURRICULUM REQUIREMENTS AT KEY STAGE 2 ▶

The programmes of study (general) which apply to athletics are as follows:

1. To promote physical activity and healthy lifestyles, pupils should be taught:
   a to be physically active;
   c to engage in activities that develop cardiovascular health, flexibility, muscular strength and endurance;
   d the increasing need for personal hygiene in relation to vigorous physical activity.

2. To develop positive attitudes, pupils should be taught:

a to observe the conventions of fair play, honest competition and good sporting behaviour as individual participants, team members and spectators;

b how to cope with success and limitations in performance;

c to try hard to consolidate their performances;

d to be mindful of others and the environment.

3. To ensure safe practice, pupils should be taught:

a to respond readily to instructions;

b to recognise and follow relevant rules, laws, codes, etiquette and safety procedures for different activities or events, in practice and during competition;

d how to lift, carry, place and use equipment safely;

e to warm up for and recover from exercise.

4. Athletic activities

Pupils should be taught:

a to develop and refine basic techniques in running, *eg over short distances, over longer distances, in relays*, throwing, *eg for accuracy/distance*, and jumping, *eg for height/distance*, using a variety of equipment;

b to measure, compare and improve their own performance.

TEACHING ATHLETICS AT KEY STAGE 2 ▶

The process of teaching through the three main athletic activity themes of running, jumping and throwing will enable the end of key stage statements to be met. The programme of study which is specific to athletic aactivity provides the teacher with some detail of the material that will be presented in the lesson, and through the units of work. The programmes of study in general provide the basis of teaching method which reflect broader aims for the delivery of physical education. All three components provide clear but flexible guidelines for the teaching of athletic activities at key stage two.

The units of work at Key Stage 2 provide a range of running, jumping and throwing experiences that are progressive in form and nature. Most of the early lessons in each key stage focus on one of these activities, aiming to develop motor co-ordination through a series of challenging or reinforcing activities. These challenges become progressively more advanced through the unit of work, with both units culminating in a number of multi-activity lessons where running, jumping and throwing activities previously taught in the unit are combined, with pupils allowed greater independence in their choice of activity. The key here is to guide the children into progressively more difficult but attainable challenges, both against themselves and others. Children will perhaps in this area recognise strengths and weaknesses in each other, and it is important that these are rationalised by the teacher. A number of the activities such as long-jumping your armspan or height, or handicapping races, help children recognise individual differences and how equality of success in athletic activities and competitions may be achieved.

In relation to the three strands of achievement in the National Curriculum, namely planning, performing and evaluating, it should be made clear that the national curriculum document recommends greater emphasis on the performing strand in Key Stages 1 to 3. Much of the emphasis in these units of work is therefore concentrated on the performance strand. However, there are many opportunities for pupil planning and evaluating in both units of work. The following model lessons from each unit of work have been written to help your understanding and application of the brief lesson outlines in the units of work.

Model lesson: unit 1, lesson 4 ▷

Theme: Hurdling

Purpose: PoS a, b

Activity bank: Activities 13: Hurdling, Activity 14a: Shuttle relay

Resources: One set of marker cones, 12 canes, 24 cones/wire skittles, 6–12 skipping ropes, bean bags

Activity	Organisation	Teaching points
Introduction: Run at a medium pace around the work area.	Ensure pupils are well spaced out.	
Stop on command.		Is your heart beating faster. Are you breathing more quickly and heavily? Do you feel warmer.
Stretch the legs carefully.	Teacher demonstrates.	Remember to hold the stretch for a count of 6. We are stretching the muscles we are going to use shortly for hurdling.
Start running again. Jump on the sound of a clap of the hands, then continue to run. Jump from the left foot to the right, and then try jumping from the right foot to the left.	Make sure you jump into a space. Be careful not to jump at or into other people.	
		Which foot do you like taking off from best?
		Stick to that one.
Development: Run around for 60 seconds, jumping over the marker cones. Take off from your preferred foot.	Use marker cones set out at random in the work area. Emphasise safety.	Imagine you are jumping over a wide river, so you have to reach out with your front foot to land on the other side.
Pupils set out hurdling lanes (see diagram on p. 146).	Get the pupils to set out four to six lanes, using marker cones, with low and medium level barriers (about 3 metres apart), i.e. skipping ropes and skittles with canes on top. Next to each lane with barriers should be a lane without any barriers.	Explain the use of the hurdling lanes, and that once you have reached the end of the lane, you should return to the starting line down the lane to your right which has no obstacles in it.
Pupils run down the lanes aiming to clear the obstacles. Break to think about the footwork pattern, then continue. Once the pupils have gained confidence over skippng ropes, they can progress to skittles with canes across the top.	Break the class into groups. Set them off in waves down the lanes. Use only the low level barriers (skipping ropes) at first.	Look for a pupil with 'good rhythm' between hurdles. Stop the class, bring them in close and ask them to close their eyes and listen to this pupil's footwork pattern (1–2–3). Emphasise keeping the head down and the front leg up.
Conclusion: Using a bean bag as a change-over baton between runners, set up a relay between groups so that they hurdle on the way out, and return down the lane to their right that has no barriers in it.	Decide whether to have the same barriers in all lanes, with mixed ability groups, or whether to split the groups according to ability, with the more-able pupils hurdling over the medium barriers and the less-able over lower barriers.	Use one group to demonstrate the relay. Point out that you must start behind the line, run out over the obstacles, turn right at the end and come back down the empty lane. Emphasise *handing* (not throwing) the bean bag to your team mate, who must be behind the starting line. Runners sit down when they have finished.
Repeat the relay and give the final positions of the teams.	Award points, e.g. 100 for first, 70 for second and so on.	Emphasise fair play and disqualify those who cheat. Praise those who worked hard.
Put away the equipment.	Give each group a different task of putting equipment away.	

ATHLETICS ACTIVITY BANK ▶

Activity 1: Crows and cranes

In pairs, start back to back in the middle of the court.

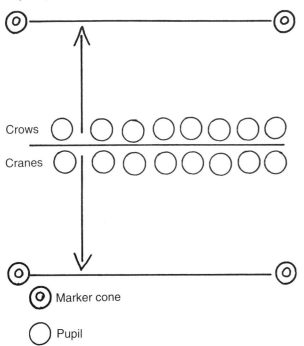

Crows

Cranes

◎ Marker cone

◯ Pupil

One line are 'cranes' the other are 'crows'. On the command 'Crows', the crows try to sprint to the line they are facing before the cranes can turn and catch them. Repeat, varying the 'Crows' or 'Cranes' command.

Activity 2: Shuttle runs

Working individually, the class all run together. Each pupil runs to a line designated by the teacher. They put their foot over the line, bending the leg, turning the head and pushing hard to return to where they came from. The pupils count how many shuttle runs they can do in 10 seconds (to the line and back is counted as two runs). Repeat this three times. Each pupil attempts to beat their own score.

Activity 3: Tail tag

Each pupil has a band placed down the back of their shorts. One pupil is designated the 'catcher' and they have to see how many 'tails' they can take out of the shorts of the other pupils. You must limit the chase to a suitably sized grid for the age of the children. When a pupil has their 'tail' taken, they join in with the chaser to catch as many tails as possible.

A variation on this activity is 'skipping tail tag'. Here the chaser and the chased have to skip (without a rope) instead of running. The teacher needs to ensure that all pupils do skip and not run!

Activity 4: Shadow chase

This activity is performed in pairs. One pupil is at the front with the partner behind. The leader aims to lose the follower; the follower aims to keep up. On the command 'Stop', the follower aims to be close enough to touch the leader. Each pupil should have two or three attempts in each role.

Activity 5: Chain tag

One pupil is the 'catcher'. They have to catch another member of the group within the designated playing area. When someone is caught, they join hands with the catcher and the two pupils move around together, attempting to catch other pupils. This is repeated until the line becomes four pupils long. At this point, the pupils divide into two groups of two and the game continues.

Activity 6: Stick-in-the-mud

6a Stick-in-the-mud
One or two pupils are chosen to be the 'catchers' and have to touch other members of the group within the designated playing area. When pupils have been touched, they adopt a stationary position, with legs apart. The remainder of the group, as well as trying to avoid the catchers, attempt to release the stationary players by crawling through their legs. Safety – ensure pupils always crawl from the back to the front.

6b Fast walking stick-in-the-mud
As above; however, both the catchers and the others are not allowed to run, but have to move around the playing area using a fast walk.

6c Sprint start stick-in-the-mud
In this version, when the runners are touched by a catcher, they have to adopt a sprint start position, i.e. crouched position.

Activity 7: Single file follow-my-leader

The leader, who is at the front, finds many different ways of travelling, e.g. running with knees high, skipping, galloping, side stepping. Each follower copies the leader. On command, the first follower runs to the front and then becomes the leader. The original leader goes to the back of the line. Continue until each pupil has had a chance to be the leader. (The class can be divided up into groups of 4 or 5.)

Activity 8: Timed runs

Pupils run over predetermined distances and are given their time in seconds. This may be done individually or in groups.

Activity 9: Traffic lights game

Pupils react to the following commands:
red – stop,
amber – walk/jog slowly,
green – sprint.

Activity 10: Magic islands

Use chalked areas, coned area, hoops or mats as islands. The pupils are required to travel from island to island using a predetermined method of locomotion, e.g. two-footed jumps, hopping.

Activity 11: Cops and robbers

The robbers line up on two opposite sides of the playing area, and the cops line up on the other two sides, as shown. Each cop has a soft foam ball. The robbers try to run to the opposite side without being hit by the balls thrown by the cops.

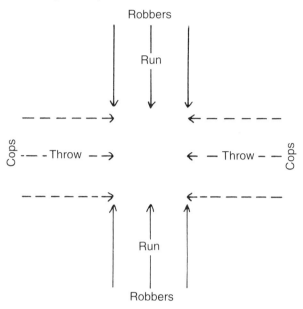

Activity 12: Dodgeball

Four to five pupils start with medium size foam balls in the centre of the work area. The rest of the group spread themselves around the space. On the command 'Go', the pupils with the balls throw them and try to hit the other pupils below the waist. Once hit below the waist, the pupil joins the team with the foam balls and assists in catching those who have not been hit. The game is over when all pupils have been caught.

Activity 13: Hurdling

Set up four to six lanes of hurdles using different barriers. Skipping ropes and skittles with canes balanced on top are suitable; the former is suitable for novice hurdlers, the latter as a progression. Place the barriers close together in the first lane; in the other lanes extend the distance between the barriers gradually.

Activity 14: Relays

14a Shuttle relay

A shuttle relay is performed in teams of three to five pupils. Each pupil takes it in turn to run out to the designated line and return to the rest of the team. They may carry an object, e.g. a bean bag or baton, to hand over to the next pupil or they may touch the next pupil to allow them to set off.

14b Pick-up-put-down shuttle relay

As above, but instead of running straight to the line and returning to the remainder of the team, each member has to collect items, e.g. bean bags, quoits, from a central position in front of the team line. They then have to place each of the items in a designated position before returning to the team.

One player may be asked to place the items (one at a time) on the way out and then collect them on the way back, or alternatively the first pupil may place them down on the way out, whilst the second member of the team may be asked to collect them on their way back.

14c Hurdle shuttle relay

For hurdling activities, the pupil hurdles on the way out to the line and returns back down the (empty) lane on their right-hand side. It is important for safety reasons that the pupils see a demonstration of this before starting the activity.

14d Square relay

The members of each team start one behind the other, as in the above shuttle relays, but this time they run around a square shape. The pupils waiting should stand inside the square, next to the start marker. Each pupil completes one circuit of the square. (Ensure that the square is large enough for the pupils to be able to run around it smoothly.)

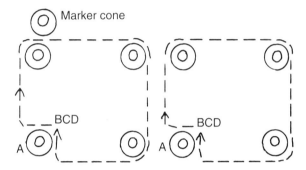

Activity 15: Basic jumps

1) Start the jump on two feet and land on two feet (rabbit)
2) Start the jump on two feet and land on one foot (kangaroo)
3) Start the jump on one foot and land on two feet (hare)
4) Start the jump on one foot and land on the same foot, i.e. a hop (squirrel)
5) Start the jump on one foot and land on the other, i.e. a step (wallaby).

Activity 16: More jumps

16a Standing two footed jump

Pupils start behind a designated line. They begin stationary with two feet shoulder width apart behind the line and swing the arms to gain momentum for a two-footed jump.

16b Consecutive two footed jumps

As above, but continue with the two-footed jumps, using the arms for momentum. Instruct the pupils how many jumps they are to perform consecutively.

16c Three spring jumps

As in 16b, but the pupils are informed that they will perform three standing two footed jumps consecutively. The final measurement is where the pupil's heels land on the third jump.

16d Standing long jumps

As in 16a, but beginning stationary behind the designated line on one foot.

Activity 17: Five stride run-up for long jump

The long jump is performed taking off from one foot and landing on two feet. The pupil is allowed a five stride run-up before taking off from a chosen foot. If the pupil chooses to take off for the jump on their right foot, they must begin the five stride run-up also on their right foot.

Activity 18: Combination jumps

Using the five basic jumps as described in Activity 15, pupils combine these jumps in any sequence they choose. To begin with, allow them a sequence of three jumps. As they progress, they can combine more jumps. For example, hop (one foot to same foot), jump (one foot to two feet), jump (two feet to two feet).

Activity 19: Long jump in relation to height

Each pupil in turn lies flat on the floor with the feet behind a starting line. Each pupil then attempts to jump his/her own height, by jumping from behind the starting line past his/her own marker.

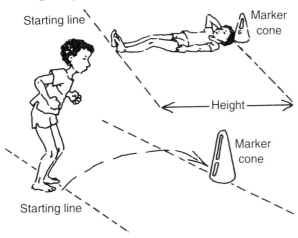

Activity 20: Standing triple jump

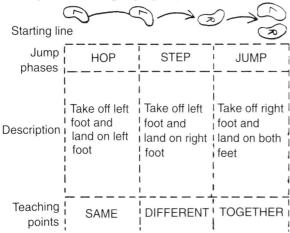

Jump phases	HOP	STEP	JUMP
Description	Take off left foot and land on left foot	Take off left foot and land on right foot	Take off right foot and land on both feet
Teaching points	SAME	DIFFERENT	TOGETHER

Activity 21: Jumping high into hoops

Work in small groups of two or three. Pupils start behind a line and run towards a hoop placed 4–5 metres away. Just before the hoop, the pupil jumps up high, landing in the hoop. A progression from this is for the pupil to jump before the hoop, turning in the air and landing facing the way they came from.

It is important that the arms swing high for momentum. On landing in the hoop, the knees should bend to take the impact. A key safety point is that pupils should take off for the jump before the hoop to avoid slipping on it.

A progression of this is to place a small barrier (0.5 metres high) in front of the hoop. The pupil has to clear the small barrier before landing in the hoop. Raise the height of the barrier to challenge the more able pupils. They could also try turning in the air to land facing the opposite direction.

Activity 22: Standing high jump

Attempt the standing high jump jumping from one foot to the same foot, then one foot to the other foot, then two feet to two feet.

Activity 23: Push throw

23a Two handed push throw

Use a soccer ball or netball. Hold the ball with two hands against the chest with the fingers facing the body. The feet should be behind the designated line. The feet should start parallel but move apart as the ball is 'pushed' forwards. One foot comes forwards, but without stepping over the line.

23b One handed push throw

Again, use a soccer ball or netball. The starting position is with the ball in the favoured hand and positioned under the chin. The opposite foot is placed forwards behind the designated line. The weight is placed over the back foot and, without bringing the ball out from the neck, the ball is pushed forwards.

Activity 24: One handed overarm throw

The pupil starts the throw by standing sideways on with the weight on the back foot. The throwing arm should be bent behind the head. The throw is made by turning the shoulders and straightening the arm as it is brought forward. The non-throwing arm should be pointed in the direction of the throw as well as aiding balance. The elbow of the throwing arm leads as the arm is brought forwards. When the standing overarm throw has been mastered, progress on to a three stride run-up before sending the ball. If the pupil is right handed, then the run-up should begin on the left foot, i.e. left, right, left, throw.

Activity 25: Two handed overhead throw

Use a large soccer or netball for this activity. Use both hands to send the ball. This activity can be carried out from the following positions: lying, sitting (seated soccer ball throw), kneeling, standing and moving. In each case, the pupil must be behind the designated throwing line before they begin the throw. This activity is more suitable for partner work as the partner can field the ball as well as marking the distance that it has been sent.

Activity 26: Side arm sling

The implement is thrown like a discus with a slinging action. The arm is approximately at shoulder height and slightly bent. The hand moves behind the line of the shoulders and then moves forward releasing the implement in a straight line forwards, usually in the direction in which the opposite shoulder is pointing.

142

Activity 27: Sprint start

The following commands should be used when performing sprint starts:

'On your marks'.

The pupil should adopt the crouched position shown.

Pupils place their hands behind the designated line, while their knees are placed approximately 0.7 metres behind the line, slightly apart, with the back foot turned under in order to gain some grip. The pupil will have to decide which foot they prefer to place forwards. The foot placed forwards is flat on the ground. The hands make a bridge position and are placed shoulder width apart. The pupil's body remains still after settling into this position.

'Set'

When you give this command the pupil raises their hips, ensuring that the back leg is positioned at an angle of 120 degrees. The eyes should be focused on a point on the floor, to ensure the head is in line. The hands should remain on the ground.

'Go'

On this command, the pupil pushes off the back leg, driving their arms as they do so. They attempt to get into their running as quickly as possible.

Activity 28: Reaction starts

These are designed to encourage a good reaction to the commands 'On your marks', 'Set', 'Go'. The positions that the pupils are asked to start the race in are not linked to the sprint start that was described in Activity 27. This activity is designed for fun!

The group are given different 'starting positions' behind a designated line. For example, sit cross-legged with back to direction of running, hands on head, eyes shut, or lie on tummy, facing the direction of running, with the hands behind the head and the legs crossed.

Give the commands 'On your marks', 'Set', 'Go'. On the word 'Go', or a whistle command, the group get up from the set starting position as quickly as possible, racing to get to the 'finish line' positioned approximately 20 metres away.

Repeat this a number of times, making up different unusual starting positions.

Activity 29: Running whilst kicking bottom

This should be carried out over 15–20 metres. The aim is not for forward momentum, rather for rapid movement almost on the spot. The legs move quickly whilst the heels kick the bottom. The arms should also move rapidly in time with the legs.

Activity 30: Running with high knees

This should be carried out over 15–20 metres. Again, the aim is not for forward momentum, rather for rapid movement almost on the spot. The legs move quickly whilst the knees are driven up towards the chest as quickly as possible. The arms should also move rapidly in time with the legs.

Activity 31: Handicapped 30 metres race

The idea is for the slower pupils to begin ahead of the quicker pupils.

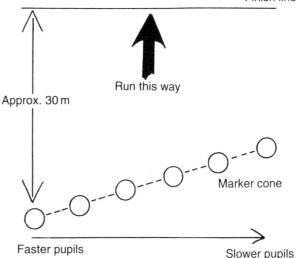

Each pupil works with a partner who has a marker cone and stands where he expects his/her partner to get to in 3 seconds (the time limit could be up to 10 seconds). The teacher shouts go and starts the clock.

Partner A starts behind a line and sprints as far as he can until the teacher shouts stop after 3 seconds. Partner B puts down the marker cone at the spot that A reached at the stop command. Partner A goes back to the line and has two more attempts to try and beat his mark, which is adjusted accordingly.

Partners swap over and the activity is repeated.

At the end of this stage of the lesson, each pupil should go and stand by his/her marker. The markers will be different distances from the start line. The start line now becomes the finish line for the race. The race is now perfectly handicapped if all pupils start from their marker.

Activity 32: Relay change-over

The correct way of handing over a relay baton is shown below.

LESSON PLANS FOR YEARS 3 AND 4

Unit 1, lesson 1

Theme: Running fast/accelerating

Purpose: PoS a, b

Activity bank: Activity 1: Crows and cranes, Activity 2: Shuttle runs

Resources: Stopclocks/watches; one set of marker cones

Introduction:
Run slowly around the work area, changing direction and changing pathway.

Play a warm-up game 'Crows and cranes' (see Activity 1).

Development:
On the teacher's command, try 10 metre shuttle runs as fast as you can (see Activity 2).
How many can you do in 10 seconds?
Teacher gives the children key points about 'turning quickly', e.g. 'Run to the line, put your foot over the line, bend your leg, turn your head, and push hard to return to where you came from'.

Try again. Can you do more than your first score in 10 seconds?
How many do you think you can do in 20 seconds?
All try.
Did you do more or less than you thought you could? Why?
Now repeat the above, starting from a lying position.

Conclusion:
Find a partner who had the same (or similar) score as you. Challenge them to two races over the number of shuttles that you scored in 20 seconds.

Use 'Ready, steady, go!' to start the race. Take it in turns to start each of the races.

Unit 1, lesson 2

Theme: Middle distance type running

Purpose: PoS a, b

Activity bank: Activity 2: Shuttle runs, Activity 3: Tail tag

Resources: One set of marker cones, stopclocks/ watches

Introduction:
Play 'Tail tag' (see Activity 3).

Development:
In a group of four, run five 30 metre shuttles (see Activity 2). All the group must stay together when running.
Compare this running with the running you did in the last lesson. Why is it slower or faster?

Can you run ten 30 metre shuttles without stopping (all the group)? Try it. This is not a race!!
Are you breathing faster now? Do you feel warm? (Explain the principle of warming up.)
How many 30 metre shuttles can your team run without stopping? Award 100 points for each shuttle run.

Conclusion:
Which group can complete fifteen 30 metre shuttle runs the quickest?

The winner receives 500 points.
Total up the points each group has earned throughout the lesson. The group with most points wins.

Unit 1, lesson 3

Theme: Longer distance running

Purpose: PoS a, b

Activity bank: Activity 8: Timed runs

Resources: One set of marker cones, stopclocks/watches

Introduction:
Running to warm-up.
The whole class run a set distance (approx. 200 metres), staying together and not racing. The teacher times the run. The pupils should run at a slow to moderate pace. How do you feel after the run? Look at the colour of each other's faces. What does it tell you?

Development:
Break into groups of four to six and try to run 200 metres as a group in the same time as the whole class time.

Repeat, but try and run 200 metres as a group in the fastest possible time.
Can your group run 400, 600, 800 metres without stopping? Try it.

Conclusion:
Two groups combine together and run a race (eight to twelve pupils).

Give points for individual places, e.g. 12 points for first place down to 1 point for last place.

Unit 1, lesson 4

Theme: Hurdling

Purpose: PoS a, b

Activity bank: Activity 13: Hurdling, Activity 14a: Shuttle relay

Resources: One set of marker cones, 12 canes, 24 cones/wire skittles, 6–12 skipping ropes, bean bags

Introduction:
Run around the work area. Jump on the sound of a clap of the hands, then keep running. Jump from the left foot to the right, and then try jumping from the right foot to the left. Which one do you like taking off from best? Stick to that one.

Development:
Using marker cones set out as shown in the work area, the pupils run around for 60 seconds, jumping over the marker cones (emphasise safety), taking off from their preferred foot.

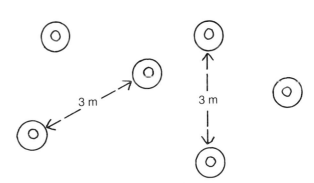

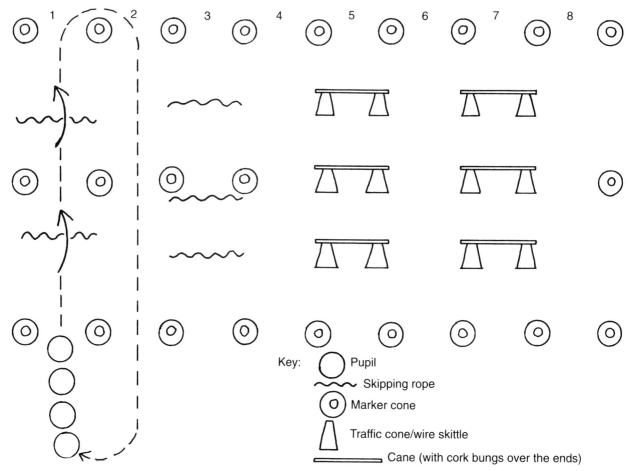

Key:

◯	Pupil
∿	Skipping rope
⊙	Marker cone
△	Traffic cone/wire skittle
▭	Cane (with cork bungs over the ends)

In a different space, get the pupils to set out four to six lanes as shown, using marker cones, with low and medium level barriers (about 3 metres apart) i.e. skipping ropes and skittles with canes on top. Next to each lane with barriers should be a lane without any barriers (as shown). The children should run down the lanes, hurdling each barrier as they come to it. They should progress from low to higher barriers.

Conclusion:
Using a bean bag as a change-over baton between runners, set up a relay between groups so that they hurdle on the way out, and return down the lane to their right that has no barriers in.

Repeat the relay and give the final positions of the teams.

Unit 1, lesson 5 ▷

Theme: Jumping for distance

Purpose: PoS a, b

Activity bank: Activity 13: Hurdling, Activity 15: Basic jumps

Resources: One set of marker cones and/or bean bags

Introduction:
Try and use a softer work area (e.g. dry grass area).
Revise the hurdling technique by getting pupils to run around in the work area at half speed hurdling on a clap of the hands. Continue this until the pupils feel that they are warm (get them to look at the colour of each other's faces and ask 'Can you feel your heart beating faster?'). Now make sure that the pupils do some simple stretching exercises.
Continue the hurdling exercise but after pupils have landed from the jump, they should immediately change direction.

Development:
Pupils slowly run around the work area and perform the following actions on the commands:
'Rabbits' – take off from two feet to land on two feet
'Kangaroos' – take off from two feet and land on one foot
'Hares' – take off from one foot and land on two feet
'Wallabies' – take off from one foot and land on the other
'Squirrels' – take off from one foot and land on the same foot.
Give each pupil a bean bag or marker cone. They put the marker down on the floor one arm span away from the start line. (Note: arm span is approximately equal to standing height.)
Which of techniques practised can they use to jump as far as their arm span, i.e. rabbit, kangaroo, hare, wallaby or squirrel? All jumps should take place from a stationary position on the start line.

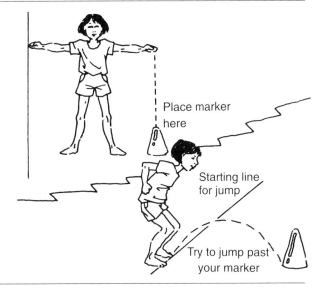

Place marker here

Starting line for jump

Try to jump past your marker

Conclusion:
Match the pupils in pairs as closely as possible for jumping distance. They then have a jumping competition using each of the five techniques.

Emphasise the rule that all jumps should start from behind the line.

Unit 1, lesson 6 ▷

Theme: Jumping for height

Purpose: PoS a, b

Activity bank: Activity 21: Jumping high into hoops,
Activity 22: Standing high jump

Resources: 12 hoops or chalk circles, canes, wire skittles

Introduction:
Run slowly around the grid. On a clap of hands, jump as high as you can.

Try taking off from your left foot, then try your right foot.

Development:
Lay out a row of 12 hoops (or chalk circles) as shown. The pupils get into groups of two or three and start behind a line.

The first pupil runs toward the hoop, jumps as high as possible and lands in the hoop and then returns to the line and the next pupil goes.

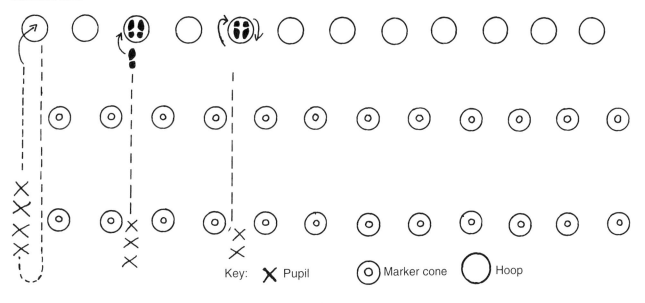

Key: ✗ Pupil   (o) Marker cone   ◯ Hoop

147

The first pupil runs toward the hoop, jumps as high as possible and lands in the hoop and then returns to the line and the next pupil goes.

Repeat until all pupils have had at least two attempts. Now ask the group to repeat, but this time they should try and turn in the air, so that on landing they face the direction from which they came.

Now place a small barrier 0.5 metres in front of the hoop. The pupils now repeat the previous two exercises over the barrier. Raise the barrier to provide an appropriate challenge for the pupils.

Conclusion:
Jog around the area slowly to remove the stiffness from your legs. Play 'Follow my leader' at a fast walking or jogging pace.

Unit 1, lesson 7 ▷

Theme: Combination jumping

Purpose: PoS a, b

Activity bank: Activity 3: Tail tag, Activity 16b: Consecutive two footed jumps, Activity 16d: Standing long jump, Activity 17: Five stride run-up for long jump, Activity 18: Combination jumps, Activity 22: Standing high jump

Resources: One set of markers and/or one set of bean bags

Introduction:
Play 'Skipping tail tag' (see Activity 3).

Development:
Work in groups of four or five on a jumping circuit, as follows:
standing two footed high jump
standing long jump
three consecutive standing long jumps
jump from one foot to one foot to two feet
five stride run-up for long jump
standing long jump with hands behind your back.

Conclusion:
Play 'Walking tag' to warm down.

Unit 1, lesson 8 ▷

Theme: Throwing (1)

Purpose: PoS a, b

Activity bank: Activity 4: Shadow chase, Activity 25: Two handed overhead throw

Resources: One large ball (football/foam ball) between two pupils, one set of bean bags, one set of marker cones

Introduction:
In pairs play 'Shadow chase' (see Activity 4). Try and follow your partner as closely as possible. Repeat three times, changing roles. Can you touch your partner after the command 'Stop'?

Development:
Work in pairs. Use a large ball and try to throw it two handed, overhead as far as you possibly can (organise the space appropriately).
Repeat this from sitting, kneeling (do not kneel on a cold hard surface), standing and moving positions. Have two attempts at each position. Your partner should mark the distance the ball travels with a bean bag/marker cone.

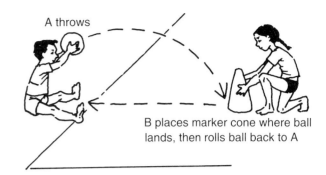

A throws

B places marker cone where ball lands, then rolls ball back to A

Conclusion:
Challenge your partner to a throwing contest from your favourite throwing position, e.g. lying or moving. See who can throw further from this position.

Unit 1, lesson 9

Theme: Throwing (2)

Purpose: PoS a, b

Activity bank: Activity 5: Chain tag, Activity 23a: Two handed push throw, Activity 24: One handed overarm throw

Resources: Tennis balls (one between two pupils), one set of marker cones

Introduction:
Play 'Chain tag' (see Activity 5).

Development:
In groups of three, form a triangle. Number yourselves 1, 2 and 3.
Using a tennis ball, throw the ball with a two handed push from the chest, as high as you can. Number 1 throws to 2 who throws to 3, who in turn throws back to 1. Make the triangle as big as you can.
Repeat the above by throwing the tennis ball as far forward as you can.
Repeat the above using a one handed throw (emphasise safety here).
Have four or five attempts at each technique.

Conclusion:
Using the one handed overarm throw, which one of your group can bounce the ball the highest off the floor? Who can make the ball rebound the furthest off a wall (use a marker cone to mark the rebound distance)?

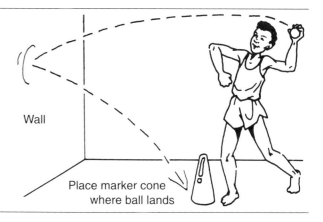

Wall

Place marker cone
where ball lands

Unit 1, lesson 10 ▷

Theme: Multi-activity (1)

Purpose: PoS a, b

Activity bank: Activity 6a: Stick-in-the-mud, Activity 27: Sprint start, Activity 31: Handicapped 30 metres race

Resources: One set of marker cones, large balls

Introduction:
Play fast walking 'Stick-in-the-mud' (see Activity 6a).

Development:
Split the class into four groups and rotate them around the following activities:
(a) Using a large ball (football) push the ball with two hands as far from your chest as you can. Mark the distance with a bean bag. How much can you improve your throw over three attempts?
(b) How many 30 metre shuttle runs can your group do without stopping?

(c) Who can standing long jump the furthest in your group?
Who can standing long jump the furthest with their hands behind their back?
(d) New activity: the teacher teaches the sprint start or crouch start (see Activity 27).

Conclusion:
Finish with a 30 metre handicap race (see Activity 31).

Finish line

Run this way

Approx. 30 m

Marker cone

Faster pupils

Slower pupils

Unit 1, lesson 11

Theme: Multi-activity (2)

Purpose: PoS a, b

Activity bank: Activity 7: Single file follow-my-leader, Activity 13: Hurdling, Activity 14a: Shuttle relay, Activity 24: One handed overarm throw

Resources: One set of marker cones, one set of skittles and canes, tennis balls, bean bags/batons, stopwatches/clocks

Introduction:
Play running/jumping games in small groups, e.g. copy the leader, run in single file, person at the back runs to the front on command. Run with knees high, skip, gallop, side-step.

Development:
Work in four groups, rotating around three activities.
(a) Low level hurdles: three lanes with a free lane to the right of each lane with hurdles in it. Each lane should be 30 metres long.
Work in pairs within each group. Partners count time in seconds or use a watch. How fast can you run 30 metres 'on the flat'?
How much slower is your 30 metre time travelling over three hurdles?
(b) In twos or threes, throw a tennis ball overarm to a group member so that he/she can catch it without it bouncing (emphasise safety).
(c) Work in twos or threes. Teacher will teach the relay change-over using bean bags or batons.

Conclusion:
Have a 30 metre relay race with a relay change-over using bean bags or batons.

Unit 1, lesson 12

Theme: Multi-choice activity

Purpose: PoS a, b

Activity bank: Activity 6c: Sprint start stick-in-the-mud, Activity 13: Hurdling, Activity 14a: Shuttle relay, Activity 16d: Standing long jump, Activity 22: Standing high jump, Activity 23a: Two handed push throw, Activity 24: One handed overarm throw, Activity 27: Sprint start

Resources: One set of marker cones, tennis balls, large balls, skittles, canes

Introduction:
Play 'Sprint start stick-in-the-mud' (see Activity 6c).

Development:
Pupils work in threes and choose to have three attempts at some of the following activities (all of which have been covered in this unit of work). Other members of their group observe and they try to help each other improve.
(a) Sprint start to 30 metre sprint
(b) Sprint start to 30 metre hurdles (three low level hurdles)
(c) Standing long jump
(d) Standing high jump
(e) How far can you run continuously as a three (30 metre shuttles)?
(f) How far can you push a football using two hands from the chest?
(g) How far can you throw a tennis ball?

Conclusion:
Have a relay, including sprint starts and baton/bean bag change-overs.

LESSON PLANS FOR YEARS 5 AND 6

Unit 2, lesson 1

Theme: Running fast

Purpose: PoS a, b

Activity bank: Activity 14a: Shuttle relay, Activity 28: Reaction starts, Activity 29: Running whilst kicking bottom, Activity 30: Running with high knees

Resources: Stopclocks/watches, one set of marker cones

Introduction:
Run – on the spot, to the right, to the left, in a figure of eight.

On command, change speed and pathway.

Development:
Run as fast as you can. Run without using the arms, using the right arm only, using the left arm only. Are your arms important?
Run as fast as you can. Run with the legs straight, with the knees high. Does lifting the knees make you faster?
Start behind a line and run fast for three seconds. Place a bean bag at the point you reached. Try to beat the marker next time (have three attempts).
Repeat the above with a partner. Try to beat their marker.
Try out some reaction starts (see Activity 28). On command, find the quickest way of getting to the finish (15–20 metres away).

Conclusion:
Have a shuttle relay.
Have a race using a reaction start (see Activity 28).
Run kicking the bottom with the heels for 15 metres.

Run with the knees up high for 15 metres.
Working in pairs, make up an activity that involves sprinting.

Unit 2, lesson 2

Theme: Running for distance

Purpose: PoS a, b

Activity bank: Activity 7: Single file follow-my-leader, Activity 8: Timed runs

Resources: Stopwatch/clock

Introduction:
Run around and on command, change the leg stride. Repeat.

In pairs play 'Follow-my-leader'. A changes leg stride, B keeps in stride. Change roles and repeat.

Development:
Play 'Single file follow-my-leader' (see Activity 7).
In a line of four or five, run around the 'track'. On command, the person at the back sprints to the front. When they are there, the next person at the back repeats and so on.

Work on timed runs (see Activity 8) over 120 or 150 metres. Set out markers 10 metres from the finish. Aim to finish in 25–30 seconds (depending on the ability/age of the pupils).

Conclusion:
The whole class spreads out around the 'track'. Run for 5–7 minutes. How many people can you pass within the given time?

Unit 2, lesson 3

Theme: Relay races

Purpose: PoS a, b

Activity bank: Activity 9: Traffic lights game, Activity 32: Relay change-over

Resources: Batons/bean bags, one set of marker cones

Introduction:
Jog around the work area. Play the 'Traffic lights game' (see Activity 9).

Development:
In pairs, practise change-overs using batons or bean bags. Try to change over when you are both running quite fast.
Introduce changing the baton over between two markers 10 metres apart. Partner A sprints from the start line for 20 metres to the first marker where partner B starts from. As A approaches the first marker, B starts sprinting. The baton should be changed over before the second marker is reached.
Practise at jogging speed initially, then build up speed in line with improvement.

Join two pairs together and practise baton change-overs as a group of four.

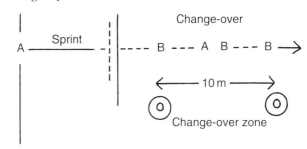

Conclusion:
Use three markers, one on the starting line, the second 10 metres away from the first and the third 20 metres away from the second. Work in groups of four. Pupil A runs from the starting line out around marker number 3, back to the starting line around marker number 1, and then changes the baton with runner B between markers 1 and 2.
Have a relay race (Race 1) in your groups of four. Then evaluate and work out the best order for your runners before having a second relay race (Race 2).

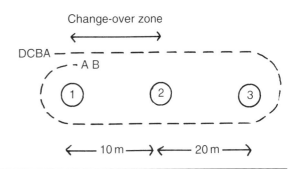

Unit 2, lesson 4

Theme: Hurdling

Purpose: PoS a, b

Activity bank: Activity 8: Timed runs, Activity 13: Hurdling, Activity 14a: Shuttle relay

Resources: Ropes, skittles, canes

Introduction:
Arrange the ropes randomly spaced out in the work area. Run around, leaping or jumping over ropes.

Do some stretching exercises as a preparation for hurdling.

Development:
Set out five lanes with 'hurdles' different distances apart in each lane (see Unit 1, lesson 4 on pp. 145 6). To start with, use lines chalked on the floor to represent the hurdles.

Hurdle each line. Try leading first with the left leg, then with the right. Which do you find easier?
Repeat the above replacing the chalk lines with skipping ropes and then with skittles with canes across the top

Conclusion:
Have a shuttle relay (see Activity 14a).
Work in twos, hurdling over ropes.
Still in twos, try timed runs over 120 metres (see Activity 8).

Work alone, hurdling over canes.
Make up an activity that involves running for 5 minutes.

Unit 2, lesson 5

Theme: Jumping for distance

Purpose: PoS a, b

Activity bank: Activity 10: Magic islands, Activity 14b: Pick-up put-down shuttle relay, Activity 15: Basic jumps, Activity 16d:

Standing long jumps, Activity 18: Combination jumps, Activity 20: Standing triple jump

Resources: Mats, bean bags, skittles, canes, hoops, markers

Introduction:
Play 'Magic islands' (see Activity 10). Spread the mats around the work area. Run around the edge of the area.

On command, jump from one mat to the other jumping from two feet to two feet.

Development:
Practise the five basic jumps given in Activity 15.
Work in pairs. Stand just behind a line, then lie down and get your partner to put a bean bag where your nose is. Attempt to jump from two feet to two feet to pass the mark. Move the mark forward by the length of one of your feet after every successful attempt. Partners watch the jumps and tell each other if they have been successful.

Using the five basic jumps practised earlier, make up a three jump combination, e.g. jump, hop, step.
Demonstrate it to your partner, who describes your combination jump and then copies it. Change roles and repeat.
Have a competition to see whose combination jump covers the most ground. Measure each jump using one person's foot paces.

Conclusion:
Practise standing long jumps (see Activity 16d). How do you measure the jump?
Have a pick-up-put-down shuttle relay (see Activity 14b).

Practise the standing triple jump (see Activity 20). Use hoops to land in.
Working individually, make up a combination jump.
Using hoops/markers/skittles/canes, make up a jumping activity.

Unit 2, lesson 6

Theme: Jumping for height

Purpose: PoS a, b

Activity bank: Activity 8: Timed runs, Activity 13: Hurdling, Activity 16d: Standing long jump, Activity 22: Standing high jump

Resources: Skittles and canes

Introduction:
Run around the space. On command, jump and stretch.

Development:
Revise the five basic jumps you worked on in lesson 5.
Use two skittles with a cane across the top. Begin at a low height, progress after each successful attempt by

raising the cane. Practise the standing high jump from:
two feet to two feet,
one foot to the same foot,
one foot to the other foot.

Conclusion:
Work in teams of four to six on the following activities:
team standing long jump,
hurdles competition,
make up a group shuttle relay,

timed runs over 120 or 150 metres,
standing combination jump – team choice,
two feet to two feet standing high jump.
Award points for the fastest/furthest/highest team in each case.

Unit 2, lesson 7

Theme: Push throw

Purpose: PoS a, b

Activity bank: Activity 22: Standing high jump,
Activity 23a: One handed push throw,
Activity 23b: Two handed push throw

Resources: Bean bags, medium foam balls, tape measure

Introduction:
Work in teams of three or four. Teams A and B stand at opposite sides of a grid, as shown.
Team A throw bean bags (or balls) in an attempt to send them over team B's line.

Team B throw their bean bags (or balls) in the opposite direction.

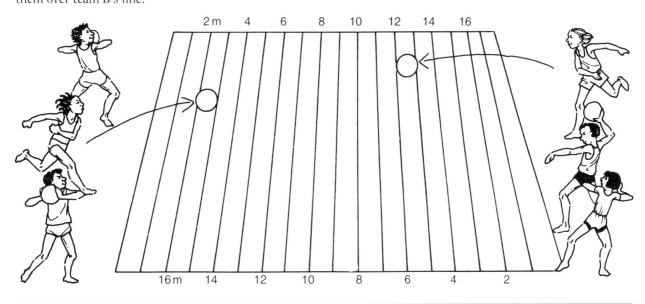

Development:
Practise using a two handed 'push' throw. Start from the following positions:
seated,
kneeling,
standing.
Start behind a specified line. Work in pairs. Pupil A throws and partner B fields the ball. Use markers set out at 2 metre intervals to help pupils judge distances.
Partner B indicates where the ball landed.
Practise the one handed push shot:
kneeling,
standing.
Work in pairs again. Watch your partner and evaluate their throw. Indicate and record the distance.

Conclusion:
Try the two handed push throw, kneeling.
Try the one handed push throw, standing.
Make up a team throwing game, throwing for distance.

Unit 2, lesson 8 ▷

Theme: Overarm throw

Purpose: PoS a, b

Activity bank: Activity 11: Cops and robbers, Activity 16c: Three spring jumps, Activity 23b: One handed push throw

Resources: Bean bags, large and small balls

Introduction:
Play 'Cops and robbers' (see Activity 11). Cops and robbers change roles after 3 minutes.

Development:
Use a large ball. Practise the two handed overhead throw:
lying,
seated,
kneeling,
standing.
Use a small/medium ball. Practise the one handed overarm throw:

kneeling (on two knees),
kneeling (on one knee),
standing (feet forwards),
standing (feet sideways).
Work in pairs. Partners throw from the same direction. Pupil A throws first, pupil B retrieves and judges how far A has thrown. Use markers set out at 2 metre intervals to help pupils judge distances.

Conclusion:
Work on the overarm throw, in pairs, each person fielding and measuring the other's throws.
Practise throwing a soccer ball with two hands from a seated position.
Make up a group relay.

Working in teams, perform three spring jumps (see Activity 16c). Add up the distances to give the team's score.
Make up a jump for height.
Work on the one handed push shot, in pairs, each fielding and measuring the other's throws.

Unit 2, lesson 9 ▷

Theme: Side arm sling

Purpose: PoS a, b

Activity bank: Activity 13: Hurdling, Activity 14d: Square relay, Activity 23b: One handed push throw, Activity 26: Side arm sling

Resources: Quoits, rugby balls, large balls, skittles, canes

Introduction:
Work individually, with one quoit per pupil. Roll the quoit, chase after and retrieve it.

Work in pairs, one behind the other. Pupil A rolls the quoit for B to retrieve, and vice versa.

Development:
Use a rugby ball (size 4). Introduce the side arm sling (see Activity 26). Practise it with:
feet forwards,
feet sideways.

Work in pairs. Each person fields and measures the other's throw. Use markers set out at 2 metre intervals. Repeat the above, using a quoit. Watch your partner's throw and offer guidance from the points given earlier by the teacher.

Conclusion:
Have a square relay race (see Activity 14d).
Make up an activity that uses the overarm throw.
Make up a combination jump for distance.

Have hurdles races in pairs over skittles with canes on top. Practise the side arm sling using a quoit or a rugby ball. In teams, throw for distance using a one handed push shot. Add up the distances to give the team's score.

Unit 2, lesson 10

Theme: Multi-activity (1)

Purpose: PoS a, b

Activity bank: Activity 6c: Sprint start stick-in-the-mud, Activity 13: Hurdling, Activity 26: Side arm sling, Activity 27: Sprint start

Resources: Canes, skittles, marker cones, quoits, stopwatch/clock

Introduction:
Play 'Sprint start stick-in-the-mud' (see Activity 6).

Development:
Work in six groups, two per activity and rotate around. The activities are as follows:
(a) 40 metre hurdles, with barriers at medium and low level. Use the sprint start to start. Give points for times, as appropriate to the ability of the class.

(b) Side arm sling quoits for distance. Use three markers for distance and award 1–3 points per throw.
(c) High jump over skittles and canes at three levels, low, medium and high (0.5 m, 0.8 m, 1.1 m). Award 1 point for low, 2 points for medium, 3 points for high. How many points can you get in 5 minutes?

Conclusion:
Finish with a team hurdle relay (two hurdles in each lane). Award points for team placings.
The team with most points throughout the lesson wins.

Unit 2, lesson 11

Theme: Multi-activity (2)

Purpose: PoS a, b

Activity bank: Activity 12: Dodgeball, Activity 14a: Shuttle relay, Activity 17: Five stride run-up for long jump

Resources: Tennis balls and marker cones

Introduction:
Play 'Dodgeball' (see Activity 12).

Development:
Six groups rotate around each of the following activities:
(a) How many laps of a 40 metre shuttle can you and a partner do without stopping (1 point for each lap)?

(b) Five stride run-up to long jump. Set markers at 0.8 m (10 points), 1.6 m (20 points) and 2.4 m (30 points).
(c) How far can you throw a tennis ball? Set markers at 10 m (10 points), 30 m (20 points) and 50 m (30 points).

Conclusion:
Have a team jumping competition. Award 50 points for the team with the longest standing long jump.

Total up the points gained by each team throughout the lesson.

Unit 2, lesson 12

Theme: Multi-activity (3)

Purpose: PoS a, b

Activity bank: All activities

Resources: As required for the activities chosen

Introduction/Development/Conclusion:
Have a team heptathlon competition. Teams enter six activities chosen by themselves the week before or by the teacher. Each child attempts three of the activities on offer. Pupils gain points to go toward their final team score.

SWIMMING

ABOUT SWIMMING

Swimming has an important place in the National Curriculum. It is an activity which, according to the Sports Council's figures, 'is the country's most popular participant sporting activity'. It can play a major part in the health and fitness of young people and, once mastered, it can open up opportunities such as speed swimming, synchronised swimming, water polo and participation in outdoor aquatic activities. However, it is considerably more significant than this – it can also be a life saver. For this reason alone it is essential that every opportunity is taken to teach people to swim and where better to start than in the Primary School.

Quite rightly therefore, swimming is one of the six programmes of study in the National Curriculum for Key Stages 1 and/or 2. Cross-curricular study plays an important part in the learning process at these stages of the educational process and swimming lends itself easily to this with teachers being able to pick up links to many other areas, such as science, maths and geography.

Learning to swim should be an exciting and stimulating experience and one which is fun and will be of lasting enjoyment. For this to happen, however, the teacher needs to plan carefully so that the learner can progress in an interesting, yet meaningful, way and at a pace that is mindful of the individual's confidence, level of ability and limitations. So often people take a dislike to swimming because of an early disappointing and sometimes frightening experience.

NATIONAL CURRICULUM REQUIREMENTS

The programme of study (activity specific) for this area of PE is as follows:

1. To promote physical activity and healthy lifestyles, pupils should be taught:
   a to be physically active;
   c to engage in activities that develop cardiovascular health, flexibility, muscular strength and endurance;
   d the increasing need for personal hygiene in relation to vigorous physical activity.
2. To develop positive attitudes, pupils should be taught:
   b how to cope with success and limitations in performance;
   c to try hard to consolidate their performances;
   d to be mindful of others and the environment.
3. To ensure safe practice, pupils should be taught:
   a to respond readily to instructions;
   b to recognise and follow relevant rules, laws,

codes, etiquette and safety procedures for different activities or events, in practice and during competition;
   e to warm up for and recover from exercise.

6. **Swimming**
   If aspects of the swimming programme have been taught during Key Stage 1, pupils should be taught the Key Stage 2 swimming programme starting at the appropriate point.
   a to swim unaided, competently and safely, for at least 25 metres;
   b to develop confidence in water, and how to rest, float and adopt support positions;
   c a variety of means of propulsion using either arms or legs or both, and how to develop effective and efficient swimming strokes on the front and the back;
   d the principles and skills of water safety and survival.

TEACHING SWIMMING

To help them in their planning, teachers should build up a 'bank' of different practices and activities that will suit all levels and, if possible, all eventualities. By having a wide choice of examples they are more likely to sustain interest and set meaningful tasks. The practices therefore need to be appropriate to the level of ability being taught and where possible lead to further progression. Pushing and gliding activities, for example, are skills in themselves; they reinforce the importance of body shape, yet they also lead to later practices for diving.

No matter what stage of the learning process pupils are at, teachers should never underestimate the importance of sound stroke technique, or more particularly how to 'use' the water. The more efficient an action, the less tiring the activity, the more simple it is to do and the more the pupil is likely to enjoy participating. Besides, if an individual finds it difficult to travel through the water he or she will be more inhibited in terms of other aquatic activity.

The ability to swim efficiently can be enhanced through an individual's understanding of the fundamentals of movement in water, such as flotation, resistance to propulsion and streamlining. With primary school children, however, the subject matter need not be laboured and can be covered easily alongside the basic teaching material. Newton's Third Law of Motion, for example, can be translated simply into instructions such as 'Push back to send yourself forwards', 'Press upwards to send yourself down', or, better still, demonstrated by asking the class to experiment with activities which illustrate this for them.

In the preparation of lessons, teachers should carefully consider their choice of equipment. There are so many different items on the market these days that people can be forgiven for feeling confused as to which are most suitable. To help, thought must be given to the *reason* for use – safety, support/buoyancy, to stimulate interest, as a challenge, as part of a progression, or simply to disguise the difficulty of a task. Buoyancy aids, for example, are essential to help the non-swimmer but care must be taken to obtain the right balance between the amount of support and the desired freedom of movement.

Children need to be taught how to use equipment and to understand why certain pieces are being used and used in that particular way. Teachers should also ensure that sufficient time is given for the class to feel the value of the aid and to determine whether or not it is appropriate. Too often, equipment is removed because on the first attempt the pupil seems to struggle or be ill at ease.

All teachers understand the need for variety in lessons. Selection and use of equipment go some way to achieving this, but so can the use of imagery and stimuli. For example, in encouraging children to submerge, the task can be much more fun if linked to 'waterholes' or 'underwater caverns'. Sculling practices come to life if performed to music or the beat of a drum.

In preparing for lessons, teachers should ensure that there is a balance between the development of skill or technique, the introduction of new skills and the reinforcement of previous material. The format recommended by the National Curriculum in terms of introduction, development, contrasting activity and conclusion lends itself to this, but swimming material should be seen within an integrated framework rather than as a series of separate skills, bolted on to each other. For example, the ability to perform synchronised swimming figures may seem to be advanced, but the fundamentals of the activity are present in almost every stage of the learning curve, such as the effective use of the limbs (especially the hands), an awareness of body shape and an understanding of floating, propulsion and resistance and the control of breathing. In preparing each section of the lesson, therefore, teachers should be mindful of the components of a whole range of activities/skills and use these in a progressive way throughout the programmes of study, rather like a child who gradually learns through the use of building blocks.

In addition to the child's ability to perform a particular task, the National Curriculum requires the individual to be able to plan and evaluate. Whilst it is important to ensure that activity levels remain high within a swimming lesson, the subject lends itself to the development of these particular more theoretical skills.

In terms of planning, for example, children could be encouraged to assist in the preparation of their class swimming gala or to plan and prepare a short sequence of movement that can be developed with a partner. In evaluating, they could help each other with basic corrections or be able to explain why a certain stroke is slower or faster than another, for example. Working with a partner in each of the lessons is a system which enables the teacher to help the pupils to plan and evaluate the other's activity, whilst simple questions beginning with 'Why does ….; What if ….; Where should ….; How can …?' etc. help the teacher to stimulate the class into lively thinking. If this is followed up by 'Show me' or 'Show your partner', then this thought process is very quickly translated into action.

In using the lesson plans which follow it is very important to remember that they are meant as a *guide* only. It is impossible for any teacher to predict how quickly one child will or will not progress, let alone a whole class. It is highly probable therefore that some children could be on lesson 4 for instance, when some are still struggling with the level of material in lesson 2. It is assumed therefore that the teacher will quickly subdivide his or her class accordingly and select appropriate practices from the Activity Bank.

The following model lesson will provide guidance on general strategies for swimming lessons.

Model lesson

Level of ability: Improver

Theme: Backcrawl: The full stroke

Purpose: PoS: c

Activity bank: 14, 15, 16, 17, 18, 19, 20

Resources: Music, sinking objects, floats/discs

Activity	Organisation	Teaching points
Introduction: Mini aqua aerobics.	Work individually, spaced out, at the shallow end, with water no higher than waist level.	
Peel each foot off the floor alternately.		Both feet in contact with the floor the whole time; 'peel' from heel to toe. Hands supporting at the sides just under the water.
Develop into small running step on the spot, sideways, forwards, backwards etc.	Depending on space – teacher may need to direct direction of movement.	Keep the body upright. Feel the water pressure as you move.
Develop into jump, kick, jump, kick etc. Move forwards, back, to side etc.		Establish use of arms (and hands in kicks in particular) to aid balance. Feel the water pressure for the bigger movements.
Develop by bringing in use of the arms and *reach* with one, as you kick with a leg. Change. Now pupil decides which steps to use.		Keep trunk upright.
Development: a) Widths on front paddle, without floats *if possible*.	Work in pairs, A and B. A goes first. When A reaches the other side, B goes. If you need to, stop, rest briefly, then lean and push to continue.	Use big flat hands, with finger tips leading. Reach out. Push *back*. Chin on surface.
b) Kicking on back, arms at side. If pupils are not confident, use floats. Arms outstretched over thighs.	As above. Keep going until told to stop.	Body long and flat with head back and chin in as if lying on a pillow. Use of hands to support if not using float. Hips up to surface. **Stretch**.
c) Kicking with hands on thighs. Kick fast, kick slowly etc.	As above.	Kick from hip. Concentrate on flicking feet up to surface. What happens when you kick fast/slow?
d) Full stroke – pupils to try after demonstration from teacher.	As above.	Same body position as above – why? Continuous windmill action with arms.
e) Try one arm at a time, with the other holding a float in the hand across the chest.	As above. Do one width using the left arm, next using the right.	Enter little fingers first. Brush ears with arms. Keep hands big and flat. Push water towards feet – why? Finish pull with palm on thigh. Reach to ceiling on lift (recovery).
f) Full stroke – all try again, without floats if possible.	As above.	Emphasis on continuous action. Lie back, hips up, body lies flat and straight – why? Keep head still. Brush ears with arms. **Stretch**.
Contrasting Activity: a) Push and glide in a long thin shape at the surface of the water.	Pupils on either side of pool, pushing to centre. If space is limited, work in twos, pushing towards a space. (Could be developed into a meeting and parting theme.)	Start with one foot on the wall, one on the bottom of the pool. Lift the standing foot to join the other and *push* back. Arms covering ears, hands together, palm on top of the back of the other hand. *Stretch* whole body and count to 5.

Activity	Organisation	Teaching points
Contrasting Activity (Contd): b) Push and glide and open out into a star shape.	As above.	What happens when you open out?
c) Push from both feet and glide along surface. Long thin shape. See how far you can go.	As above. Partner to climb out (if time).	Partner to look at body shape and give feedback on position of arms, legs and head.
d) Push and glide underwater.	As above.	Breathe in. Slide down the wall with the feet, tip/roll on to front and *push*. Head between outstretched arms, squeeze ears and hands. **Stretch.**
e) Push and glide and crawl kick.	As above.	Bring in kick after you have been gliding for 5 seconds. Keep top half of body streamlined – why?
Conclusion: Pick up objects from the bottom of the pool with your hands. How many can you collect?	Scatter objects. Count how many there are. Pupils to place on side.	Breathe in before you submerge. Blow out as you come up. Keep eyes open.

SWIMMING ACTIVITY BANK

Activity 1: Getting in

1   2   3   4

Activity 2: Basic turning
Crouch down, with the chin on the water. Turn round using your hands. Push to the right, turn to the left. Try this again while sitting on a float.

Activity 3: Regaining standing from prone position
Lie down, sit up, stand up.

**Activity 4: Regaining standing from prone position –
use of floats**
Lie down, sit up, stand up.

Activity 5: Regaining standing from supine position
Lie down, sit up, stand up.

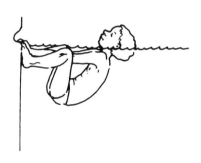

**Activity 6: Regaining standing from supine position –
use of floats**
Lie back, sit up, stand up.

Activity 7: Double support: front kick

Activity 8: Floating shapes

Activity 9: Crawl kick at rail

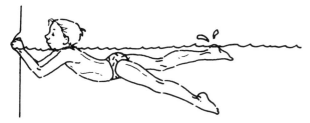

Activity 10: Double support, back kick

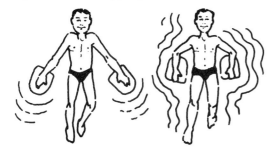

Activity 11: Basic jump

Step off. Enter feet first. Bend the knees on landing. Keep the head up and the eyes open.

Activity 12: How to hold the float

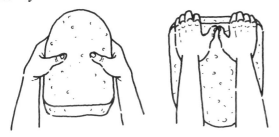

Activity 13: Kicking on back with float support

Activity 14: Front paddle

Keep the hands in front of the chest. Kick the legs up and down. Reach and pull with the hands, keeping them big and flat.

Activity 15: Back paddle

Keep the hands at the side of the hips, 'sculling' like a fish's fins. Legs kicking continuously.

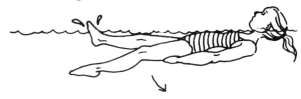

Activity 16: Backcrawl – one-arm practice

Keep moving with the arm straight. Pull the palm to the thigh.
Reach to the ceiling.
Brush the ear with the arm.

Activity 17: Push and glide (one foot)

Stand as shown, with one foot on the bottom and the other against the wall. Push off using the foot against the wall and glide away.

Activity 18: Push and glide (two feet)

This time use both feet against the wall. Push off and *stretch*. Squeeze the ears with the arms.

Activity 19: Sink, push and glide

Take a deep breath before submerging. Keep the upper body upright on the way down. Roll on to your front and push from both feet.

Activity 20: Angled push and glide

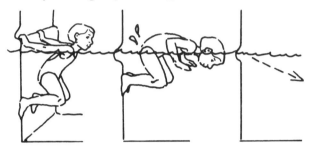

Activity 21: Over and under bridges

Activity 22: Basic sculling – use of hands

Keep the hands big, flat and firm. Move them inwards and outwards. The little finger is raised and leads on the outward movement and the thumb is raised and leads on the inward movement. Each hand should describe a flat figure of eight.

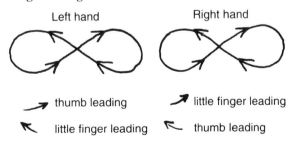

Activity 23: Basic support scull

Palms face the bottom of the pool.

Activity 24: Back layout scull

Hands near the hips. Palms face the bottom of the pool.

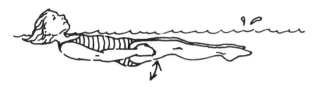

Activity 25: Extended front paddle

Reach forwards. Recover underwater.

Activity 26: Backcrawl arms – standing practice

Activity 27: Body shape in the air

Activity 28: Felling trees

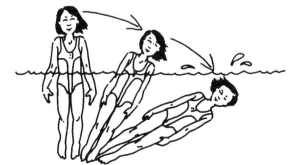

Activity 29: Complete front paddle
Face in water. Reach out. Pull to hip. Recover underwater.

Activity 30: Front crawl – no breathing
Face in water. Pull to hip. Elbow out first. Arms over water. Finger tip entry.

Activity 31: Handstand
Spring and tuck. Arms above head. Reach for the floor. Hands wide and firm.

Activity 32: Front crawl arms – standing practice

Activity 33: Reach rescue

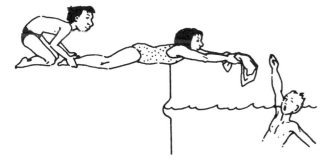

Activity 34: Spring feet to hands

Activity 35: Diving over partner

Activity 36: Sitting dive

Activity 37: Scull and turn
The hands should be flat like paddles. Turn the palms in the opposite direction to where you want to go.

Activity 38: Inverted breaststroke – land practice
Drop the heels. Turn the feet out, like a penguin. Push them round and back together.

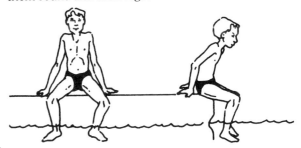

165

Activity 39: Inverted breaststroke – use of floats
Start with the legs together. *Drop* the heels and turn the feet *out*. Push the water round and finish with the feet together.

Activity 40: Breaststroke kick – two floats

Activity 41: Breaststroke arm action – standing practice

Activity 42: Kneeling dive

166

LESSON PLANS

Unit 1, lesson 1

Level of ability: Non-swimmer

Theme: Water confidence: To experience different situations in water

Purpose: PoS b

Activity bank: Activities 1–8

Resources: Arm bands, discs, floats, 'egg flips'

Introduction:
Enter the pool. Walk down the steps backwards or sit on the side, twist to place both hands on the side, turn and slide in facing the wall (see Activity 1).

Development:
a) Work on travelling activities such as ordinary walking, hopping, skipping, walking on different surfaces of the feet, e.g. heels, tip toes, sides of feet. 'Walk tall', 'walk small'. Walk in different directions. Crouch and turn to the left/right by using your hands (see Activity 2).
b) Learn to stand from a prone position. From lying on the front: hold on to the rail, kick the legs up and down behind, stop and then sit up and stand up, still holding the rail (see Activity 3).
Repeat this away from the side – sit up, then stand up (see Activity 4).
From lying on the back: hold on to the rail, with the feet on the wall, near to the hands. Lie back, with the arms straight and the head as if on a pillow. Keep the eyes open and look at the ceiling. Lift the head up, sit up, then stand up (see Activity 5).
Repeat by gently pushing and stretching away from the wall; float on the back, then lift the head, sit up and stand up.
Repeat away from the wall, holding a float and kicking the legs up and down – sit up, then stand up (see Activity 6).
c) Front kicking to the wall: hold a float under each forearm. Face the wall, with the shoulders down; lean, push and stretch and kick to the wall using an up and down kick. (See Activity 7).
Repeat, taking a step further back each time. See how far from the wall you can start.

Contrasting activity:
Work without floats but with arm bands or discs if necessary.
Float on your back for 10 seconds.

Try different shapes, e.g. wide, thin, twisted and tucked (see Activity 8).
Work with a partner. Mirror or copy their shapes.

Conclusion:
Blow 'egg flips' across the pool.

Unit 1, lesson 2

Level of ability: Beginner

Theme: Water confidence: To introduce up and down kicks

Purpose: PoS b, c

Activity bank: Activities 1, 7, 9, 10, 11

Resources: Arm bands, discs (if necessary), floats

Introduction:
Sit on the side of the pool and slide in (see Activity 1).
Travel in different ways, using different levels, different directions etc.

Development:
Practising kicking – up and down kicks.
a) Face the wall, hold on to the rail. Keep the chin on the surface and kick the legs up and down, with long legs and floppy feet (see Activity 9).
b) Back to the wall, feet on the bottom – lean, push and glide, then kick as far as you can before standing and making your way to the other side.
c) Try this on your back. Hold on to the rail, with the feet on the wall and the knees bent. Release the hands

Contrasting activity:
Jump in; jump in and submerge; jump in, submerge and then kick to the other side either on the front or the

Conclusion:
Work in groups. Play 'Ring a Roses'.
Pretend to be 'Melting ice creams' (sink slowly into the water).

and push and kick as far as you can. Make your way to the other side.
d) Try using floats, with or without arm bands or discs. Kick as far across as you can on your front, holding a float under each forearm (see Activity 7).
Repeat on your back, holding a float under each forearm as if in an armchair, then with the arms straight (see Activity 10).
Encourage a stretched shape, with long legs and floppy but pointed feet. Blow out as you kick.

back; jump in, submerge and then kick on the front to half way across, turn over and kick on the back to the other side (see Activity 11).

Unit 1, lesson 3

Level of ability: Beginner

Theme: Front and back paddle: To build up confidence for front and backcrawl

Purpose: PoS b, c

Activity bank: Activities 12, 13, 14, 15

Resources: Balls, floats

Introduction:
Jump in and push a ball with the chin, then with the nose, then with the forehead. Blow out before breathing in.

Development:
Work on the front and back kick, with or without discs, but use two floats, as in Lesson 2.
Work on the front and back kick using one float:
Front – arms out straight, with the hands either holding the sides of the float or over the top of it (see Activity 12).
Back – arms out straight, hold the float at the sides, keep the float above the hips (see Activity 13).
Emphasise long legs, floppy feet, splashing from feet.

Work on the front paddle (see Activity 14). Try this without floats or arm bands, if possible.
Push and glide, then, with the chin on the surface, reach out alternately with the hands and pull back to the chin. Make this a continuous action. Keep the hands big and flat and the legs kicking continuously behind.
Work on the back paddle (see Activity 15). Try this without floats or arm bands, if possible.
Push and glide on the back. Kick the legs, with the hands at side of the hips, sculling like a fish's fin.

Contrasting activity:
Jump in and submerge.
Jump as high as you can.
Jump as far out as you can.

Conclusion:
Float using different shapes. Work in pairs. Your partner counts how long you can stay in that shape.

Unit 1, lesson 4 ▷

Level of ability: Beginner/improver

Theme: Introduction of backcrawl: To continue building confidence for front and backcrawl

Purpose: PoS a, c

Activity bank: Activities 16, 17, 18, 19

Resources: Music, sinking objects

Introduction:
Mini aqua aerobics to music.

Development:
a) Work on the front paddle as Lesson 3.
b) Kicking on the back, with the arms at the sides, then with the arms over the thighs. If possible, extend the arms behind the head (start with the hands behind the head).
Stress a long flat body shape, keeping the hips up, the head back and the chin in. If pupils are not too confident, go back to the use of floats.
c) Attempt the full stroke, with alternate arm action, after a demonstration from the teacher on the pool side.

d) Concentrate on one arm at a time, but with the legs kicking.
Hold the float with one hand over the top and across the tummy (for support) (see Activity 16). Use the other arm to pull and recover. Enter with the little finger, brush the ear with the arm, keep the head still, the eyes open and pull down the side until the palm hits the leg. Reach to the ceiling and lift (recovery).
Change arms and repeat.
Try the full stroke once more.

Contrasting activity:
Work on pushing and gliding, linked to the body shape, streamlining and resistance, and to diving.
a) Glide along the surface, pushing from the wall. Start with one foot on the wall and the other foot on the floor. Lift the standing foot to join the other foot and push, stretch and count to 5 (see Activity 17).
b) Repeat the above, pushing from both feet (see Activity 18).

c) Push and glide under water (see Activity 19).
Slide down the wall, roll on to the front and push (take a deep breath before you submerge).
Stress a long, stretched body shape, with the arms squeezing the ears, the legs together and the toes pointed.
Bring in the crawl kick after gliding for a count of 5.

Conclusion:
Pick up objects from the bottom of the pool with your hands.
How many can you collect and put on the pool side?

Unit 1, lesson 5 ▷

Level of ability: Improver

Theme: Backcrawl continued: To improve backcrawl leg action

Purpose: PoS a, c

Activity bank: Activities 13, 15, 20

Resources: Small coloured balls, floats

Introduction:
Play 'Mini volleyball' in groups of four. Use small coloured balls. Keep the ball up in the air as much as possible.

Development:
a) Widths, alternating back paddle and front paddle. Refer to Lessons 3 and 4.
b) Kicking practices on the back.
Start with one float held under each arm.
Then try one float held over the hips (see Activity 13).
Back paddle – use the hands at the side of the hips (see Activity 15).

Contrasting activity:
a) Push and glide for as long as possible.
b) Push from the wall towards the bottom of the pool and touch the bottom. Keep the eyes open.

Conclusion:
Play 'Tick'. Three people are 'on'. Go into a floating position when 'ticked'.

Kick, with the hands on the thighs: kick hard, kick quietly and gently, kick hard, etc.
c) Try the full stroke. Teacher demonstrates the alternating action of the arms.
Keep the arms straight, brush the ears with the arms (revert back to the back paddle when necessary).

Unit 1, lesson 6 ▷

Level of ability: Improver

Theme: Sculling: To improve body position for backcrawl

Purpose: PoS a, c

Activity bank: Activities 21, 22, 23, 24

Resources: Floats, hoops, sinking hoops, stopwatch

Introduction:
Jump in.
Work in pairs, numbered 1 and 2. No. 1 stands with legs apart and/or with arms straight out across the surface of the water. No. 2 travels under each 'bridge' and over where appropriate (see Activity 21).

Development:
a) Front paddle: swim for 1 minute without stopping. Keep the chin on the surface, the hands firm and the finger tips leading.
b) Sculling – introduction to the correct method.
Stand in the shallow end, with the hands outstretched and figures together at the surface. Move the hands out and in with a small sweeping figure of eight movement (see Activity 22). Press out with the little finger leading, sweep in with the thumb leading. Imagine stroking a dog or cleaning a window.
c) Begin to bring the feet up into a crouched position, using the sculling action to support you (see Activity 23).

Feel the need to work harder and slightly faster and to bring the hands out towards the sides of the body.
d) Lie flat out on your back and use the sculling action to stay up and on the same spot. Stretch into a long thin shape, with the toes and hips at the surface and the head as if on a low pillow (see Activity 24). The hands should be at hip level.
e) Backcrawl: try the stroke, with a body position like the sculling position just practised. Use a float to try one arm at a time. Hold the float across the tummy for support. Concentrate on little finger entry, brushing the ears with the arms and finishing the pull at the thigh. Repeat using full stroke.

Contrasting activity:
Arrange floating hoops on the surface and sinking hoops upright in the water.
Pass through, over and under the hoops.

Conclusion:
Use a sculling action to support you whilst adopting and holding different shapes.

Unit 1, lesson 7

Level of ability: Improver

Theme: Backcrawl: To improve arm action

Purpose: PoS a, c

Activity bank: Activities 25, 26, 27

Resources: None

Introduction:
Swim across the width of the pool changing from front to back by rolling, i.e. horizontal roll. Use an up and down kick and the front and back paddle. Work on smooth changes and on breathing out.

Development:
a) Work on the front paddle. Introduce a longer pull to the tummy. Reach out as far as possible, with the finger tips leading; pull back with big flat hands (see Activity 25).
b) Work on the backcrawl with the emphasis on the arm action.

Stand at the shallow end and practise the arm action in the air. Concentrate on alternate action, little finger entry, thumb leading recovery, brushing ears with arms (see Activity 26). Pull to the thigh.
c) Widths of the full stroke backcrawl, with the arm action as in b) and also keeping the head very still.

Contrasting activity:
Jump in: jump high, jump far.
Jump and show different body shapes in the air (see Activity 27).

Conclusion:
Play 'Felling trees'. The teacher is the tree feller and the pupils 'fall' depending on the side of the cut (see Activity 28). Keep the body rigid until the shoulders are submerged.

Unit 1, lesson 8

Level of ability: Improver

Theme: Front paddle: Stepping stones for front crawl

Purpose: PoS a, c

Activity bank: Activities 29, 30, 31

Resources: Floats, music or drum

Introduction:
Swim for 2 minutes using backcrawl. Use a long slow pull with a matching recovery. Remember to blow out.

Development:
a) Swim widths using the front paddle, pulling to the tummy.
b) Work in pairs. Hold the float and kick for two widths, then hand float to partner, who repeats. Kick fast and hard. See how fast you can do this, with each pair going through it twice (if necessary pairs could use two floats).
c) Work on the front paddle (face in the water without breathing), pulling the hands to the hips and recovering under water, as before. (See Activity 29). When you need to breathe, roll over on to your back and finish using backcrawl.

Hold the head steady, with the water at the hair line and take long pulls with big flat hands.
d) If pupils are comfortable with this, introduce recovery *over* the water. Keep the head still, with the face in the water, pull to the hip, then elbow out and sweep the hand back to the entry point beyond the head (see Activity 30).
(The basic rule is: face *out*, hands *in*; when face is comfortable *in*, hands can recover *out* of water.)

Contrasting activity:
Head first sculling:
a) Revision of 'flat' scull. Use a long body shape, lying flat on the water surface, keep the hands near the hips, with the palms facing the bottom of the pool.
b) Lift the hands up a little by tilting them at the wrists.

The palms should face towards the feet. Use the same action as before, out and back making a figure of eight, but this time as you travel head first.
c) To music or the beat of a drum, alternate between head first travel and staying still.

Conclusion:
Try handstands in the shallow end (see Activity 31).

Unit 1, lesson 9

Level of ability: Improver

Theme: Front crawl arm action: To encourage recovery action over the water

Purpose: PoS a, c

Activity bank: Activities 32, 33

Resources: T-shirts brought by the pupils

Introduction:
Swim widths using any method, wearing a T-shirt. Encourage the class to change stroke to experience the effect of wearing a garment.

Development:
a) Swim widths, alternating between front paddle pulling to hip and attempting recovery over the water.
b) Introduction of arm action for front crawl. Standing in the shallow end, bent forward at the hips, practise the front crawl arm action: finger tip entry, in front of shoulder, elbow up as if going over a barrel, hands big and flat, pull to hip, recover elbow first, hands recover low over surface (see Activity 32). Go back to the entry point.
Try the full stroke – without breathing – across a width. Breathe only at the sides of the pool if you can. If you cannot, roll over on to your back and complete the width using backcrawl.
The water level should be at the hair line, with the eyes looking diagonally forwards and downwards.

Contrasting activity:
Stage a simple rescue. Work in groups of three. One person struggles in the water, the second uses T-shirts to reach and pull them in and the third holds the reacher's legs (see Activity 33).

Conclusion:
Swim from deeper water to shallow water, keeping close to the side and using any stroke. Those who are not confident should start much closer to the shallow end, but focus on moving down the pool, not across it.

Unit 1, lesson 10

Level of ability: Improver

Theme: Beginning of diving: To build up confidence to enter water head first

Purpose: PoS b

Activity bank: Activities 34, 35, 36

Resources: Floats, stopwatch

Introduction:
Timed distance – pupils see how far they can swim in 2 minutes, using either front or back action.

Development:
Introduction of diving.
a) Shallow end practices. Jump as high as possible, feet to feet. Jump and 'land' on different parts, e.g. seat, one shoulder, other shoulder.
b) Spring from feet to hands (see Activity 34). Aim to get movement over the surface. Push the hips up and stretch the arms above the head, squeezing the ears. The hands should be one on top of the other, with the palms

downwards. Imagine you are 'diving' over a barrel.
c) Work in pairs, labelled A and B. A holds arm outstretched, B 'dives' over it (see Activity 35). Keep the hips up, stretch the legs after the push, with a slight pike at the hips.
d) Those who are comfortable with this try a sitting dive (see Activity 36). Lean, push and stretch, with the arms squeezing the ears and the hands one on top of the other.

Contrasting activity:
Sculling – revision of stationary and head first scull (see Lesson 8).
Try feet first scull. Concentrate on keeping the same action, except for the change in the hand angle at the wrist.

Sit on a float and use the hands to turn left and right (see Activity 37).
Try this without a float, in a tucked position.
Put together a sculling sequence, choosing from moving head first, being stationary, moving feet first and turning left and right.

Conclusion:
Try the front crawl, full stroke, no breathing. Try one width without stopping.

Unit 1, lesson 11

Level of ability: Improver

Theme: Introduction to breast stroke: To familiarise class with the position of the feet and the pathway of the kick

Purpose: PoS a, c

Activity bank: Activities 38, 39, 40

Resources: Music, floats, large light balls

Introduction:
Work on a continuation of the sculling sequence from Lesson 10, using phrasing of music in relation to the changes of scull and body shape.

Development:
a) Walk at the shallow end, using different surfaces of the feet, ending with walking on the heels.
Walk, turning the feet out, still walking on the heels (Charlie Chaplin walk).
b) Sitting on the pool side, practise the sitting kick (see Activity 38). Check the feet are turned out, like a penguin. Drop the heels and circle with the heels.
c) In the water, close to the side, hold two floats out in front and walk with the feet turned out. Lean forwards and keep the feet turned out. Draw a circle with the heels. With the chin on the surface, bring the heels to the seat and kick round and *back*.

d) Inverted breaststroke (see Activity 39). Take up a position in the water as if sitting in a deck chair, with one float under each arm. Start with the legs together, drop the heels and turn the feet out. Sweep round and finish with the feet together.
e) Try this again on the front, using one or two floats (see Activity 40). Keep the shoulders square, the feet turned out and bring the heels up to the seat. Kick round and *back*; finish with the legs long and straight.
f) Practise kicking, concentrating on the kick *back* and breathing out as this happens. (Note: do not attempt the full stroke at this stage.)

Contrasting activity:
Play a mini volleyball game (3 v 3).

Conclusion:
Work in pairs, with one pupil watching the other for safety.

Sit on the bottom of the pool.
Lie on the bottom of the pool, if you can. Breathe out to help you sink.

Unit 1, lesson 12

Level of ability: Improver

Theme: Introduction of arm action for breaststroke:
To enable class to attempt full stroke

Purpose: PoS a, c

Activity bank: Activities 41, 42

Resources: Floats

Introduction:
Revision of feet to hands 'diving' in the shallow end.
Thrust and extend the legs and get the hips up, with a
slight pike. Work on streamlined entry.

Link three of these movements together.

Development:
a) Revision of breaststroke leg kick.
Start by walking on heels, holding floats.
Progress to leaning and kicking.
Try front and back kicks.
Progress to using one float.
b) Introduction of arm action (see Activity 41).
Standing in the shallow end, bend forwards at the hips.
With the forefingers gently together, stretch forwards
and turn the palms outwards at 45°, then circle around
an imaginary bowl. The hands should reach the prayer
position. Cut through the water, back to the start, with
the finger tips first and the hands flat.
Try this action whilst walking but still bent at hips.
c) Try the full stroke (if possible, after watching a
demonstration).
Stress the rhythm: pull, then kick; pull, then kick, etc.
Stretch between strokes, finish with the legs together.

Contrasting activity:
Revision of the sitting dive (see Activity 36).
Introduce the kneeling dive (see Activity 42) and, if
there is time, an appropriate crouching dive.
Stress starting with the toes over the edge, then lean,
push and *stretch*.
(Note: Teacher must check the depth of the pool,
according to ASA recommendations, and be aware of the
pool's rules for diving.)

Conclusion:
Swim down the pool to the shallow end using front
crawl, without breathing. When you need to breathe,
roll on to your back and finish using backcrawl.

OUTDOOR AND ADVENTUROUS ACTIVITIES

ABOUT OUTDOOR AND ADVENTUROUS ACTIVITIES ▶

Outdoor and Adventurous Activities extend through all key stages of the National Curriculum as one of the six areas of the foundation subject of PE. The frequently held belief that outdoor education is mainly concerned with outdoor pursuit activities, such as rock climbing, white water canoeing, caving and strenuous mountain walks, has meant that many teachers, particularly in the primary sector, have been reluctant to become involved. However, we now have to consider outdoor activities for all age ranges and outdoor education must be considered as a cross-curricular medium at all levels.

With a little imagination, the scope for a stimulating and creative area of learning is limitless. Throughout the key stages, Outdoor and Adventurous Activities encourage the learning of skills and knowledge to explore and investigate the potential for physical activities in our rich and varied environment, with safety and enjoyment. Understanding and recognising opportunities for physical activity in the immediate and distant environment are essential if we are to provide a rounded Physical Education experience. By the time pupils finish their school education, it is essential that they appreciate the frailty of our environment and are aware of how an individual can play a role in helping to preserve it for future generations, yet continue to use it for healthy and challenging physical activity. Outdoor and Adventurous Activities should enable pupils to develop this not alone, but in a cross-curricular context, as part of their whole education.

NATIONAL CURRICULUM REQUIREMENTS AT KEY STAGE 2 ▶

The majority of statements from the programme of study (general) are relevant to Outdoor and Adventurous Activities and these are listed below.

1. To promote physical activity and healthy lifestyles, pupils should be taught:
   a to be physically active;
   c to engage in activities that develop cardiovascular health, flexibility, muscular strength and endurance.
2. To develop positive attitudes, pupils should be taught:
   b how to cope with success and limitations in performance;
   c to try hard to consolidate their performances;
   d to be mindful of others and the environment.
3. To ensure safe practice, pupils should be taught:
   a to respond readily to instructions;
   b to recognise and follow relevant rules, laws, codes, etiquette and safety procedures for different activities or events, in practice and during competition;

c about the safety risks of wearing inappropriate clothing, footwear and jewellery, and why particular clothing, footwear and protection are worn for different acivities.

5 Outdoor adventurous activities

Pupils should be taught:

a to perform outdoor and adventurous activities, eg orienteering exercises, in one or more different environment(s), *eg playground, school grounds, parks, woodland, seashore;*
b challenges of a physical and problem-solving nature, *eg negotiating obstacle courses,* using suitable equipment, *eg gymnastic or adventure play apparatus,* whilst working individually and with others;
c the skills necessary for the activities undertaken.

All of the above will occur naturally in most activities.

It is also important to bear in mind the end of key stage statements (see page 4).

175

TEACHING OUTDOOR AND ADVENTUROUS ACTIVITIES AT KEY STAGE 2

For practical reasons, model lessons and units of work are not included for this area of PE. Outdoor and Adventurous Activities does not fit comfortably within a regular school time-table and schools will invariably adopt different approaches to this area of the curriculum. Although it would be possible to suggest some lessons that would meet both the criteria for the programmes of study (activity specific) and be incorporated in a time-table, most of the activities will fall outside. Resources, finance, travel time and staff experience in this area will dictate the approach adopted.

Within the Activity Bank there are many activities that could be included at this key stage. Initial introductory lessons in most activities should be in the school environs; however, it is desirable that excursions are made outside the school environment at a later date. Whether this be on a daily basis or for an extended period of a week or more will again be determined by each school.

One approach may be to condense the Outdoor and Adventurous Activities area, to make an Outdoor Education Week. This could be residential, under canvas or even consist of a series of single day trips. A cross-curricular theme is the obvious development, to include environmental investigation related to other subject areas. Personal and Social Development is another area that should be considered when designing such a programme.

Another approach may include introductory lessons in the classroom followed by regular weekly, half-day sessions outside the school, culminating with an overnight camp locally.

The majority of work at this key stage should focus around orienteering, campcraft and low level walks.

There should also be an element of problem solving and adventure/challenge designed activities. However, certainly towards the end of this key stage, pupils should have the opportunity to experience at least one of the more traditional outdoor pursuits of climbing, canoeing or gorge scrambling.

Apart from the limiting factors of school location, finances and resources, the area of safety will be clearly of most concern to teachers. Outdoor pursuit qualifications are not necessary for many of the activities, but a good level of experience is essential for the activity to be taught effectively. For this reason, many schools may opt to employ outside agencies and instructors or possibly visit their Local Authority Outdoor Education Centre.

Whatever route is taken, a thorough understanding of the safety issues, rules and regulations is necessary. In addition to the numerous instructional and safety books specific to the activities, all Authorities are required to provide their own Safety Regulations and Guidelines document for Outdoor Activities and 'out of school visits'. A thorough understanding of these safety documents is a pre-requisite before planning any Outdoor and Adventurous Activity scheme, whether the school plans to run an 'in-house' programme of activities or to employ outside agencies to work in this area of the curriculum.

Outdoor and Adventurous Activities are not dangerous. Many of the perceived risks are not real. If an individual makes a mistake there can be dire consequences. If we plan ahead thoroughly and adhere to the established safety guidelines and regulations, Outdoor and Adventurous Activities should be an instrumental element of a pupil's educational development.

OUTDOOR AND ADVENTUROUS ACTIVITY BANK

Activity 1: Orienteering

Orienteering is an activity that uses a map or plan to follow a series of checkpoints to complete or explore an area of ground. It is often competitive, but not necessarily so, and is usually completed at speed when the skills are learnt. As the individual improves, the compass is introduced and when this is combined with the map, more difficult routes can be undertaken. Generally recognised as one of the most educational sports, orienteering has a great following and can be undertaken by people of all abilities, whether young or old. There should be a structured progression, starting in the classroom (hopefully at Key Stage 1) of simple orientation activities within the school environs, leading to established courses in local parks and woodlands. Orienteering is a running sport that encourages healthy participation and competition in many varied environments, which can provide for possible cross-curricular themes at appropriate stages. Map-reading skills, environmental observation, the development of self-confidence and teamwork are clear objectives in this area of outdoor activity.

Activity 2: Low level walks

Woodland rambles, easy hill walks and beach combing are but a few examples of activities that should be included in any programme. The choice of venue will usually be determined by the location of the school and the resources available. A greater emphasis on environmental observation can be made to include recognition and recording of features (wildlife, trees and shrubs, flowers, etc.), whilst still providing a physical challenge. Pupils should be encouraged to participate in the selection of appropriate clothing and footwear and should recognise and understand the ground rules with regard to personal and group safety.

Activity 3: Campcraft

Most pupils are enthusiastic to camp and experience the adventure and assume a degree of self-sufficiency and independence. This should be encouraged, but needs to be well managed. Initial lessons could be classroom-based, e.g. investigating and examining the variety and suitability of shelters which can be constructed in different environments. Alongside this, investigating the additional equipment required to spend a comfortable night out can provide stimuli for cross-curricular topics. This should lead to building and erecting tents and shelters, with whatever equipment is available, within the school grounds or in other suitable locations nearby. The care and maintenance of the equipment used should be emphasised at all times. The introduction and use of cooking stoves (if included) should be strictly supervised, taking care to select suitable stoves for this age range. Much preparation will be required before a group should experience a night out, cooking for themselves, but with a well-structured schedule, the experience of this outdoor activity will be well worth the effort.

Activity 4: Gorge scrambling

This is an activity that combines fun with personal and group challenge, which can be designed to suit the level of the group. Scrambling up or down a suitable river or stream-bed, jumping from boulder to boulder, walking along fallen logs and swinging across pools from suspended ropes will provide an adventure in an educationally stimulating terrain. Teamwork should be encouraged, with both the least and most able pupils being challenged. An element of problem solving can be included to develop initiative and co-operation within a relatively controlled environment.

Activity 5: Rock climbing

This is a physically and mentally challenging activity and safety concerns should be paramount. Safety concerns are obvious; less obvious, and quite subtle, are the consequences of an unstructured and poorly taught introduction to this area of activity. Initial experiences can often deter a pupil from showing further interest in climbing for the rest of his life. At this stage in the pupil's development, it should be seen as fun, challenging and, above all else, safe, providing that stringent safety procedures are followed. The first experience could include a visit to a local climbing wall, top-roping on short single pitch crags and the understanding of simple knots and the equipment used. Abseiling could also be included, but should be seen as part of the whole climbing experience and not as a separate activity. It is not envisaged that this will be much more than a very brief introduction to this activity.

Cross-curricular themes could include an investigation of rock types and vegetation, as well as providing stimuli for imaginative writing.

Activity 6: Canoeing

By the time a pupil nears the end of Key Stage 2, he or she should be feeling comfortable in water and the introduction of canoeing should not prove to be a problem. Initial experience on a swimming pool is desirable (but not essential), as this allows the pupil to become confident in a kayak or canoe in a familiar environment. The use of the necessary equipment should be clearly understood and the procedures adopted before entering the water should be emphasised. At this stage, outdoor experience should not go beyond flat-water on small lakes and pools, providing an opportunity to attempt very basic paddling techniques and games.

Activity 7: Problem solving, adventure games and challenge courses

These can be integrated or individual activities, being school based, without the necessary financial expense encountered in some of the other activities outlined. Short rope lengths, wooden planks, barrels, tyres, blindfolds and similar inexpensive items can be collected relatively easily. These can be incorporated into short problem-solving activities and courses, which can be undertaken by individuals, pairs or groups of children in a competitive or non-competitive manner. The activities need not be physically challenging; rather they may require a degree of initiative and teamwork to be successful. The teacher will need to have vision and a creative imagination to anticipate the likely outcomes and design the activity to achieve the chosen objectives. A selection of games and activities follow, some of which may be familiar under a different name or with minor variations. These games and activities have been selected to give an idea of the scope and variety available to the teacher.

'City gates'

There are many variations of this. One of the simplest is to arrange four benches in cross formation and select four teams, one to each bench. The teams run round the outside of the bench formation (or move in any way) until the whistle is blown and then each team finds its own bench. The first team to adopt the agreed finishing position, e.g. balancing on seats, hands joined, wins.

'Chinese wall'

Two parallel lines ten feet apart are drawn across the ground in the centre of the playing area – this forms the wall. One or more players stand on the wall to defend it. The other players try to cross the wall without being touched. If they are touched, they either join the defenders, or count the number of times they are successful in running to and from the boundaries within the time limit of the game.

'Names on planks'

Ask the group(s) to line up on a plank or bench. Now ask them to re-arrange themselves (without getting off) into various orders, e.g. alphabetical, age, birthdays, height. Try a non-verbal version.

'Untangle the knot'

Each group (six to ten pupils) stands in a tight circle. Everyone puts their left hand in the circle and holds someone's hand. Then everyone puts their other hand in, to hold someone else's hand. Then, without letting go, they must untangle the knot into its simplest form, e.g. a circle or a figure of eight.

'Skis'

For this exercise you will need a pair of 'skis' (two lengths of wood with rope attached, as in the diagram). The task for the group (four to seven pupils) is to use the 'skis' to transport the whole group to a destination of your choice. Once the group are fairly well co-ordinated they should try reversing or turning.

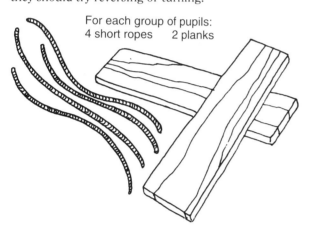

For each group of pupils:
4 short ropes   2 planks

'Electric fence'

A rope is suspended between two objects (between three and four feet above ground level) and it is explained to the groups (each of six to eight pupils) that the rope is electrified and if anyone touches it they are either out of the game or their whole group must start again. The objective is to transport the group over the fence, without touching it, using only themselves and a conductive beam (short plank).

Raft building

This activity could be combined with a swimming lesson, but would obviously have to be strictly controlled and supervised. Using apparatus available in the swimming pool, a group could be asked to build a raft that could be used to carry an object to the other side of the pool, yet keep it dry.

SOME USEFUL REFERENCES ▶

Safety
Safety in Outdoor Education, 1989, D.E.S., H.M.S.O.
In addition to the above, all Local Education Authorities produce regulations and guidelines for outdoor activities and visits.

Orienteering
McNeill, C., Ramsden, J. and Renfrew, T., 1987. *Teaching Orienteering; A Handbook for Teachers, Instructors and Coaches,* Harveys in conjunction with the British Orienteering Federation.
McNeill, C. and Renfrew, T., 1989. *Start Orienteering,* Harveys (a collection of four books with schemes of work for Primary Teachers).
McNeill, C., Martland, J. and Palmer, P., 1992. *Orienteering in the National Curriculum.*

Hill walking and rock climbing
Langmuir, E., 1984. *Mountaincraft and Leadership,* British Mountaineering Council.
Barry, J. and Shepherd, N., 1988. *Adventure sports: rock climbing.*
British Mountaineering Council, 1988. *Mountain Code.*

Canoeing
Good, G.C., 1983. *Canoeing Handbook,* British Canoe Union.
Ruse, D., 1986. *Canoe games.*

Campcraft
Brown, T. and Hunter, R., 1976. *Spur book of lightweight camping.*

Problem solving, adventure games and challenge courses
Rohnke, K., 1986. *Silver Bullets: A guide to initiative problems, adventure games and trust activities.*
Roberts, C., 1989. *Go For It (P.E. Activities for the Classroom Teacher).*

SOME USEFUL ADDRESSES ▶

British Orienteering Federation, Riversdale, Dale Road North, Darley Dale, Matlock, Derbyshire DE2 2HX.

British Mountaineering Council, Crawford House, Precinct Centre, Booth St. East, Manchester M13 9RZ.

British Canoe Union, Mapperley Hall, Lucknow Avenue, Nottingham NG3 5FA.